Cambridge Studies in Philosophy and Law

Some other books in the series:

New Essays in the Legal and Political Theory of Property

Edited by

Stephen R. Munzer

University of California, Los Angeles

PUBLISHED BY THE PRESS SYNDICATE OF THE UNIVERSITY OF CAMBRIDGE
The Pitt Building, Trumpington Street, Cambridge, United Kingdom

CAMBRIDGE UNIVERSITY PRESS
The Edinburgh Building, Cambridge CB2 2RU, UK
40 West 20th Street, New York, NY 10011-4211, USA
10 Stamford Road, Oakleigh, VIC 3166, Australia
Ruiz de Alarcón 13, 28014 Madrid, Spain
Dock House, The Waterfront, Cape Town 8001, South Africa

http://www.cambridge.org

First published 2001

Printed in the United States of America

Typeface Times Roman 10/12 pt.   *System* MagnaType™ [AG]

A catalog record for this book is available from the British Library.

Library of Congress Cataloging in Publication Data
New essays in the legal and political theory of property / edited by Stephen R. Munzer.
p.   cm. – (Cambridge studies in philosophy and law)
Includes index.
ISBN 0-521-64001-6
1. Property. 2. Right of property. I. Munzer, Stephen R. II. Series.
K720 .N49 2001
330.1'7–dc21   00-063046

ISBN 0 521 64001 6 hardback

Contents

Contributors

WILLIAM FISHER   Harvard Law School

J. W. HARRIS   Keble College, Oxford University

EDWARD J. MCCAFFERY   University of Southern California Law School and California Institute of Technology

STEPHEN R. MUNZER   School of Law, University of California at Los Angeles

SEANA VALENTINE SHIFFRIN   Department of Philosophy and School of Law, University of California at Los Angeles

JEREMY WALDRON   Columbia University Law School

Preface and Acknowledgments

This book collects new work in the legal and political theory of property. No volume of this length could be representative of recent developments in this field. Yet I hope that these essays will give some idea of the variety and vitality of recent work on property. The contributors to this collection range in age from their early thirties to their late fifties, represent many institutions, and have varied moral and political points of view.

Some who started this project had to leave for one reason or another, but the stalwarts who remain helped me and each other. I did not ask the contributors to write on any particular topic but rather invited them to prepare an essay on a topic in the theory of property that interested them. From the start this was a collaborative project. Each contributor was asked to comment on the drafts of their comrades at two different stages. In a procedure that may be unusual for a collection of this sort, I circulated the penultimate drafts of my fellow authors for blind review. Gerald J. Postema, the General Editor of Cambridge Studies in Philosophy and Law, sent out my contribution for blind review. If the essays of my comrades bear the marks of responses to objections, this quality derives not from my modest editorial skills but in significant part from the detailed comments of outside readers. Anonymous reviewers contributed enormously to the improvement of my own essay; any remaining defects are my sole responsibility. I am deeply grateful for the time that all of the outside readers put into preparing careful criticisms and suggestions.

Of those whom I am permitted to name, I wish to thank Jules Coleman, who invited me to assemble this collection, and his successor, Gerald J. Postema, who saw it through to completion. Emily Mah helped immensely with production and indexing. Above all I thank my secretary, Margaret Kiever, who brought these essays together and handled more correspondence than she or I care to contemplate. For material support I am indebted to the Dean's Fund in the School of Law and to the Academic Senate at UCLA.

STEPHEN R. MUNZER
Los Angeles, California
June 12, 2000

Introduction

STEPHEN R. MUNZER

Never in the history of Western political theory has property been ignored. Among classical and medieval thinkers, Plato, Aristotle, and Aquinas all had something to say about property. In the modern period, Grotius, Pufendorf, Filmer, Locke, Hume, Rousseau, Kant, Hegel, Marx, Bentham, and Mill all assigned property a central place in their speculations on human values and society.

The twentieth century saw some remarkable contributions to thinking about property. Especially notable are essays by individuals who were or are professionally situated in schools of law rather than in departments of philosophy, politics, or economics. The work of Wesley Newcomb Hohfeld and A. M. Honoré, for example, exerted great influence on how philosophers as well as lawyers understand the concept of property.[1] Robert Lee Hale, an academic lawyer as well as an economist, formulated a view on property, its distribution, coercion, and the modern state that has formed a major tributary of critical legal studies.[2] Economists as well as lawyers played a major role in other segments of contemporary writing on property. For instance, R. H. Coase's essays illuminated the law of nuisance and the nature of the business firm, and Berle and Means's treatment of the separation of ownership from control in the modern corporation continues to reverberate in the literature on corporate governance.[3]

---

1 See Wesley Newcomb Hohfeld, *Fundamental Legal Conceptions as Applied in Judicial Reasoning*, ed. Walter W. Cook and foreword by Arthur L. Corbin (Westport, Conn.: Greenwood Press, 1978 [1919]); A. M. Honoré, "Ownership," in A. G. Guest, ed., *Oxford Essays in Jurisprudence* (Oxford: Clarendon Press, 1961), pp. 107–47. The influence of Hohfeld on academic lawyers is especially evident in the American Law Institute, *Restatement of the Law of Property* (St. Paul, Minn.: American Law Institute Publishers, 1944).
2 See, for example, Robert L. Hale, "Bargaining, Duress, and Economic Liberty," *Columbia Law Review,* 43 (1943): 603–28; Robert L. Hale, "Coercion and Distribution in a Supposedly Non-Coercive State," *Political Science Quarterly,* 38 (1923): 470–94.
3 See R. H. Coase, "The Problem of Social Cost," *Journal of Law & Economics,* 3 (1960): 1–44;

Philosophers have hardly been absent from twentieth-century contributions. John Rawls and Robert Nozick have each left a significant mark. Although Rawls has written little that specifically addresses property, his two principles of justice have important implications for property and its distribution. His first principle applies to "basic liberties," which include "the right to hold (personal) property."[4] The first part of his second principle requires that the social institutions concerning other kinds of property, such as the means of production, be structured so that any social and economic inequalities are "to the greatest benefit of the least advantaged."[5] Later writers have explored tensions between the two principles as applied to property and criticized Rawls's views from the perspective of a broad theory directed specifically to property, and Rawls has modified some aspects of his earlier views.[6] If Rawls offers an egalitarian political philosophy, Nozick provides a libertarian alternative. Nozick's sole book on political philosophy contains not only a critique of Rawls on justice but also, and more importantly, a dazzlingly clever historical-entitlement theory of justice.[7] Pretty much single-handedly, Nozick gave academic respectability to libertarianism and influenced a new generation of libertarian thinkers.[8] He also played a large role in reviving interest in Locke's views on property.

It is chiefly in the last three decades that theoretical writing on property has displayed the variety, rigor, and insight equal to that of, say, philosophical work on criminal law and constitutional law. Much recent writing is self-consciously interdisciplinary. The penetration of neoclassical economics into schools of law has advanced clear, useful thinking about property, as the abiding influence of Guido Calabresi and A. Douglas Melamed makes plain.[9] The absorption of Locke, Hegel, and the legal realists by philosophers, political theorists, and academic lawyers has reworked older speculation in the light of

R. H. Coase, "The Nature of the Firm," *Economica,* 4 (1937 (n.s.)): 386–405; Adolf A. Berle, Jr. and Gardiner C. Means, *The Modern Corporation and Private Property* (New York: Commerce Clearing House, 1932).

4 John Rawls, *A Theory of Justice* (Cambridge, Mass.: Harvard University Press, 1971), p. 61. Rawls gives a full statement of both principles, including priority rules, on pp. 302–03.

5 Ibid., p. 302.

6 See, for example, Norman Daniels, "Equal Liberty and Unequal Worth of Liberty," in Norman Daniels, ed., *Reading Rawls: Critical Studies of A Theory of Justice* (Oxford: Basil Blackwell, 1975), pp. 253–81; J. W. Harris, *Property and Justice* (Oxford, Clarendon Press, 1996), pp. 258–62; Stephen R. Munzer, *A Theory of Property* (Cambridge: Cambridge University Press, 1990), pp. 233–41. For adjustments to his earlier theory, see John Rawls, *Political Liberalism* (New York: Columbia University Press, 1996 [1993]) (paperback ed. with new introduction), especially pp. 298, 338–39.

7 Robert Nozick, *Anarchy, State, and Utopia* (New York: Basic Books, 1974), pp. 149–231.

8 See, for example, Loren E. Lomasky, *Persons, Rights, and the Moral Community* (New York and Oxford: Oxford University Press, 1987), Ch. 6.

9 Guido Calabresi and A. Douglas Melamed, "Property Rules, Liability Rules and Inalienability: One View of the Cathedral," *Harvard Law Review,* 85 (1972): 1089–128.

new problems and new techniques.[10] At the same time, work that integrates political theory and a deep understanding of property law has continued.[11]

Given this embarrassment of riches, a major contributor to the resurgence of interest in the theory of property has intimated, perhaps tongue in cheek, that there may be a surfeit, if not of property, at least of writing about it.[12] I hope that this is not so. At all events, I have a stake in its not being true. Thus, I need to explain why the essays in this volume advance the ball.

In "Property, Honesty, and Normative Resilience," Jeremy Waldron poses the following question: What is the relation between property and honesty? An appealing, if overly quick, answer is that to be honest (in a broad sense of integrity and upright conduct) is to respect the rules of property law. Thus, stealing would be dishonest because it violates rules of property. Yet this answer leads one to push the inquiry more deeply, for some might question whether stealing is dishonest in *all* legal systems. Perhaps some legal systems are so egregiously unjust that in them stealing is neither dishonest nor other-wise wrong.

Waldron breaks new ground in suggesting that the key to a deeper and more satisfactory answer lies in a phenomenon that he calls normative resilience. This phenomenon rests on a distinction between two types of judgments. Type 1 judgments concern the justification of an institution. Type 2 judgments concern individual conduct in relation to that institution. Waldron then defines normative resilience as the phenomenon whereby judgments of type 2, al-though they are predicated upon the institution, nevertheless remain unaffected by judgments of type 1 that are adverse to the institution.

Two central theses advanced in his paper are the following. First, *property* is a normatively resilient institution. For example, someone could make the type 1 judgment, "The property system in El Salvador is unjust," and still make the type 2 judgment, "It was dishonest of the poor villager to take the landowner's car." Waldron reminds us, though, that resilience and normative force can be matters of degree. Thus, if a property system is *egregiously* unjust, then per-haps taking someone's car is "not really dishonest." The second thesis is that the more normatively resilient an institution is, the more harm it may do if it is unjust, and so the heavier is the burden that must be discharged in its initial justification. As applied to the specific case of property, the second thesis

10 In a vast literature, see, for example, Seyla Benhabib, *Natural Right and Hegel: An Essay in Modern Political Philosophy* (Ann Arbor, Mich. and London: University Microfilms International, 1978) (Yale Univ. Ph.D. dissertation, May 1977); G. A. Cohen, *Self-Ownership, Freedom, and Equality* (Cambridge: Cambridge University Press, 1995); Margaret Jane Radin, *Contested Commodities* (Cambridge, Mass. and London: Harvard University Press, 1996); Joseph William Singer, "The Reliance Interest in Property," *Stanford Law Review,* 40 (1988): 611–751; Jeremy Waldron, *The Right to Private Property* (Oxford: Clarendon Press, 1988).
11 See, for example, Harris, *Property and Justice.*
12 See Lawrence C. Becker, "Too Much Property," *Philosophy & Public Affairs,* 21 (1992): 196–206.

would have the following corollary: If property is an especially normatively resilient institution, then the initial burden of justifying it is quite heavy.

If Waldron is right that institutions of property law are generally highly normatively resilient, then it becomes more important than ever to make sure that institutions of property are justified. He explores some explanations of the phenomenon of normative resilience, and here focuses on the theories of David Hume and Jeremy Bentham. Waldron also pursues some further implications of the normative resilience of property.

In "Property as Social Relations," I aim to bridge a gap between two groups of thinkers who write about the legal and political theory of property. The first group consists of some legal realists and some critical legal scholars who, along with a few others, understand property relations as a set of social relations. This group includes Felix S. Cohen, Robert L. Hale, Duncan Kennedy, and Joseph William Singer. It also includes the Canadian political theorists C. B. Macpherson and Jennifer Nedelsky. The second group consists of just about everyone else. Libertarians, traditional Marxists, and analytic philosophers of whatever political persuasion say almost nothing about social-relations theorists. I think that we need more cross-talk. So, as an academic lawyer whose philosophical training comes from the Anglo-American analytic tradition, I try to offer a critical and constructive discussion of various social-relations views.

It is not easy, however, to say what a social-relations theory of property *is,* for thinkers in the first group differ significantly among themselves. Yet the following themes are central, though perhaps not indispensable, to most of the views offered by the first group: an emphasis on coercion or the exercise of power by those who have property against those who lack it, or at least do not have much of it; the presence of the state as a nonneutral party, because it specifies and enforces property rights; the self as a nonindividualistic entity that arises from social relations; and the idea that property rights grow out of social relations that are highly contextualized.

I argue that social-relations theories contain both insights and flaws. The insights include an awareness of the many ways in which market forces, the distribution of income and wealth, and especially government regulation affect all who engage in commercial transactions. A salient flaw is that no theory examined shows which social relations are, or help to constitute, property. In addition, social-relations theories frequently rest on flawed accounts of coercion, power, and freedom. They often adopt as well unsatisfactory positions on autonomy and the self.

My argument unfolds not as a dry assault on one proposition after another ascribed to social-relations thinkers, but from a careful consideration of their texts. This way Cohen and Hale, Kennedy and Singer, Macpherson and Nedelsky get to speak in their own words, not mine. There is also a political dimension to my argument. Contemporary social-relations theorists are associated almost entirely with the radical left. I endeavor to show that there is less distance between them and Rawlsian political liberals than either group has imagined.

So far as I am aware, this essay is the first effort by someone outside social-relations approaches to property to examine their writings as a more or less coherent and distinctive set of views about property. To be sure, my inquiry is incomplete.[13] And social-relations thinkers may not appreciate the problems I seek to put on their agenda at the end of my essay. Yet I shall have achieved one of my main aims if others pursue the mutual engagement of quite different approaches to property.

It is a commonplace to think of property as something that one may use during life and then upon death transmit it by will or intestate succession to others. The next two essays explore the living and dead sides of property – waste and inheritance – respectively.

As long as one lives, may one use one's property *ad libitum* – even to the point of frittering it away or destroying it? Edward J. McCaffery addresses this question in "Must We Have the Right to Waste?" He begins by observing that Anglo-American law has long permitted owners to do pretty much whatever they want with their property, right down to the limiting case of using it all up or wasting it. He calls this broad permission the *jus abutendi*. Thinkers as different as Blackstone, Pound, and Honoré have taken this right to waste to be one of the salient rights in the "bundle of rights" that has come to symbolize property.

On reflection, McCaffery suggests, this affirmative right to waste is – or ought to be – as puzzling as it is entrenched. He traces the evolution of the right and lays bare its connections to an absolute, or nearly absolute, conception of ownership developed largely in the context of an agrarian society and real property. McCaffery then canvasses what is wrong with waste from the point of view of political liberalism. His subject takes on especial importance because value has moved away from land and into intangible, fungible units of value, paradigmatically money. A concern with wasting the family farm has now become, or should become, a concern with depleting large stores of nominally private capital. McCaffery concludes by proposing a revised conception of ownership with a practical law against waste, one that features a progressive consumption tax as its instantiation of an antiwaste norm.

One of the novel features of McCaffery's argument against the continuance of the *jus abutendi* is the way that it brings taxation to center stage in our thinking about property. In exploring different conceptions of waste, he makes a specific case against waste in the sense of the relatively nonurgent

---

13 For example, space did not allow me to consider Benhabib, *Natural Right and Hegel;* Carol C. Gould, *Rethinking Democracy: Freedom and Social Cooperation in Politics, Economy, and Society* (Cambridge: Cambridge University Press, 1988); Richard Dien Winfield, *The Just Economy* (London: Routledge, 1988); Ross Zucker, *Democratic Distributive Justice* (Cambridge: Cambridge University Press, 2001).

expenditure of resources – a conception different from the law's customary sense of destruction or dissipatory waste. McCaffery would put in place a progressive cash-flow consumption tax to reduce such nonurgent spending. A far-reaching intellectual and practical consequence of his essay is to presage a substantially trimmed conception of property, which he calls a life-estate conception of ownership.

J. W. Harris considers the other side of the coin: inheritance. In "Inheritance and the Justice Tribunal," he sets up an intriguing problem. His Justice Tribunal sits in an imaginary country that resembles modern Western societies, except that there is no law of testation or intestate succession. Disputes about what should happen to a person's resources upon death are submitted to the Tribunal. Anyone may apply. The Tribunal is directed to consider any principled argument. It may assume that the justifications it gives would support decisions in a class of disputes similar to the present one. Beyond that, no kind of argument is ruled out by statute or precedent.

The case considered in Harris's essay is that of Mrs. Jones, a rich widow, who has recently died. The following submit claims to all or part of her resources: (1) her daughter, a childless woman married to a wealthy man; (2) a penniless artist patronized by Mrs. Jones; (3) an acquaintance whom Mrs. Jones promised would inherit her property; (4) a neighbor who rendered Mrs. Jones valuable help without pay; (5) the spokesperson for workers at a factory owned by Mrs. Jones that is in danger of failing; and (6) an official from the Treasury.

Three judges on the Justice Tribunal render opinions on the distribution of the estate of Mrs. Jones: Libertarian, C.J., Communitarian, J., and Egalitarian, J. Unsurprisingly, the judges disagree, and their opinions illustrate strikingly different approaches to inheritance. The opinions provide material for Harris's reflections on the case in the balance of his essay. He deals at length with two main concerns.

One is "the historical-entitlement deficit" that infects the opinion of Libertarian, C.J. Harris claims that, from the perspective of a pure historical-entitlement theory, the state is barred from first occupancy of ownerless resources. He also argues that such theories give no account of how resources, made ownerless on a death, could in practice be subject to first occupancy by private persons – especially if the resources consist of intangible items like bank accounts and shares in corporations. Here Harris offers critical assessments of the views of Richard A. Epstein and Hillel Steiner.

The other main concern is "the egalitarian crunch" that affects in different ways the opinions of Communitarian, J., and Egalitarian, J. These judges are radically at odds about which, if any, of the obligations of decedents should be taken into account when their resources are distributed. Harris uses these opinions as a jumping-off place to examine recent philosophical work on inheritance, especially that of D. W. Haslett.

Harris's essay not only is a splendid vehicle for getting students to think about inheritance but also carries a powerful message regarding the best way to think about it. He argues that single-principle or single-track approaches to inheritance are bound to fail. The stereotypical visions of the three judges show as much. The antidote to such overly simple ways of thinking, about property generally and inheritance in particular, is to recognize that one needs a mix of property-specific reasons of justice to solve problems of institutional design.

The last two essays in this volume deal with intellectual property. Seana Valentine Shiffrin uses a philosophical microscope to draw some unexpected conclusions about Lockean approaches to the subject. William Fisher employs a wide-angle legal and economic lens to give a broad picture of the current terrain of thinking about intellectual property.

In "Lockean Arguments for Private Intellectual Property," Shiffrin challenges the popular conception that Lockean justificatory foundations provide strong support for robust, private intellectual property rights. She argues that the nature of intellectual works makes them less, rather than more, susceptible to Lockean justifications for private appropriation.

As a matter of interpretation, Shiffrin explores a theory that she regards as *Lockean* but not necessarily *Locke's* own views. Those views may not be recoverable, and even if they are they may not be the philosophically soundest way of developing his core ideas. Shiffrin takes Locke's texts seriously. But she tries to construct the most promising arguments that jibe with his main ideas and motivations, and relegates to a lower place his less central views and remarks. Because her chief interest is philosophical, she deemphasizes some features of the seventeenth-century background and the ideological and theological commitments of some present-day interpreters of Locke.

She develops a Lockean theory of property that emphasizes his starting point of the initial common ownership of resources as a concrete expression of the equal standing of, and community relationship among, all people. Departures from the system of common ownership are justified, Locke argues, when private appropriation is necessary to make full, effective use of the property. While this may be true of material resources whose use depends upon exclusive use or whose effective management depends on exclusive control, it is not true of most intellectual products. They may be used simultaneously by more than one person. Furthermore, their value is usually enhanced, rather than diminished, through free, nonexclusive, shared, common use. She concludes there is a Lockean presumption *against* natural, private rights over intellectual property.

A salient contribution of Shiffrin's essay is its identification of three different possible understandings of the intellectual commons. First, the commons embraces all intellectual products; authors discover and take products out of the commons, but neither create nor refine them. Second, the commons includes only the materials – such as ideas, values, and literary and musical themes – for intellectual products; authors not only discover these materials but express them and their interconnections in publicly accessible and indeed sometimes unique ways. Third, the commons is void of intellectual products; authors invent them. Shiffrin dissects the strengths and weaknesses of each of these understandings. She also takes note of the plausible hybrid view that the best characterization of the commons pivots on the type of intellectual product under discussion.

In "Theories of Intellectual Property," Fisher examines four theories that currently dominate scholarship concerning the law governing copyrights, patents, trademarks, and trade secrets. Utilitarian theorists attempt to balance optimally the power of these laws to stimulate creativity and their concomitant tendency to curtail public enjoyment of the creations they induce. Labor theorists advocate adjustments of these laws that will properly reward artists and inventors for their intellectual labors, without worsening the positions of other people. Personality theorists justify these laws either on the ground that they shield from appropriation or modification artifacts through which authors and artists have expressed their "wills," or on the ground that they create social and economic conditions conducive to creative intellectual activity, which in turn is important to human flourishing. Finally, social-planning theorists see in these laws opportunities to foster a just and attractive culture, including a rich democratic discourse.

Fisher argues that the content and prominence of the four theories derives from a combination of three circumstances: (1) their correspondence to lines of argument that have long figured in constitutional provisions, case reports, and preambles to legislation; (2) the influence of analogous divisions within contemporary political philosophy; and (3) the popularity of comparable perspectives among legal scholars concerned with property rights in land.

He then explores gaps, conflicts, and ambiguities in the four theories. The utilitarian approach is hobbled, Fisher suggests, by the lack of information necessary to make it operational, the impracticability of simultaneously stimulating optimal amounts of intellectual creativity and optimal levels of engagement in other forms of socially valuable work, and the incompatibility of the measures necessary to reduce various types of wastefully rivalrous inventive activity. Labor theorists, in Fisher's judgment, have trouble convincingly connecting their claims to Locke's original theory of property rights, defining morally worthy "intellectual labor," identifying "the commons" from which intellectual laborers must be able to derive their raw materials, interpreting the famous Lockean "proviso," dealing with the equally notorious problem of proportionality between labor and reward, and deriving plausible recommendations for doctrinal reform from their analyses. Personality theory is hampered, Fisher thinks, by the divergence of the many different ways in which property rights in general and intellectual-property rights in particular might conduce to human flourishing, by the thinness of the conceptions of selfhood on which the theory depends, and by unresolved debates among its principal practitioners. These debates concern such issues as how much control is legitimately exercised by creators over their creations once they have been transferred to others; whether creators' rights may be legitimately alienated; and how to specify the scope of defensible privacy interests. Lastly, Fisher contends that social-planning theorists have comparable difficulties formulating a vision of a just and attractive culture and then extracting from that vision determinate recommendations concerning the ideal shape of legal rules governing the creation and use of art, music, and inventions.

Yet Fisher's vision is neither nihilistic nor unremittingly skeptical, for the final section of his essay shows that, despite these formidable difficulties, the theories are valuable for at least two reasons. First, they have proved useful in identifying nonobvious solutions to specific doctrinal problems, such as the proper scope of the "right of publicity" and the legitimacy of price discrimination in the marketing of intellectual products. Second, they help foster socially and politically valuable conversations among the various institutions responsible for the shaping of intellectual property law.

No single theme unites these essays, nor does any single political commitment animate them, but their variety and vitality make clear that much of interest resides in contemporary thinking about property.

1

Property, Honesty, and Normative Resilience

JEREMY WALDRON

I. Introduction

What is the relation between property and honesty? Fairly straightforward, one would think. In times past, "honesty" was used often as a general term for virtue or honor, encompassing chastity, generosity, and decorum. But according to the *Oxford English Dictionary,* its prevailing modern meaning is "[u]prightness of disposition and conduct; integrity, truthfulness, straightforwardness: the quality opposed to lying, cheating, or stealing."[1] So, if stealing is one of the things to which the quality denoted by "honesty" is characteristically opposed, then to that extent "property" and "honesty" are correlative terms. To steal is to take somebody's property – that is, an object that, under the rules of property, he has the right to possess – with the intention of permanently depriving him of it (what lawyers call the *animus furandi*). To be disposed not to steal means that one is disposed not to violate the rules of property in this way. To be honest – in this sense of honesty – is to respect the rules of property.

But respect *which* rules of property? The *existing* rules in society, currently in force – however unjust or oppressive? Or the rules of property in so far as they are regarded as fair? "Honesty" also has the meaning of "fairness and straightforwardness of conduct."[2] Does it pull us in two directions here? Is the man who violates an unjust property right with the intention of permanently depriving an undeserving "proprietor" of some goods he "owns" dishonest? Is this even a marginal case for the concept of dishonesty? Or do "honest" and "dishonest" go unequivocally with the positive law of property (leaving it perhaps a further question whether dishonesty is always a vice or always wrong, all things considered)?

Earlier versions of this paper were presented at conferences in Los Angeles and Wellington. I am grateful to Stephen Munzer and Maurice Goldsmith for their comments on those occasions.
1 "Honesty," I.3.d., *Oxford English Dictionary* (Internet Edition).
2 "Honesty," 2.a., *Webster's Ninth New Collegiate Dictionary* (Springfield: Merriam Webster, 1991), p. 579.

If it *is* a marginal case, then what tends to make the difference at the margin? Is the taking[3] less dishonest depending on its manner, depending on the motive, depending on the extent of the injustice, or depending on whether there is an appeal to some alternative set of existing property rights (say, from the past)? Some might say, for example, that there is necessarily something furtive or deceitful about dishonesty, so that an open taking of something when property rules are contested is to that extent less dishonest. Or they may say that even if the existing allocation of property is unfair, it matters whether or not the taker is motivated by personal greed: although he took from the rich, Robin Hood was not dishonest inasmuch as he gave what he took to the poor. Or, if one "steals" for personal use, it may make a difference whether it is personal use to satisfy a mere want or personal use to satisfy desperate need, particularly if a case can be made that the society's neglect of such need is itself the ground of the injustice. Finally, it may make a difference whether the taker is attacking existing property rights purely on the basis of his own utopian theory of justice, or whether he is attacking them in the name of some alternative set of property rights that was established and existed in the society in the recent past. In his famous study *Whigs and Hunters,* E. P. Thompson notes that a lot of what was condemned in eighteenth-century England as poaching, stealing, and trespass was regarded by the perpetrators as the vindication of traditional property:

What was often at issue was not property, supported by law, against no-property; it was alternative definitions of property-rights: for the landowner, enclosure – for the cottager, common rights; for the forest officialdom, "preserved grounds" for the deer; for the foresters the right to take turf.[4]

In this context, the defenders of traditional rights would not regard themselves as thieves nor their takings as dishonest, however much their opponents tried to stigmatize them in those terms.

2. Two Types of Judgments

We are imagining that something that is officially regarded as Y's private property is taken by another individual X, without Y's consent, in circum-stances where there is reason to question the justice of the official distribution.

In each of the aspects I have mentioned – manner, motive, need, extent of the injustice, reference to a set of traditional rights – one can imagine a scale. For example, one might locate a given taking on a scale that runs from

---

3 I use "taking" as a neutral term; it refers to any appropriation of a resource by a person other than the officially designated owner, accompanied by the intention permanently to deprive the officially designated owner of the resource, whether that appropriation is morally justified or thought to be morally justified or not.

4 See E. P. Thompson, *Whigs and Hunters: The Origin of the Black Act* (Harmondsworth: Penguin Books, 1977), p. 261.

completely deceitful takings through various degrees of furtiveness in the direction of takings that are unabashedly public. Although there may be a point on this scale at which a taking ceases to be regarded as dishonest, ceases even to be regarded as theft, there is also likely to be a range of points on the scale at which the action *would* be regarded as dishonest, notwithstanding the question about injustice. In some circumstances, it is dishonest to openly take property that is unjustly held. Or, to put it more carefully, there is a range of cases in which the condemnation of an open taking as dishonest does not depend on any judgment about the justification of the property right in question. One may withhold judgment on the latter issue, but still unequivocally condemn the taking as dishonest in the cases within this range. The existence of such a range of cases, I shall call, "*the normative resilience of property.*"[5]

Normative resilience refers here to the way in which certain normative judgments (such as judgments about honesty and dishonesty) by which property arrangements are upheld are insulated from other normative judgments about the property arrangements (such as judgments about their justice or injustice, their justification or lack of justification). The concept of normative resilience indicates a discontinuity between two types of normative judgment associated with an institution: (1) judgments concerning the justification of the institution, and (2) judgments concerning individual conduct in relation to the institution. Resilience is the phenomenon whereby judgments of type 2, although they are predicated upon the institution, nevertheless remain unaffected by judgments of type 1 that are adverse to the institution. A resilient institution continues to exert itself normatively through its type 2 judgments, notwithstanding the fact that it is discredited at the type 1 level. Thus, a resilient institution of property that everyone regards as unfair may yet support judgments of honesty and dishonesty, just as a resilient institution of punishment that everyone regards as unjust in its operations may still have the effect of stigmatizing "crooks."

III. Normative Resilience Clarified

A few general points help to clarify the concept of normative resilience. First, the phenomenon does not depend on there being different communities making the judgments of type 1 and type 2, respectively. Of course, that is very common: The people who condemn the taking as dishonest are not the same as those who condemn the property system as unjust. But I am interested, under the heading of "resilience," in cases where the judgments of both types are made by the same people. Or, rather, I am interested in cases where the type 2 judgment is made – by whoever makes it – in a way that is not dependent upon

---

5 I used the phrase "institutional resilience" to refer to something similar in Jeremy Waldron, "Property, Justification and Need," *Canadian Journal of Law and Jurisprudence,* 6 (1993: 185–215, at 186–9 and 205–06.

or vulnerable to any judgment that *they* may make of type 1. Moreover, I am interested in cases where this is not simply a failure of inference. A person may believe that all theft is dishonorable but fail to draw the conclusion that burglary is dishonorable (because they forget that burglary is a form of theft.) Maybe in the end that is the proper explanation of normative resilience – too many people are failing to draw appropriate conclusions from the judgments of type 1 that they make. But it may not be the best explanation: It is possible or arguable that there is really is a logical gap between judgments of type 1 and judgments of type 2. An exploration of normative resilience is an exploration of that hypothesis (and of what would follow from it).

Second, the judgments of type 1 that interest us here may be either general judgments or particular judgments. In *Punishment and Responsibility,* H. L. A. Hart distinguished between the general justifying aim of an institution and the particular distributive rules by which it operates. He thought, for example, that an institution of punishment might be utilitarian in its general justifying aim but still operate by retributive principles. And he offered a similar analysis of property:

[I]n the case of property we should distinguish between . . . the question why and in what circumstances it is a *good* institution to maintain, and the question in what ways individuals may become *entitled* to acquire property, and *how much* they should be allowed to acquire.[6]

Hart criticized John Locke – unfairly in my view[7] – for thinking that the same considerations ("the labor theory") could be used to answer both questions. The interdependence or otherwise of these two questions in the case of property is an interesting issue (as it is also in the case of punishment),[8] but this is not what interests me under the heading of "normative resilience." For these purposes, I am classifying both of Hart's questions under type 1. That is, I am interested in the way in which judgments of honesty and dishonesty are insulated from a general judgement that a whole system of property is unjustified (a communist argument, for example, against private property), and from a general judgment that the distribution of private property in a particular society is inequitable, and from a particular judgment that the distribution of some specific object or resource is unjust.

This explains why a famous passage from David Hume should not be regarded as an illustration of normative resilience. Hume asked us to consider that

---

6 H. L. A. Hart, *Punishment and Responsibility: Essays in the Philosophy of Law* (Oxford: Clarendon Press, 1968), p. 4.
7 See Jeremy Waldron, *The Right to Private Property* (Oxford: Clarendon Press, 1988), pp. 331–2.
8 See Waldron, *Right to Private Property,* pp. 323–42.

A single act of justice is frequently contrary to public interest; and were it to stand alone, without being follow'd by other acts, may, in itself, be very prejudicial to society. When a man of merit, of a beneficent disposition, restores a great fortune to a miser, or a seditious bigot, he has acted justly and laudably, but the public is the real sufferer. . . . But however single acts of justice may be contrary, either to public or private interest, 'tis certain, that the whole plan or scheme is highly conducive, or indeed absolutely requisite, both to the support of society, and the well-being of every individual. 'Tis impossible to separate the good from the ill.[9]

Certainly Hume will figure in the account I want to offer (in Section IV). But this passage concerns the sort of looseness between general and particular justificatory judgments that Hart was talking about, not the sort of looseness between justificatory judgments, on the one hand, and judgments pertaining to individual conduct, on the other. Hume's case would indicate a case of normative resilience if one were to conclude that in fact there is *no* justification for returning the fortune to the miser, but *still* felt dishonest about keeping it.

What about generality at the level of the type 2 judgment? Is what I am calling "normative resilience" anything more than a reflection of our tendency to apply judgments of honesty, dishonesty, and so on without regard to the circumstances of particular cases? Certainly we *may* make our type 2 judgments in this coarse-grained way. But whether such judgments are resilient in the sense that interests me will depend on what happens when attention is focused insistently on particular details.[10]

Third, although I have concentrated so far on the relation between justificatory judgments directed toward an institution (what I call type 1 judgments) and judgments that relate to the conduct or character of those who are constrained by the institution (what I call type 2 judgments), the latter class is broader than I have so far indicated. Under the type 2 heading, I am interested in any judgments that pertain to individual conduct, character, or condition that appear to be derived (in some sense) from an institutional arrangement (such as property), but that exhibit a certain looseness in that derivation relationship that enables them to survive despite the discrediting of the institutional arrangement from which they are supposedly derived. "Honest" and "dishonest" have been our paradigms of type 2 judgments in relation to the institution of private property. Terms such as "theft," thief," "stealing," "pilfering," and so on, fall into the same class: Like "dishonest," they seem appropriately to characterize actions that violate property rules even when those property rules are thought to lack moral justification. But it is not only terms of condemnation that have this resilience. Also some of the terms connoting ownership seem to work this way as well. I may think of a piece of land as "mine" or as "belonging to me," and think of myself as its "owner," without thinking that the rules that designate me as the owner have any moral justification.

9 David Hume, *A Treatise of Human Nature,* ed. L. A. Selby-Bigge (Oxford: Clarendon Press, 1888), p. 497 (Book III, Part 2, Section ii).
10 I am grateful to Jim Harris for this point.

The general characteristic of type 2 judgments is that they apply to individuals (or their actions, relations, or circumstances) what are sometimes referred to as "thick" moral predicates – in this case predicates whose descriptive meaning is related to certain institutional arrangements.[11] We have been working with predicates of this kind associated with property. But we can list other such predicates related to other institutions. For example:

Table 1

Type 1	Type 2
I. *Private property* is morally justified.	X is a *thief, dishonest,* etc. Object O *belongs* to Y.
II. There is a moral justification for *the state*.	X is a *traitor,* or a *terrorist.* Y has *authority.*
III. C is the *true religion.*	X is a *heretic.*
IV. *Traditional marriage* is a good institution.	S is a *fornicator.* H is an *adulterer.* G *deserted* W.
V. There is a justification for *aristocracy.*	Y is of *noble birth.* That man is not Y; he is *Sir* Y. X does not know *his place.*
VI. There is a justification for *military discipline.*	Y *orders* X to do A. X is *insubordinate.*
VII. The *criminal justice* system works fairly.	X is a *crook.* Y is *innocent.*

In each case the type 2 predicates cannot be understood without reference to the institution denoted in the type 1 judgments. Yet, in each case it is an open question how resilient the type 2 judgments are, that is, the extent to which their proper use does not depend upon the speaker's acceptance of (something like) the corresponding type 1 judgment. In line III, for example, the judgment that someone is a heretic does not seem to be normatively resilient. It is not a judgment that would be made except by someone who accepted the truth of the orthodoxy relative to which the alleged "heresy" was defined. Sometimes one term associated with a given institution may figure in resilient judgments,

---

11 Not all thick moral predicates have these institutional connections. In some, the descriptive element refers to types of actions and responses to situations that are being commended or condemned (e.g., virtue words such as "courage"). For doubts about the ability to isolate the descriptive meaning of a thick term from its normative force, see John McDowell, "Noncognitivism and Rule-Following," in S. Holtzman and C. Leich, eds., *Wittgenstein: To Follow a Rule* (London: Routledge, 1981), pp. 141–62, especially pp. 144 ff.

while others do not. In line V, a person who rejected the legitimacy of the aristocratic class system might well refuse to talk of someone's "not knowing his place." But he might continue nevertheless to refer to a person who has been knighted as "Sir John," or whatever.

The other point I want to stress at this stage is that the type 2 predicates that interest us are normative or evaluative predicates, used in a way that carries their ordinary normative or evaluative force. I am not interested in ironic or what are sometimes referred to as inverted-commas uses of type 2 predicates,[12] as when Martin Luther talks of "we heretics" or a social rebel acknowledges with bitter irony that he has forgotten "his place." The resilience of ironic or inverted commas uses of type 2 predicates is definitional and uninteresting. What is challenging, however, is a type 2 judgment retaining its ordinary evaluative force in circumstances where the corresponding type 1 judgment has been repudiated or discredited.

Table 2

(1) The private property system around here is just.
(2) Taking that food would be stealing.
(3) X's baby needs that food or it will die.
(4) All things considered, X ought to take the food.

Notice I say *"ordinary"* evaluative force; I do not say that the evaluation implicit in the type 2 judgment must be conclusory. One could judge some action dishonest without concluding that it was the wrong thing to do, all things considered. Maybe there are circumstances in which one *ought* to be a thief. There is some complication here depending on how one analyzes prima facie judgments and moral conflict. For example, consider the four judgments in Table 2. Normative resilience concerns the relation between 1 and 2. Somebody who rejects 1 might nevertheless accept 2; but such a person may also accept 4. There are two ways to understand the relation between 2 and 4. First, one might say that the evaluative force of 2 is merely provisional, pending the final judgment 4; once 4 is adopted, one abandons the condemnation implicit in 2. Alternatively, one might say that even if 4 is adopted, 2 still retains some of its evaluative force. Moral conflicts such as those between 2 and 4 are not always neatly resolved, without moral remainder, so to speak.[13] One may appropriately feel bad about doing A, even while acknowledging that A is, all things considered, the appropriate thing to do. On this second analysis, there is

12 See R. M. Hare, *The Language of Morals* (Oxford: Oxford University Press, 1952), pp. 124 and 167 f.

13 See Bernard Williams, "Ethical Consistency," in *Problems of the Self* (Cambridge: Cambridge University Press, 1973), pp. 166–86.

no particular problem in specifying *ordinary evaluative force* so far as normative resilience is concerned. The ordinary moral force of "stealing" includes *inter alia* its propensity to hang over as a moral remainder in moral conflicts such as that in our example. But suppose one adopts the first pattern of analysis, giving evaluative force to 2 only provisionally, pending the final judgment 4. Then, whether 2 should be regarded as normatively resilient in our sense depends on whether the rejection of 1 is decisive in yielding 4. If one says "On the one hand this would be stealing, but on the other hand, the system of property is unjust; therefore 4," then 2 is not normatively resilient. But if 4 is based on something like 3, understood as a moral consideration of independent force, then what I have called the resilience of 2 is undefeated. On this analysis, its resilience consists not in its always having evaluative force, but in its evaluative force being liable to be canceled out only by independent considerations of a certain weight.

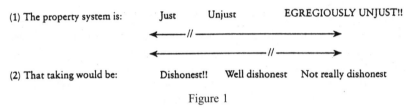

Figure 1

Also, resilience and normative force may be matters of degree. Remember that in the first paragraph of section 2, I stressed the existence of a *range* of cases in which the force of a type 2 judgment might vary, dwindle and finally peter out, depending on factors like motivation, openness, and so on. Some of these scalar considerations are independent of the relevant type 1 judgment. (They concern, for example, the manner in which the conduct in question is performed.) Others may *not* be independent of the type 1 judgment: We might say, for example, that if the injustice of the institution is really egregious, then the corresponding type 2 judgment must eventually be withdrawn. Thus, it is possible that the evaluative force of the type 2 judgment does vary in a way that depends on variations in the type 1 judgment. But the type 2 judgment may *still* be regarded as resilient if the two scales fail to line up perfectly, as, for example, in Figure 1. In Figure 1, the judgment about dishonesty is somewhat resilient, because although it fades depending on how unjust the property system is, it is not simply abandoned as soon as the property system is condemned.

III. Positivism and Normative Resilience

The examples given in Table 1 included many in which the type 1 institution is a legal institution. And the analysis we are giving raises certain issues in regard to our understanding of the normative ramifications of positive law. Consider, for example, the judgments in Table 3. Clearly the type 2 judgments in Table 3

Table 3

VII.A: Our *laws* are in general just.	This case is a *binding precedent.*
VII.B: It is good to have a *legal system.*	That act would be *illegal.*
	This is a *valid* will.
	Properly interpreted, the statute means . . .
	X is a *criminal.*

are in *some* sense resilient, relative to judgments like VII.A. Even in a legal system, most of whose provisions are unjust, we can still distinguish (by the system's own lights) between valid and invalid wills, binding and nonbinding precedents, lawful and unlawful acts, and proper and improper interpretations of legal sources.[14]

In a rather crude sense of legal positivism, normative resilience is simply a consequence of legal positivism. Positivism is often caricatured as the thesis that human laws have a claim to our respect simply because of their existence as social phenomena. Existing positive law is to be obeyed, whether we judge it morally right or wrong, according to this (caricatural) form of positivism. To discover that something is *the law,* on this account, is to discover something that has immediate normative consequences for action, whatever independent judgment we might make about it from a moral point of view. Most modern positivists do not hold this version. They know that it is a theory attributed to them by some of their opponents, but they think that in general their opponents err (both in the opponents' own jurisprudence and in the theories they attribute to positivists) by investing concepts like law and legal validity with too much moral weight. Critiques of positivism, said H. L. A. Hart, are often based on "an enormous overvaluation of the importance of the bare fact that a rule may be said to be a valid rule of law."[15] The implication of a positivist jurisprudence, on Hart's view, is not that propositions are to be *respected* or *deferred to* as law by virtue of their social existence, but that they are to be *identified* as law on that basis, leaving it a further question – an independent moral question – what respect, if any, is due to them on that ground or any other.

It follows that although sophisticated legal positivists in the Hart camp might accept the resilience of the type 2 judgments in Table 3, some of them might want to deny that this is to be understood as *normative* resilience. They might say that the type 2 judgments have no normative force whatsoever. They

14 Cf. Ronald Dworkin, *Law's Empire* (Cambridge: Harvard University Press, 1986), pp. 101–08.
15 See H. L. A. Hart, "Positivism and the Separation of Law and Morals," reprinted in his collection *Essays in Jurisprudence and Philosophy* (Oxford: Clarendon Press, 1983), p. 75 (criticizing Lon Fuller's jurisprudence). See also H. L. A. Hart, *The Concept of Law,* 2nd ed. (Oxford: Clarendon Press, 1994), pp. 203–07.

tell us about the law, or they express legal conclusions, but they are not used to commend, condemn, evaluate, or prescribe. The positivist's judgment that some action is illegal, for example, tells us nothing about whether he thinks that, from the moral point of view, it ought to be done. Moreover, to use it in this purely descriptive way – to indicate what the law is – is not to use the term "illegal" ironically or in inverted commas or in any other way that varies from its ordinary use. The claim of these positivists is that terms like this are not ordinarily used to express moral judgments.

Four issues need to be untangled here. First, it is arguable that some of the judgments that I have listed on the right-hand side of Table 3 as type 2 judgments in fact belong on the left (with the type 1 judgments). They may stand in the same relation to VII.A or VII.B as – in our earlier discussion – principles of property distribution (or particular distributions) stand to the general justifying aim of property. I am not sure what to think about this.

Second, although it is true that terms like "illegal" are not normally used to express moral judgments, that does not mean that their use has no normative aspect at all. Participants in a legal system usually deploy type 2 judgments in a conduct-guiding way, by which I mean that there is characteristically what H. L. A. Hart called an *internal aspect* associated with the use of terms like "illegal," "valid," and so on, and that aspect is certainly normative.[16] An outsider – an anthropologist or a comparative lawyer, for example – may not use these terms normatively. But they could not function in legal judgments unless they were used normatively by a community of participants in the legal system;[17] and the anthropologist and comparative lawyer could not infer that they were legal terms unless they noticed them being used normatively in such a community.

Third, some modern legal positivists hold a view that is called *normative positivism*. They believe that it is (morally) a good thing that judgments of legal validity and invalidity, lawful and unlawful conduct should be able to be made without using moral judgment.[18] (Bentham certainly fell into this category, and so, I think, did Hobbes.) That belief is presumably dependent upon a type 1 judgment such as VII.B in Table 3. The normative positivist view is roughly this: It is (morally speaking) a good thing that we have a system of positive law, for that enables us to judge statutes, wills, and so on as valid or invalid without making moral judgments. Now, it is unlikely that type 2 judgments grounded in *this* way would be very resilient. Once one abandons VII.B,

---

16 See Hart, *The Concept of Law,* pp. 88 ff.
17 Ibid., pp. 110–17. But as Hart emphasizes, they need not be used normatively by *all* participants in the legal system. Their normative use among a corps of officials may be sufficient. Ibid., pp. 116–17. See also the account of "detached" uses of legal terminology in Joseph Raz, *Practical Reason and Norms* (London: Hutchinson, 1975), pp. 170–77.
18 For normative versions of positivism, see Gerald J. Postema, *Bentham and the Common Law Tradition* (Oxford: Clarendon Press, 1986), pp. 328–36.

one is likely to divest the type 2 judgments in Table 3 of any specifically moral content. If they have any normative content left at all, it will be that discussed in the previous paragraph (i.e., the ordinary internal aspect).

Fourth, whether we are talking about the normativity associated with the internal aspect of law, or the moral normativity that is associated with legal judgments in a jurisprudence of normative positivism, it is unlikely to be an all-things-considered normativity. There will be a further question of how much respect, ultimately, is owed to the law as such.[19] In other words, the issues that arose with regard to the judgments set out in Table 2 will also arise with regard to legal judgments. Consider, for example, the following variation on Table 2:

Table 4

(1) Our laws are just and it is a good thing that we have a legal system.
(2) Action A is illegal.
(3) Action A is required by my religion.
(4) All things considered, I ought to perform action A.

Someone may accept 1 and 2, and yet follow 4 because of 3. Or someone may accept 2 but not 1, and yet still follow 4 because of 3. The hypothesis of normative resilience with regard to positive law would require that, in this sort of case, there must be a looseness between 1 and 2 which is quite independent of whatever looseness there is between 2 and 4. For someone who accepts 4, 2 can have a normative force independent of 1 only if 4 is based on 3 and 3 is not the reason for rejecting 1.

This tangle of considerations – particularly the third consideration, about normative positivism – has convinced me that it would be unwise to attempt to establish any *general* hypothesis of the normative resilience of legal judgments.

It seems that some legal or legally based judgments are normatively more resilient than others. In Table 1, for instance, the difference we noted between example I ("justified property"/"honesty") and example III ("true religion"/ "heresy") would seem to work whether or not law is involved in example III. Even in countries with a legally established religious orthodoxy, religious dissenters did not regard themselves as heretics, and probably not even as "guilty of heresy." Similarly with example II: In countries with antiterrorist legislation, those whom legal officials designate as terrorists usually regard themselves as "freedom fighters," not terrorists, once they reject the legitimacy of the existing state and legal system.

19 See Dworkin, *Law's Empire*, pp. 96–8 and 108–113.

In the present paper, I want to concentrate particularly on the normative resilience of judgments associated with property. Although private property is a legal institution and has a legal existence, and although the resilience (such as it is) of positive law no doubt contributes something to the resilience of judgments about "stealing," "dishonesty," and "belonging," there seems to be something particular about property that lends it extra resilience in a way that is not associated with all legal institutions or all the normative judgments that they generate.

V. Justifying the Normative Resilience of Property

In this section, I shall explore a possible line of justification for the normative resilience of property, a line of justification that may also help explain the distinction noted above between property and some of the other legal examples we have been considering. In the final section – section VI – I shall consider what (justified) normative resilience would imply in regard to the overall enterprise of type 1 justification in political philosophy.

First, a preliminary point about justification, explanation, and ideology. An explanation of the normative resilience of property may or may not justify it. The explanation may be purely psychological, in which case what appears to be normative resilience will still seem like a sort of mistake unless some other, justifying explanation is forthcoming. A purely psychological account may tell us something about the way an ideology works; but it will tell us nothing in itself about the rights and wrongs of property. However, it is also possible that a psychological explanation – though in itself incomplete as a justification – is nevertheless part of an account that justifies normative resilience. Alternatively, it is possible that a psychological account of what appears to be normative resilience tells us something about the tasks of justificatory theory. It may tell us that those tasks are impossible and fatuous, perhaps because almost everything that we think of as justification turns out to be the psychological residue of ideology. Or (as I shall argue at the very end of the paper) it may tell us that the burden of justification is actually heavier than we thought and the task of justifying such an institution against its critics harder than that of justifying an institution that lacks this apparent resilience. That is, the more resilient an institution, the more harm it may do if it is unjust; so the heavier the burden that must be discharged in its initial justification. That will be my thesis.

It is not hard to think of a psychological explanation for the resilience of a judgment like "This farm belongs to me." Someone who has been designated officially as the owner of a given piece of land is likely to have actual control of the land: He will know it intimately, he may inhabit it with his family, cultivate it, earn his living from it, care about it, and regard it as part of the wealth that he relies on for his own security and that of his descendants. He will be able to point to features of the land where his work and his initiative have made a difference, so that the land will not only seem like his; it may even look like his (in the way that a work of art looks like the artist's). These effects are likely to accrue to him by virtue of the operation of the system of property as positive law quite independently of whether it is just or unjust, or whether he or anyone else regards it as just or unjust.[20]

There is some interesting discussion of this phenomenon in David Hume's *Treatise of Human Nature.* In Book III of the *Treatise,* Hume noted that the effects we have just been discussing are likely to produce something like a sense of "mine" and "thine," which is not simply a cloak for mere utility or advantage.

Such is the effect of custom, that it not only reconciles us to anything we have long enjoy'd, but even gives us an affection for it, and makes us prefer it to other objects, which may be more valuable, but are less known to us. What has long lain under our eye, and has often been employ'd to our advantage, that we are always the most unwilling to part with; but can easily live without possessions, which we never have enjoy'd, and are not accustom'd to.[21]

It is, as one would expect Hume to say, a matter of constant conjunction and its effect on the imagination:

When two objects appear in a close relation to each other, the mind is apt to ascribe to them any additional relation, in order to compleat the union; and this inclination is so strong, as often to make us run into errors (such as that of the conjunction of thought and matter) if we find that they can serve to that purpose. . . . Since, therefore, we can feign a new relation, and even an absurd one, in order to compleat any union, 'twill easily be imagined, that if there be any relations which depend on the mind, 'twill readily conjoin them to any preceding relation, and unite, by a new bond, such objects as have already an union in the fancy.[22]

Hume uses this in the *Treatise* to explain why it is natural to associate the artificial relation of property to the relation between a person and thing established by mere possession and occupancy in a state of nature.[23] But it may also

---

20 These effects are probably less likely to accrue, however, or likely to accrue to a lesser extent, if the property system seems precarious on account of its (perceived) injustice – that is, if its (perceived) injustice means that some officials are beginning not to treat the provisions of positive law, in this regard, as normative for them in any sense at all. This may happen in an advanced revolutionary situation, where crucial players are beginning to defect from the established legal system.

21 Hume, *Treatise,* 503 (Book III, Part 2, Section iii).

22 Hume, *Treatise,* p. 504 n (Book III, Part 2, Section iii).

23 Hume, *Treatise,* pp. 504–5 (Book III, Part 2, Section iii): "And as property forms a relation betwixt a person and an object, 'tis natural to found it on some preceding relation; and as property is nothing but a constant possession, secur'd by the laws of society, 'tis natural to add it to the present possession, which is a relation that resembles it." See also Jeremy Waldron, "The Advantages and Difficulties of the Humean Theory of Property," *Social Philosophy & Policy,* 11, no. 2 (Summer 1994): 85–123.

be used to explain why a relation of affection established by law (without regard to the law's moral content) may also be associated with – in Hume's terms, be completed by – a sense of righteous possession, which often goes together with property systems when they *are* morally justified.[24]

Jeremy Bentham noticed something similar in explaining why a system of escheat was better, psychologically, for those who suffered under it than a system of estate duties:

Under a tax on successions, a man is led in the first place to look upon the whole in a general view as his own: He is then called upon to give up a part. . . . His imagination thus begins with embracing the whole: then comes the law putting in for its part, and forcing him to quit his hold. This he cannot do without pain. . . .[25]

If, by contrast, we "keep from him the whole, so keeping it from him that there shall never have been a time when he expected to receive it," then there is no disappointment and no hardship.[26]

Try the experiment upon a hungry child: give him a small cake, telling him after he has got it, or even before, that he is to give back part of it. Another time give him a whole cake, equal to what was left to him of the other and no more, and let him enjoy it undiminished – will there be a doubt which cake afforded him the purest pleasure?[27]

In Bentham's discussion, we begin to edge the psychological account in the direction of a justification. For Bentham, it is not just a matter of the imagination embracing what positive law guarantees, it is also a matter of pleasure and pain, which of course are the currency of moral justification in Bentham's utilitarian theory. The child with the smaller cake gets more pleasure than the child with a larger cake that is vulnerable to confiscation. The person who has to give up what he expected to hold cannot do so, Bentham says, without pain. And that pain accrues whether or not the giving-up is morally required. What matters is that he expected to be able to hold it; that is what hurts when property is overturned. We are dealing here, in other words, with expectations – utilities projected into the future:

[W]e must consider that man is not like the animals, limited to the present, whether as respects suffering or enjoyment; but that he is susceptible of pains and pleasures by

24 See also Hume's observation in Book II of the *Treatise:* "If justice . . . be a virtue, which has a natural and original influence upon the human mind, property may be look'd upon as a particular species of *causation;* whether we consider the liberty it gives the proprietor to operate as he please upon the object, or the advantages, which he reaps from it. 'Tis the same case, if justice, according to the system of certain philosophers, should be esteem'd an artificial and not a natural virtue. For then honour, and custom and civil laws supply the place of natural conscience, and produce, in some degree, the same effects." Hume, *Treatise,* p. 310 (Book II, Part 1, Section x).
25 Jeremy Bentham, "Supply Without Burthen," in *Jeremy Bentham's Economic Writings,* ed. W. Stark (London: George Allen and Unwin, 1952), vol. 1, p. 291.
26 Ibid.
27 Ibid., p. 292n.

anticipation; and that it is not enough to secure him from actual loss, but it is necessary also to guarantee him, as far as possible, against future loss.[28]

Property, says Bentham, is entirely a matter of expectations: "In matters of property in general, . . . *hardship* depends upon *disappointment; disappointment* upon *expectation; expectation* upon the dispensations, meaning the *known* dispensations of the law."[29]

The justificatory edge of Bentham's argument works as follows. The pains of disappointment that are likely to ensue when something a person has regarded as his property is taken away are much greater than the corresponding pleasures that someone receives when the property is redistributed fairly. Sure, the new owner gets some enjoyment from the resource; but then the old owner lost his enjoyment. Sure, the new owner's enjoyment may be greater than that of the old owner, if we have moved in the direction of a more equal distribution: The law of diminishing marginal utility shows that that is probable.[30] But that extra utility has to be balanced against the specific pains of disappointment, coupled with the impact of the redistribution on others' enjoyment of other resources, which is rendered correspondingly less secure:

To regret for what we have lost is joined inquietude as to what we possess, and even as to what we may acquire. . . . When insecurity reaches a certain point, the fear of losing prevents us from enjoying what we possess already. The care of preserving condemns us to a thousand sad and painful precautions, which yet are always liable to fail of their end. Treasures are hidden or conveyed away. Enjoyment becomes sombre, furtive, and solitary. It fears to show itself, lest cupidity should be informed of a chance to plunder.[31]

As a result, industry is deadened, incentives collapse, and long-term schemes of production become psychologically impossible. It follows, says Bentham, that from a utilitarian point of view, existing property rights must be respected, no matter how unjust or unequal they appear.

When security and equality are in conflict, it will not do to hesitate a moment. Equality must yield. The first is the foundation of life; subsistence, abundance, happiness, everything depends upon it. Equality produces only a certain portion of good. . . . [I]f

28 Jeremy Bentham, "Security and Equality of Property," an extract from Jeremy Bentham, *Principles of the Civil Code,* excerpted in C. B. Macpherson, ed., *Property: Mainstream and Critical Positions* (Oxford: Basil Blackwell, 1978), pp. 41–58, at p. 50. See also Stephen R. Munzer, *A Theory of Property* (Cambridge: Cambridge University Press, 1990), pp. 194–5 and Ryan, *Property and Political Theory,* p. 98.

29 Bentham, "Supply Without Burthen," p. 291 (emphasis in original). Bentham also ventures this observation in "Security and Equality of Property," p. 51: "It is proof of great confusion in the ideas of lawyers, that they have never given any particular attention to a sentiment which exercises so powerful an influence upon human life. The word *expectation* is scarcely found in their vocabulary."

30 For Bentham's discussion of the utilitarian case for equality, see Bentham, "Security and Equality of Property," pp. 46–7.

31 Ibid., p. 54.

property should be overturned with the direct intention of establishing an equality of possessions, the evil would be irreparable. No more security, no more industry, no more abundance! Society would return to the savage state whence it emerged.[32]

So we get a dissonance of the sort we are looking for – between type 2 judgments that are dependent on existing property arrangements, and type 1 judgments that hold that those arrangements are unjust. A system of property may be unjust in the sense that it was an outrage to justice when it was set up, unjust in the sense that it ought to have been set up on a different basis. But once established, the rights and relations it generates take on a moral life of their own. Now it becomes morally wrong to interfere with them, even though it would not have been morally wrong to set up the system of justice on a different basis altogether.

Someone might object that Bentham's argument goes further than driving this wedge between type 1 and type 2 judgments about property. It not only gives type 2 judgments independent support; it establishes in fact a different sort of type 1 argument in favor of existing arrangements, namely, a conservative argument. For, surely, conservative arguments are one class of type 1 argument. Some theories of property are inherently conservative. They argue that private property holdings ought to be respected, not because this is the most efficient way of dealing with material resource, nor because it is an appropriate way of rewarding moral desert, nor because it is required by respect for Lockean entitlements, but because any attempt to change the existing system would be profoundly disruptive. There is something to this. Certainly, the propositions supported by Bentham's principle of respecting established expectations are propositions that apply to governments, legislators, and would-be reformers, and not just to the ordinary beneficiaries of the property system or other private individuals constrained by its rules.

[W]hat ought the legislator to decree respecting the great mass of property already existing? He ought to maintain the distribution as it is actually established. It is this which, under the name of justice, is regarded as his first duty. This is a general and simple rule which applies itself to all states; and which adapts itself to all places, even those of the most opposite character. There is nothing more different than the state of property in America, in England, in Hungary, and in Russia. Generally, in the first of these countries, the cultivator is a proprietor; in the second, a tenant; in the third, attached to the glebe; in the fourth, a slave. However, the supreme principle of security commands the preservation of all these distributions, though their nature is so different, and though they do not produce the same sum of happiness. How make another distribution without taking away from each that which he has? And how despoil any without attacking the security of all?[33]

32 Ibid., p. 57.
33 Ibid.

Still there is a difference between Bentham's position and a purely conservative position. When the opportunity arises to vary property arrangements in a
way that does not produce pains of disappointment, Bentham is in favor of
doing so, and doing so on the basis of principles of justice that are not conservative at all. His proposal to abolish collateral inheritance is a clear example of
this;[34] and Bentham was infuriated by any suggestion that his plan would be
opposed on the grounds of a more pervasive conservatism.

The account we have given is purely utilitarian. But one could imagine
developing a similar account using nonutilitarian ideas. In a number of influential essays, Margaret Radin has argued that respect for existing property rights
is bound up with respect for persons:

Most people possess certain objects they feel are almost part of themselves. These
objects are closely bound up with personhood because they are part of the way we
constitute ourselves as continuing personal entities in the world.[35]

Radin uses the idea to distinguish between claims to property of different
kinds – the claims of landlords and tenants, for example, in disputes about
residential rent control.[36] But clearly it can be used also as an account of
normative resilience: In Radin's example, even if a system of residential rent
control is unjust, particular persons may be so bound up with the tenancies that
they have established on this basis that it would be disrespectful now to them as
persons to expose that identification (of them with their homes) to the vicissi-
tudes of market pricing. And Radin's argument would have the additional
interesting feature that, if the link between property and personhood is established by something long-lived and intimate like residential occupation, landlords cannot claim the benefit of similar resilience for the property rights that
they have at stake in the matter.[37]

Radin seems to think that this personhood argument is Hegelian in prove-
nance:[38] It is an application, she says, of Hegel's argument in the *Philosophy of
Right* about the importance of embodying one's freedom in the external
world.[39] I have argued elsewhere that Hegel's discussion is more like a type 1
argument about property.[40] But clearly there is enough of a conservative edge
to Hegel's political philosophy in general (and enough doubt expressed in his

---

34 See Bentham, "Supply Without Burthen." For a discussion of Bentham's proposal, see Jeremy
    Waldron, "Supply Without Burthen Revisited," *Iowa Law Review,* 82 (1997): 1467–85.
35 Margaret Jane Radin, "Property and Personhood," reprinted in her collection *Reinterpreting
    Property* (Chicago: University of Chicago Press, 1993), pp. 35–71, at p. 36. Note that Radin's
    account also includes a discussion of the fetishistic implications of this at pp. 43–4.
36 Margaret Jane Radin, "Residential Rent Control," in Radin, *Reinterpreting Property,* pp.
    72–97.
37 Radin, "Residential Rent Control," p. 79.
38 Radin, "Property and Personhood," pp. 44–8.
39 G. W. F. Hegel, *Elements of the Philosophy of Right,* ed. Allen Wood (Cambridge: Cambridge
    University Press, 1991), pp. 73 ff. (esp. paragraphs 41–64).
40 See Waldron, *Right to Private Property,* pp. 344–51.

work about the whole business of mounting type 1 arguments), that it would be wrong to neglect this connection.[41] (We will return to Hegel in section V.)

Intriguingly, there is room for a similar argument about personhood in the utilitarian tradition. David Hume pointed out in Book II of the *Treatise,* that "the mention of property naturally carries our thought to the proprietor,"[42] and the constant conjunction account of possession that we considered earlier can easily be associated with Hume's account of personal identity.[43] The connection is made explicit in Bentham's discussion. Expectation, for Bentham, is not just a matter of pleasure or pain projected forward into the future. It is crucial to our being, as selves extended in time:

It is hence that we have the power of forming a general plan of conduct; it is hence that the successive instants which compose the duration of life are not like isolated and independent points, but become continuous parts of a whole. Expectation is a chain which unites our present existence to our future existence. . . .[44]

And he continues, in language worthy of Radin's account or that of Radin's Hegel:

Everything which I possess, or to which I have a title, I consider in my own mind as destined always to belong to me. I make it the basis of my expectations, and of the hopes of those dependent upon me; and I form my plan of life accordingly. Every part of my property may have, in my estimation, besides its intrinsic value, a value of affection – as an inheritance from my ancestors, as the reward of my own labor, or as the future dependence of my children. Everything about it represents to my eye that part of myself which I have put into it – those cares, that industry, that economy which denied itself present pleasures to make provision for the future. Thus our property becomes a part of our being, and cannot be torn from us without rending us to the quick.[45]

Once again, property arrangements will tend to have this effect in constituting people's sense of themselves, whether or not they are justified. It is enough that the property rights in question are established and officially supported. Once that is the case, people will tend to think of the things assigned to them (even the things assigned unjustly to them) as *theirs* and as *belonging to them.* And those claims will seem to the people concerned not just echoes of the positive law, but claims with independent moral force inasmuch as positive property rights have become connected with the basis of their personhood.

So far in this section we have concentrated on a particular kind of type 2 judgment about property – namely, possessors' judgments of things *belonging*

41 See Hegel, *Elements of the Philosophy of Right,* pp. 9–23 (Preface).
42 Hume, *Treatise,* p. 310 (Book II, Part 1, Section x).
43 See Hume, *Treatise,* pp. 251 ff. (Book I, Part 4, Section vi) and 277 ff. (Book II, Part 1, Section ii).
44 Bentham, "Security and Equality of Property," p. 51.
45 Ibid., p. 54.

to them. What about the other end of the stick – people's sense of the distinction between honesty and dishonesty, and the wrongness of stealing? How do we explain and justify the resilience of these judgments in relation to a set of perhaps unjustified property rights?

David Hume offered an account of sorts. Considerations like the ones outlined earlier in this section will explain why those who benefit from existing property rights will develop various terms and modes of vehement condemnation of acts that tend to interfere with those rights. Others will join them in that to the extent that they foresee what they have to lose from a general deadening of industry following from such violations (along the lines that Bentham indicated). That will happen whether or not the system of property was initially justified. Beyond that, Hume reckoned, even when the violation and its effects are quite remote, "it still displeases us; because we consider it as prejudicial to human society, and pernicious to every one that approaches the person guilty of it. We partake of their uneasiness by *sympathy*."[46] Together interest and sympathy will explain the development of virtue- and vice-concepts whose role it is to sustain the existing order of property.

Hume considers the extent to which this may be supplemented by purely political indoctrination. But he doubts that that does much work on its own:

Any artifice of politicians may assist nature in the producing of those sentiments, which she suggests to us, and may even on some occasions, produce alone an approbation or esteem for any particular action; but 'tis impossible it should be the sole cause of the distinction we make betwixt vice and virtue. For if nature did not aid us in this particular, 'twou'd be in vain for politicians to talk of honourable or dishonorable, praiseworthy or blameable. . . . The utmost politicians can perform, is, to extend the natural sentiments beyond their original bounds; but still nature must furnish the materials, and give us some notion of moral distinctions.[47]

The connection between particular property rights and our natural sympathies is for Hume the best explanation of our tendency to mold our own sentiments and those of our children into dispositions of probity and honesty.

We need not accept Hume's particular account of the origin of moral distinctions of course. Maybe moral distinctions are developed not merely by interest and sympathy, but by all sorts of methods of social construction, according to the direct power of the moral considerations at stake. So, for example, if Bentham is right, one might expect moral concepts, like those used in type 2 judgments condemning theft, dishonesty, and expropriation to be forthcoming in society, just as one expects that in general moral ideals will follow considerations of social utility. And the same sort of case may be made on Radin's account. Any sensibility that values respect for persons will tend to

46 Hume, *Treatise,* p. 499 (Book III, Part 2, Section ii).
47 Hume, *Treatise,* p. 500 (Book III, Part 2, Section ii).

develop modes of evaluation appropriate to the specific vulnerability of personhood in relation to existing property rights and – this is the important point – to develop them in a way that does not connect them too tightly to the modes of evaluation used for the overall assessment of the property regime.

One further point. At the very beginning of this paper, I noted that "honest" tends to be a quite general term of moral appropriation. It used to mean virtue and honor of all sorts, encompassing chastity, generosity, and decorum; and even now it includes "[u]prightness of disposition and conduct; integrity, truthfulness, straightforwardness" as well as "the quality opposed to lying, cheating, or stealing."[48] More than almost any other virtue word, "honesty" connotes a thesis about the unity of the virtues; it connects refraining from others' property with a general willingness to act truthfully, rightfully, and straightforwardly. It connects with virtues like industriousness, as when we talk of "an honest day's work." It connotes incorruptibility ("honest politicians"), neutrality ("honest broker"), sexual respectability ("make an honest woman of her"), and genuineness ("honest-to-God goodness"). These are not just ambiguities. There is a real tendency to think that someone who is honest in any of these regards is more likely to be honest in the others as well. The fact that honesty has all these ramifications is interesting, for it echoes what we might think of as the social pervasiveness of property. An established system of property is not simply one aspect, among others, of the social structure. It is quite all-encompassing, for it establishes much of the context in which we deal with others, relate to them, trade with them, work for them, and compete with them. Whether we like it or not, we all have to learn how to get by in the prevailing system of property.[49] We have to learn which things are *ours* and which not; how to acquire something we do not already possess; under what circumstances we will gain the benefit of others' work with the resources *they* possess; and in general how industry, commerce, and social intercourse are carried on in a world composed of objects and places designated as items of property. One who shows himself incompetent in this regard, even in one instance, is a kind of general menace: If he does not take property seriously *here,* we may say, he may not take it seriously anywhere. (After all, we do rely to an enormous extent on people's voluntary willingness not to just run off with things they covet or break into whatever places they like.) And if this person does not take this part of the social fabric seriously, he may not take any of it seriously. If we cannot trust him not to steal a towel from a hotel, can we trust him with our accounts or with our children? Can we trust him to tell the truth or keep his engagements or do the work that he promises to do?

48 See note 1, above.
49 Cf. the account of "Layman's Property" in Bruce Ackerman, *Private Property and the Constitution* (New Haven: Yale University Press, 1977), pp. 116 ff. See also Waldron, *The Right to Private Property,* pp. 42–3.

Once again, all this holds whether or not the established system of property is itself morally justifiable. If it is the established system, then it is the pervasive basis of social context in the way I have been describing. It is not surprising, then, we would develop concepts like "honesty" and "dishonesty" whose purpose it is to convey this point, that someone who violates existing property rules in one regard is in general not to be trusted. It is not surprising, either, that these concepts would develop quite independently of any thoughts about overall justification. There may be innumerable just alternatives to the existing system of property, many of them much more just than the one that presently exists. But there is room for only one of them to be established, and it is within the framework of the one that *is* established that we all have to make our lives, for better or for worse.

Incidentally, I think this also explains a couple of the connections that were explored in section I. There I said there is a connection between honesty and actions done in the open (and that therefore an open infringement of a property rule is less likely to be stigmatized as dishonest than a covert or furtive one). An action done in the open is one that can stand scrutiny in the sight of others with whom we share a social framework: one puts oneself on display, as it were, as one who has no reason to expect that he will not be trusted in general on account of the current infringement. (The logic is similar to that of the general law-abidingness which is displayed — paradoxically — in open acts of civil disobedience.) Similarly, someone whose challenge to contemporary property is grounded in some set of traditional property rights may seem less threatening to the social fabric, insofar as his deference to a tradition of property rights shows that he takes the idea of social fabric seriously.

If I am right in this hunch that the normative resilience of terms like "honesty" and "dishonesty" is explained in part by the social pervasiveness of property, then we might have a way of explaining some of the distinctions we found when we scrutinized Table 1. Remember I said that some of the examples there exhibited normative resilience while others did not. For example, there does not seem to be the same normative resilience among the following pairs — as seen in Table 5 — as there is between private property and honesty.

Table 5

Institution	Type 2 Predicate
The state	terrorist
True religion	heretic
Traditional marriage	fornicator
Aristocracy	lack of noble birth

The explanation may be that those to whom the type 2 epithets in Table 5 are likely to be applied share, for the most part, a social world with those who agree with them that the institutions on the left of the table are unjustified. For example, those whom proponents of traditional marriage would condemn as fornicators tend to share a world with people who deny that sex outside marriage is always wrong; and those whom defenders of the state label terrorists often have to confine their social relations to a small corps of trusted fellow insurgents, who of course agree with them in repudiating current state arrangements. In the case of property, by contrast, one has to be a very fortunate opponent of current property arrangements to live surrounded only by like-minded individuals. Maybe the members of extreme socialist sects can do this (though even Karl Marx paid his rent in London, and Engels inherited industrial wealth from his family); or maybe the members of utopian communities can (like the Robert Owen community in Edinburgh). But most opponents of existing property arrangements, no matter how deeply they feel about the issue, have to make a living and share a world with others who support those arrangements in a framework that they constitute.

VI. Political Philosophy and the Enterprise of Justification

So there may be something to the normative resilience of property. It may not be inappropriate to condemn theft, commend honesty, and respond sympathetically to claims of belonging in the context of an unjust system of property rights. What follows from this? What does it tell us about the enterprise of justificatory argument in political philosophy?

It may be thought that the normative resilience of property argues for a rather gloomy prospect for grand theorizing in political philosophy. By indicating the enduring importance of judgments based on existing property rights whether the property system in general is justified or not, it may be thought to weaken the case for the more general inquiry. Since we are morally bound by existing property rights anyway, what is the point of asking whether the property system is just or unjust? Perhaps normative resilience hooks up with a more general Hegelianism, which maintains (in some suitably nuanced sense) that everything is alright as it is, and that philosophers should stop going around indicting existing institutions for failing to conform to their theories and, as Hegel puts it scathingly, "issuing instructions on how the world ought to be."[50] Philosophers should stop worrying that legal reality lacks a moral justification; instead they should concentrate their energies on uncovering the rationality and justification that the normative resilience of existing arrangements shows is undoubtedly present already.

A somewhat different argument, although to a similar effect, may be made by a Marxist. The resilience of type 2 judgments – the Marxist may say – is to

---

50 Hegel, *Elements of the Philosophy of Right,* p. 23 (Preface).

be explained ultimately in terms of social psychology. It is an instance of ideological power – that is, an indication of the ability, which prevailing institutions have, to infect not just the lives, but the consciousness of those who suffer under them. It is not enough that the system of capitalist property expropriates and exploits the proletariat. It also inoculates them against any form of rebellion or resistance by stigmatizing any infringement of prevailing property rules with the shame and dishonor of dishonesty. Ideologically, an established system of property may have the effect that the proprietorial sentiments of the advantaged actually evoke an empathy and respect from the disadvantaged, which is quite isolated from the latter's opinion about the justice or injustice of the property-holding in question. This, if you like, gives an ideological spin to the Bentham/Radin thesis about the connection between property and personality. We make it *as though* attacking P's property is attacking P herself; and since clearly it would be wrong to attack P herself (whatever the distributive situation), that sense of wrongness is projected onto any encroachment on P's property even though such encroachment, considered on its own merits, might be quite justifiable.

In its ideological aspect, the normative resilience of property may also be connected with myths of equal opportunity and the equality or reciprocity of rights. We bring up our children to believe that in respecting P's property, they are according no greater respect to her than she is required to accord to them, and that if P has property (and they have none), this has to do with the way she succeeded (while they failed) in consummating opportunities that were available equally to everyone. We know all too well that such sentiments may persist, and surface in the phenomena of shame and the sense of dishonesty I have mentioned, long after the economic conditions of opportunity, equality, and reciprocal respect that thy appeal to have evaporated. On this account, the quest for a general justification (or critique of property) is not so much preempted (as it is on the Hegelian approach) as hopeless. Since the ideology of property is already firmly in possession of all the space in moral consciousness that an effective justificatory theory could possibly occupy, we should abandon the futile business of challenging that ideology on moral grounds. The normative resilience of property – as an ideological product – shows that we are bound to lose *that* battle. If we oppose property, we should devote ourselves to the direct task of overthrowing it, rather than waste energy in a futile endeavor to discredit it.

I find neither of these lines of argument (the Hegelian line or the Marxist line) convincing. I do not believe we should use the normative resilience of property as a basis for inferring pessimistic conclusions so far as the justificatory enterprise is concerned. There are a number of responses that I want to make.

First, and most obviously, any Hegelian account of the social and legal world would be inadequate if it did not mention *our existing practice of engaging in general justificatory discourse* – for that is part of reality, too – and if it did not give that a place in the overall system of social practice that is "alright as it is." Second – so far as the Marxist argument is concerned – unless we adopt a very deterministic understanding of ideology, we should understand that something is in fact being fought out at the level of moral argument that is not simply foreordained by the victory of capitalist property at a more material "level." Ideological structures have a certain autonomy from material forms that mean they are not the mere reflex of existing arrangements. Since, as we have seen, the normative resilience of property is neither perfect nor comprehensive but varies in several dimensions (e.g., according to the extent to which the system as a whole is condemned), the mere fact of resilience does not show that broader justificatory inquiry is completely futile.[51]

Third, even if we acknowledge that the normative resilience of existing private property arrangements is a sign of their ability to survive moral or philosophical critique, it does not follow that critique has no effect in the world or that it is morally insignificant. For it is important not only what we bring about in the world but also *how we inhabit the world.* Even if we are pessimistic about the likely effects on institutions of our justificatory discourse, still we need to consider justificatory arguments to ascertain whether we are entitled to live comfortably with the institutions that surround us.[52] From this point of view, we are not entitled to assume in advance (e.g., on Hegelian grounds) that everything is "alright" in the sense that we may live *at our ease* in modern society. Surely the upshot of a justificatory enquiry may be sadness and shame, concerning the immoveable institutions of our society, rather than the reconciliation that Hegel was looking for. That the resilience of certain institutions is *lamentable,* rather than something to which reason can be reconciled, is a familiar and perfectly respectable position for philosophers to adopt: it is the attitude of Plato to democratic politics in Books Six and Seven of *The Republic,*[53] of de Tocqueville to banal egalitarianism in Volume II of *Democracy in America,*[54] of Max Weber to the "iron cage" of bureaucratic rationality,[55] and of Hannah Arendt to the modern state's preoccupation with life and labor.[56] Although these theorists do not think there is much to be done about what they lament, and though they may accept (and even explain) the fact of

---

51 See also Thompson, *Whigs and Hunters,* pp. 258–69.
52 What follows in the next few paragraphs is adapted from Waldron, "Property, Justification and Need."
53 See, for example, Plato, *Republic,* trans. Robin Waterfield (Oxford: Oxford University Press, 1993), pp. 207–19 (487b–497a).
54 See, for example, Alexis de Tocqueville, *Democracy in America* (New York: Knopf, 1994), pp. 316–21 (Vol. II, Bk. IV, Ch. vi).
55 See, for example, Max Weber, *Economy and Society,* ed. Guenther Roth and Claus Wittich (Berkeley: University of California Press), vol. 2, pp. 1393–405.
56 See Hannah Arendt, *The Human Condition* (Chicago: University of Chicago Press, 1958), pp. 305–25.

resilience, that does not diminish the importance of their evaluative arguments.[57]

A smaller scale example may help here. Many people believe that the abolition of capital punishment is a political impossibility in the United States for the foreseeable future at least so long as fear of crime is bound up with racial antipathy. But they nevertheless regard the debate about its justification as a live and important one, inasmuch as it determines whether, as moral beings, we may live *comfortably* in a society of which popular enthusiasm for judicial killing is an ineradicable feature. Moreover, that question – reconciliation or discomfort – is not seen as an indulgent matter of posture, but as an issue of authenticity and understanding. So long as this is recognized, the strictures of justificatory debate lose none of their importance in view of the resilience of the institutions we are evaluating.

The fourth point I want to make is the most important; it is the point I intimated earlier (at the beginning of Section IV). It seems to me that if an institution has the sort of resilience that we have been talking about, if it has or is likely to have this sort of presence in any society in which it is established, if it carries this kind of psychological baggage, if the mere fact of its positive existence is going to generate and sustain resilient type 2 judgments, then that does not diminish the burden of justification so far as an institution of this kind is concerned: *instead it increases it.* It means that if we *do* have any opportunity to make our justificatory discourse effective – if we are poised, for example, to introduce a new system of property (as governments have been over the last decade in Eastern Europe) – then we should think very carefully about what we do, because the likely resilience of what we are instituting means that it is liable to do much more damage and be much harder to eradicate if we make wrong choices at this stage than would be the case with our setting up a nonresilient institution.

Again, an analogy may help. Consider the choices faced by a religious teacher who wants to address the question of sex with his pupils. Clearly it is important for him to tell them the truth, to get it right, and to communicate that truth in a way that will do the most good. If he makes a mistake (or, worse, tells his pupils lies), he does them a grave disservice – depriving them of harmless pleasures, leaving them ill-equipped to deal with the dangers of pregnancy or sexually transmitted diseases, making them ashamed of things they need not be ashamed of. To some extent, this damage may be reversible in later life, as they discover that what they were taught was untrue. But if his sex education teaching is resilient in the consciousness of his pupils, in the way that religious sex education often is, it will not be enough for the pupils to later become aware of his errors. Even if they are rightly convinced that he misled them (say

---

57 See also Jeremy Waldron, "What Plato Would Allow," in *Nomos XXXVII: Theory and Prac-tice,* ed. Ian Shapiro and Judith Wagner DeCew (New York: New York University Press, 1995), pp. 138–78, at pp. 153 ff.

about homosexuality or masturbation) the stigmatization of these activities as "wrong" or "dirty" might remain, resiliently, in their minds long after the underlying theories have been discredited. If this is a possibility – and I take it that one can figure out in advance that it is – then that is a reason for the teacher to approach his task more carefully, rather than less carefully. He should think to himself, "I had better be very sure that I have got this right, because to a certain extent my teachings will be resilient and uncorrectable if I am wrong." He certainly should not think (though no doubt many sex educators do), "It doesn't matter whether I am right or wrong, for even if my lies are uncovered, they will still have the psychological effect that I desire." And that would be the analogue of inferring a diminution of the justificatory burden from the normative resilience of property. In other words, the normative resilience of property may properly be said to diminish our sense of *when* justificatory discourse can have any effect in the real world; but just because of that, it increases the burden of justification we are under for those occasions when justificatory discourse *can* have some effect.

2

Property as Social Relations

STEPHEN R. MUNZER

I. Introduction

This essay considers the approach in legal and political theory that views property relations as a set of social relations – or, for short, property as social relations. The topic is not the Hohfeld–Honoré orthodoxy that treats property as an important subclass of *legal* relations among persons with respect to things.[1] Rather, the topic is the view that property is best seen as *social* relations among persons with respect to things. Among legal realists, this view of property is held, along with others, by Felix S. Cohen[2] and Robert L. Hale.[3] In critical legal studies, Duncan Kennedy[4] and Joseph William Singer,[5] among

For helpful comments I thank Toby Bordelon, Gary Chartier, William Fisher, J. W. Harris, Virginia Held, Emily Mah, Randall Peerenboom, J. E. Penner, Seana Shiffrin, Jeremy Waldron, some anonymous readers, my colleagues and seminar students, and members of the Law and Philosophy Discussion Group.

1 See Wesley Newcomb Hohfeld, *Fundamental Legal Conceptions as Applied in Judicial Reasoning,* ed. Walter W. Cook and foreword by Arthur L. Corbin (Westport, Conn.: Greenwood Press, 1978 [1919]; A. M. Honoré, "Ownership," in A. G. Guest, ed., *Oxford Essays in Jurisprudence* (Oxford: Clarendon Press, 1961), pp. 107–47. Versions of the orthodoxy include Lawrence C. Becker, *Property Rights: Philosophic Foundations* (London, Henley and Boston: Routledge & Kegan Paul, 1977), pp. 7–23.

2 See Felix S. Cohen, "Dialogue on Private Property," *Rutgers Law Review,* 9 (1954): 357–87.

3 See, for example, Robert L. Hale, "Bargaining, Duress, and Economic Liberty," *Columbia Law Review,* 43 (1943): 603–28; Robert L. Hale, "Coercion and Distribution in a Supposedly Non-Coercive State," *Political Science Quarterly,* 38 (1923): 470–94.

4 See Duncan Kennedy, "The Stakes of Law, or Hale and Foucault!," *Legal Studies Forum,* 15 (1991): 327–65 (hereinafter "Hale and Foucault!"); reprinted with very slight changes in Duncan Kennedy, *Sexy Dressing Etc.* (Cambridge, Mass. and London: Harvard University Press, 1993), pp. 83–125. Page references are to the original and reprinted texts, respectively, separated by a slash mark. Where there are differences in language, I quote the reprinted article.

5 Joseph William Singer, *Property Law: Rules, Policies, and Practices,* 2nd ed. (New York: Aspen Law & Business, 1997), pp. 20–23; Joseph William Singer, "The Legal Rights Debate in Analytical Jurisprudence from Bentham to Hohfeld," *Wisconsin Law Review* (1982): 975–1059; Joseph William Singer, "The Reliance Interest in Property," *Stanford Law Review,* 40 (1988): 611–751 (hereinafter "Reliance Interest"); Joseph William Singer, "Re-Reading Property," *New England Law Review,* 26 (1992): 711–29; Joseph William Singer and Jack M. Beermann, "The

others, take this approach to property. The Canadian political theorists C. B. Macpherson and Jennifer Nedelsky also have social-relations views of property.[6] In what follows, I use equivalently the terms social-relations "approaches" to and "views" of property.

I attempt to fill a void in the existing literature on the theory of property by examining the social-relations view. This view has been almost entirely ignored by libertarians, traditional Marxists, and analytic philosophers of whatever political stripe. At the same time, latter-day legal realists and adherents of critical legal studies have infrequently engaged other approaches to property in a fruitful way.[7] An anthropologist of the academy might well conclude that social-relations theorists and competing theorists of property have largely gone their separate ways and have not often managed to examine the others' work in a fashion that seeks to understand as well as to criticize.[8]

I pursue the following course. Section 2 describes social-relations approaches in more detail. Section 3 identifies a possible ambiguity in social-relations views between revising the concept of property and attacking justifications of property. Section 4 examines the interconnections among coercion, power, and freedom. Section 5 builds on this examination by considering several positions on autonomy and the nature of the self. Section 6 then tackles some central questions concerning the nature of social relations and their role in property. Section 7 tries to effect a rapprochement between social-relations views and one form of political liberalism. Section 8 identifies some key problems that social-relations thinkers might address in the future development of their views.

My aims are not only to evaluate critically but also to explore possible common ground. There is indeed much to criticize in social-relations views. They often rest on flawed accounts of coercion, power, and freedom. They frequently adopt unsatisfactory positions on autonomy and the self. Most

Social Origins of Property," *Canadian Journal of Law and Jurisprudence*, 6 (1993): 217–48; Joseph William Singer, "Sovereignty and Property," *Northwestern University Law Review*, 86 (1991): 1–56.

6 See, for example, C. B. Macpherson, "The Meaning of Property" and "Liberal-Democracy and Property," in C. B. Macpherson, ed., *Property: Mainstream and Critical Positions* (Toronto and Buffalo: University of Toronto Press, 1978), pp. 1–13, 199–207; C. B. Macpherson, "Capitalism and the Changing Concept of Property," in Eugene Kamenka and R. S. Neale, eds., *Feudalism, Capitalism and Beyond* (Canberra: Australian National University Press, 1975), pp. 104–24; Jennifer Nedelsky, "Law, Boundaries, and the Bounded Self," *Representations*, 30 (Spring 1990): 162–89.

7 Exceptions include Duncan Kennedy and Frank Michelman, "Are Property and Contract Efficient?," *Hofstra Law Review*, 8 (1980): 711–70, which examines law-and-economics approaches; and Singer, "The Legal Rights Debate in Analytical Jurisprudence from Bentham to Hohfeld," which, though it does not investigate normative theories of property stemming from other traditions, grapples with theorists of legal rights whom philosophers take seriously.

8 This article supersedes the remarks on social-relations approaches in Stephen R. Munzer, "The Special Case of Property Rights in Umbilical Cord Blood for Transplantation," *Rutgers Law Review*, 51 (1999): 493–568, at 562–68 (hereinafter "Special Case").

seriously, they do not provide an adequate treatment of which social relations are, or help to constitute, property.

Social-relations views also yield insights. They illuminate the manifold ways in which market forces, the distribution of income and wealth, and governmental regulation affect those who buy and sell products and services. They are alert to the difference in power between individuals and the government. Above all they drive home the point that the state is not a neutral party, for it sets up and enforces rights of property and contract.

Of necessity, this essay unfolds as a delicate balancing act. On the one side, the larger picture of social relations must be kept constantly in mind. Otherwise, the forest gets obscured by the trees (and branches on trees, and leaves on branches). On the other side, it would be a mistake to rely on what some might perceive as a cardboard version or amalgamation of social-relations views. It is, thus, important to inspect the writings of individual thinkers carefully, even at the risk of being said to go for the capillary.

II. A Synopsis of Property as Social Relations

Origins and Development. To make this essay accessible, I first summarize the views placed under the heading of property as social relations. The wellsprings of this approach to property lie in the legal realist movement that began in the early twentieth century. This movement took issue with a picture of law as a set of clear, formal rules from which judges could reach decisions in individual cases by applying the rules almost mechanically to the facts. The legal realists were skeptical of, variously, the clarity of legal rules, the knowledge of facts, and the ability of judges to reach decisions without infusing moral, political, and social values into their interpretations of both law and facts. Influential legal realists include Karl Llewellyn, Jerome Frank, Morris R. Cohen, Felix S. Cohen, and Hale.

So far as property is concerned, the Cohens occupy a special place. Morris Cohen's influential article "Property and Sovereignty" likens the power associated with property holdings to sovereignty.[9] He suggests that different sorts of property require different justifications, and that inasmuch as property confers sovereignty, justifications of property must be analogous to justifications of sovereignty. Felix Cohen's article "Dialogue on Private Property" replays a Socratic exchange in which the participants try to agree on a definition of private property. He is, to my knowledge, the first writer to use the phrase "property as social relations."[10]

Hale was educated as both a lawyer and an economist. At different points in his career, he taught in the law school and the economics department at Colum-

---

9 Morris R. Cohen, "Property and Sovereignty," *Cornell Law Quarterly,* 13 (1927): 8–30.
10 Cohen, "Dialogue on Private Property," at 361 (emphasis and initial capitals omitted).

bia University. As a legal realist, Hale lacked the towering reputation of Llewellyn and Frank, yet as an economist he had the training to wrestle with the orthodox economics of his day. Hale's writings dealt not only with property and economics but also the (dreary) subject of regulating the rates of public utilities. Hale was critical of prevailing views of neoclassical economics and the market. His work has influenced Kennedy, Singer, and other critical legal scholars, who are partly responsible for reviving interest in Hale's corpus.[11]

Kennedy is a founder of critical legal studies, and his many articles have had an impact on a significant subset of a generation of academic lawyers. At first it may seem odd to discuss some of his work in this essay, for Kennedy has no well articulated theory of property. However, his article on Hale and Foucault develops the former's account of coercion with the aid of the latter's treatment of power, and the analysis of coercion and power is central to social-relations views of property. In addition, Kennedy is an insistent critic of law and economics.[12] His criticisms increase understanding of what social-relations thinkers are trying to do in opposing law-and-economics approaches to property.

Singer, unlike Kennedy, is a theory builder. He has a distinctive interpretation of legal realism and its relation to the market, law and economics, and some forms of liberalism.[13] Of the various figures associated with property as social relations, Singer has written the most widely and systematically about property. As will emerge, he has the clearest social-relations view.

The last two thinkers who figure importantly in this essay are neither economists nor academic lawyers but political theorists. Neither thinker is directly associated with critical legal studies. Macpherson is the author of several highly regarded books on political philosophy as well as various articles.[14] He lays particular stress on revising the concept of property in terms of social relations. Nedelsky is the author of a widely read book on the nature of private property under a Madisonian perspective on the United States constitution.[15] She has a distinctive understanding of autonomy and the nature of the self in relation to property.

11 An excellent study is Barbara H. Fried, *The Progressive Assault on Laissez Faire: Robert Hale and the First Law and Economics Movement* (Cambridge, Mass. and London: Harvard University Press, 1998).
12 In addition to the articles cited in notes 4 and 7 above and note 18 below, see Duncan Kennedy, "Law-and-Economics from the Perspective of Critical Legal Studies," in Peter Newman, ed., *The New Palgrave Dictionary of Economics and the Law* (London: Macmillan Reference Limited, 1998), vol. 2, pp. 465–74, and Kennedy's articles cited in the bibliography.
13 See Joseph William Singer, "Legal Realism Now," *California Law Review,* 76 (1988): 465–544.
14 See C. B. Macpherson, *The Political Theory of Possessive Individualism: Hobbes to Locke* (Oxford: Oxford University Press, 1962); C. B. Macpherson, *Democratic Theory: Essays in Retrieval* (Oxford: Clarendon Press, 1973); and articles cited in note 6 above.
15 See Jennifer Nedelsky, *Private Property and the Limits of American Constitutionalism: The Madisonian Framework and Its Legacy* (Chicago and London: University of Chicago Press, 1990).

Eight Propositions. Perhaps there are as many social-relations views as there are proponents of property as social relations, but it helps to have a fuller description. The following eight propositions give a broad picture. Yet they are subject to different interpretations, and fall short of a systematic formulation – if, indeed, such a formulation is possible. Anyone who subscribes to all eight has a *full theory* of property as social relations. Anyone who subscribes to most of them has a *theory* of property as social relations. Anyone who subscribes to several of them and does not depart too sharply from the others espouses a social-relations *approach* to or *view* of property. After stating each proposition I explain how accepting it might contrast with other positions and might have great appeal in some quarters.

1. The self is nonindividualistic and is constructed mainly out of various social relations among human beings.

This proposition differs from the views of most libertarians and most neo-classical law-and-economics scholars. It appeals to some other scholars partly because it seems to them to be true and partly because it gives a basis for rejecting the conclusions of libertarian and law-and-economics approaches. Insofar as social-relations writers speak of the social construction of the self, it is often unclear whether they are referring to each particular *self,* the *concept* of the self, or the *understanding* of the self in various moral, political, or legal theories.

2. Social relations run the gamut from brief interactions with strangers to market transactions and business dealings to generally intimate and endur-ing ties within the family.

This proposition is a start on giving content to the view that property is not, or not just, a matter of legal relations. It attracts those who believe that law is not best seen as a tidy and determinate body of rules. Attending to *social* relations appears to show that property law is changing and indeterminate, and to provide a basis for results in litigation that differ from and are to some intuitively more attractive than the results generated by legal rules. For exam-ple, in *Local 1330, United Steel Workers of America v. United States Steel Corporation,*[16] the steel company proposed to close two steel plants. The plaintiffs sought an order requiring the company either to keep the plants open or to sell them to the plaintiff unions. The court, relying on its understanding of the law, ruled in favor of United States Steel. Singer's social-relations view maintains that enduring relations of mutual dependence between the company on the one side and the workers, their families, and the town on the other side

16 631 F.2d 1264 (6th Cir. 1980).

gave the latter property rights in the plant.[17]Recognizing those rights would have led to a different result in the lawsuit.

3. Rights of various sorts, including property rights, grow out of social relations.

If the analytic jurisprudence of the concepts of rights and of property seems dry or even sterile, an emphasis on the relevance of social relations to both rights and property appears to enliven and enrich the study of property rights. The emergence of property rights from social relations is a matter not only of history but also of normative theory. Accordingly, those who take a social-relations approach to property tend to criticize both conservative historical accounts and classical treatments of property that rest on patriarchy, natural rights, or deference to the status quo.[18]

4. Differences in power influence the relations among human beings and the property rights that result.

Although some other approaches see existing systems and distributions of property as more or less benign, power is ubiquitous in social and economic life. Property is a matter of constant pushing and shoving. So those who put power (Kennedy) – or its cousin coercion (Hale and Singer) – front and center arguably attend to a phenomenon that others have overlooked or under-estimated.

5. Variations in power and the distribution of property enable some persons to limit the freedom of, or even to coerce, other persons.

This proposition departs from most libertarian approaches to property.[19] It also departs from free market models of property (and contract), because such models overemphasize relations that are supposedly created by voluntary agreements between individuals. But a less-than-radical theorist can acknowledge that rules of property law limit the freedom of those whose conduct they constrain. The ability of individuals to satisfy their preferences depends partly on the amount of power and property they possess.

6. The existence of power, coercion, and the largely socially constructed nature of the self leaves scant room for autonomy understood as highly

17 See Singer, "Reliance Interest," at 614–23, 655–63, 701–49, and passim.
18 See, for example, Duncan Kennedy, "The Structure of Blackstone's Commentaries," *Buffalo Law Review,* 28 (1979): 205–382.
19 By libertarian I have in mind preeminently the entitlement theory of Robert Nozick, *Anarchy, State, and Utopia* (New York: Basic Books, 1974), pp. 150–82. See also Loren E. Lomasky, *Persons, Rights, and the Moral Community* (New York and Oxford: Oxford University Press, 1987), Ch. 6.

individualistic self-government, although it may point toward some different account of the self and autonomy.

This proposition signals various contrasts regarding the roles of the self and autonomy in understanding property. The full significance of these contrasts will become apparent only as this essay unfolds. As regards the self, social-relations thinkers differ not only from most libertarians and from those lawyer-economists who depict individuals as rational maximizers of preference satisfaction. They also differ, or at least seem to, from most political liberals, who allegedly underplay the way in which the self is arguably socially constituted and influenced by manifold forces.

So far as autonomy is concerned, the contrasts are trickier. In contemporary political theory, autonomy is held out by political liberals as valuable and important. But what is meant by "autonomy"? Social-relations thinkers resist a simple and flat-footed understanding of autonomy as self-government. They also tend to distance themselves from understanding autonomy as the psychological capacity to be self-governing – a capacity that is part of the foundation of a moral right to be treated as self-governing. At this point social-relations thinkers divide. Some seem to regard autonomy as a will-o'-the-wisp or perhaps not to exist at all. Others seem to view autonomy as a complicated, nonindividualistic affair that involves fettered choices and communal constraints born of social relations. The appeal of social-relations views, then, resides partly in what their advocates see as a more accurate understanding of the self and autonomy than that offered by competing libertarian, law-and-economics, and liberal thinkers.

7. The state is not a neutral party, because it specifies and enforces property rights.

This proposition may elicit a yawn now, but it was strikingly novel and controversial when asserted by the legal realists in the first half of the twentieth century. Often judges deciding cases involving property and contract wrote their opinions in such a way as to give the impression that the result reached was inevitable. For example, in *Coppage v. Kansas*[20] the Supreme Court held that an employer could fire workers who sought to form an employees' association. It recognized that employers might have more property than employees but concluded

since it is self-evident that, unless all things are held in common, some persons must have more property than others, it is from the nature of things impossible to uphold

20   236 U.S. 1 (1915).

freedom of contract and the right of private property without at the same time recognizing as legitimate those inequalities of fortune that are the necessary result of the exercise of those rights.[21]

The legal realists and their present-day successors emphasize that judges often have choices under existing law as informed by social relations. Relatedly, Morris R. Cohen stresses:

> The character of property as sovereign power may be obscured for us in a commercial economy . . . by the fiction of the so-called labor contract as a free bargain. . . . [T]here [is] actually little freedom to bargain on the part of the steel worker or miner who needs a job. . . .[22]

Moreover, the legislative and executive branches of government have choices in enacting and enforcing laws pertaining to property and contract. The making of these choices should involve an awareness of the social relations among those who are affected.

8. The reform of institutions sometimes requires changing basic rules of property law.

This proposition is amplified in various ways. One amplification is that remedying current defects cannot always be accomplished by paying money. Singer's discussion of the *United Steel Workers* case argues not for paying monetary damages to the employees but for a change, based on social relations, in existing law that would either keep the plant open or require the company to sell the plant to the employees. Another commentator argues that reform of property law is needed because tax-and-transfer redistribution "merely fulfills preexisting needs," whereas changing property rules "can resituate people in positions that allow them greater freedom."[23] Such arguments seem to give social-relations views a more radical cast than, say, many forms of political liberalism.

So ends my statement of eight propositions that summarize property as social relations. From the summary, it is evident that the topic is a family of disparate but related claims that connect property to the complexities of social forces (both external to and constitutive of the self). Of the figures I discuss,

21 Ibid. at 17. See also *Hitchman Coal & Coke Co. v. Mitchell,* 245 U.S. 229 (1917) (enjoining a union from organizing employees who had signed a yellow-dog contract with their employers); *Adair v. United States,* 208 U.S. 161 (1908) (invalidating a statute that made it unlawful for a railroad to discharge an employee who joined a union).
22 Cohen, "Property and Sovereignty," at 12. See also Fried, *The Progressive Assault on Laissez Faire,* pp. 29–107; Singer, "Legal Realism Now," at 475–503.
23 Note, "Distributive Liberty: A Relational Model of Freedom, Coercion, and Property Law," *Harvard Law Review,* 107 (1994): 859–76, at 867.

Singer is probably the only one who espouses a *full theory*. Nedelsky and perhaps Kennedy and Macpherson each offer a *theory* of property as social relations. Hale and Felix S. Cohen each have a *view* of property as social relations. I single out these figures for discussion because they offer the most provocative and influential statements of one or more of the eight propositions listed. I place in the background authors who, even if they subscribe to most of these propositions, are in the main derivative thinkers.[24] I mention only in passing authors who have original and interesting positions and show an affinity for a social-relations approach to property, but who introduce republican, pragmatist, feminist, or critical-race-theory elements or whose main concerns lie elsewhere.[25]

Approach. The following discussion is legal and political theory rather than intellectual history. It inevitably flattens out nuances in the development of the ideas considered – for example, debts to Hegel and Marx, the exact ways in which the Cohens and others unsettled the legal orthodoxy of the nineteenth and early twentieth centuries, and the emergence of Hale, a renegade "progressive" economist, as a leading influence on critical legal studies. Space does not permit tracing the history of legal realism and critical legal studies beyond the rough sketch given earlier.

The theoretical discussion does not take up each proposition in turn. That would be tedious beyond belief, and focusing on fairly abstract propositions might raise in the minds of readers doubts about whether the authors under review actually subscribe to these propositions as I have formulated them. Rather, I consider carefully the words in which they express their ideas. So the summary of property as social relations serves as a general guide and each figure discussed gets a chance to speak in his or her own words. Readers may find the following roadmap helpful. Section IV on coercion, power, and freedom discusses Hale and Kennedy (propositions (3), (4), (5) and (7)). Section V on selves and autonomy deals with Felix S. Cohen, Kennedy, and Nedelsky (propositions (1), (3), (4), (5), and (6)). Section VI concentrates on Kennedy and Singer (propositions (1) through (8)). First, however, it is necessary to identify a possible ambiguity in social-relations views and to show that it leads to an easily correctable problem.

24 As mentioned in the Introduction to this book (page 5 n. 13), limitations on space have prevented me from discussing such decidedly nonderivative thinkers as Seyla Benhabib, Carol C. Gould, Richard Dien Winfield, and Ross Zucker.
25 See, for example, William W. Fisher III, "Reconstructing the Fair Use Doctrine," *Harvard Law Review*, 101 (1988): 1659–795, at 1744–95; William H. Simon, "Social-Republican Property," *UCLA Law Review*, 38 (1991): 1335–413; Patricia Williams, "Fetal Fictions: An Exploration of Property Archetypes in Racial and Gendered Contexts," *Florida Law Review*, 42 (1990): 81–94. As to the work of Margaret Jane Radin, I have pretty much exhausted what I have to say in Munzer, "Special Case," at 560–62, and Stephen R. Munzer, "An Uneasy Case Against Property Rights in Body Parts," *Social Philosophy & Policy*, 11, no. 2 (Summer 1994): 259–86, at 263–6, 270–71.

III. Identifying a Recurring Ambiguity

The foregoing synopsis masks a possible ambiguity: whether social-relations views are an attempt to revise the concept of property, or are an attack on some familiar justifications of property. In fact, at different times they are both, though social-relations writers do not always seem clear on the matter.

On the one hand, social-relations theories sometimes appear to be conceptually revisionary: Property is not legal relations, but social relations, among persons with respect to things. From this point, however, it is unclear whether legal relations, if accepted in society, become social relations for purposes of defining property, and whether all or only some social relations are, or help to constitute, property.

On the other hand, social relations theories sometimes seem to attack other theories of property on normative grounds. Suppose that someone argues for the proposition that private property is good because it promotes the autonomy of individuals. A possible counterargument is that attending to the reality of fully situated social relations shows that this proposition is false. Private property does not promote autonomy because, perhaps, there are no separable individuals. Or, perhaps, separable individuals lack autonomy because of the power and coercion of others. Or, perhaps, because unequal distributions of private property confer more autonomy on some individuals than others, no justification of private property is sound unless it yields equal autonomy for all.

The ambiguity just described is important because the failure to notice it undermines some arguments of some social-relations thinkers. An illustration is Macpherson's criticism of the concept of property as centrally an exclusive right to something and his proposal for a new concept of property – namely as "a right to a set of social relations, a right to a kind of society."[26] But Macpherson believes that there are both good and bad social relations, and tries to redeploy the concept of property so that it includes only good social relations. He thereby manipulates the concept of property when it is normative argument that would be to the point.[27]

My point here is only that social-relations thinkers need to be clear on what they are doing. Obviously, any theorist can argue *both* that a concept of property should be revised *and* that some familiar justifications of property should be rejected. But ordinarily the grounds for these respective arguments differ. The first sort of argument usually points to some legal or social transformation – for example, that whereas the subject of property rights once was material things (land, houses, tools) it now also includes nonmaterial

26 Macpherson, "Capitalism and the Changing Concept of Property," at 121.
27 See J. W. Harris, *Property and Justice* (Oxford: Clarendon Press, 1996), pp. 154–61. Harris first drew this ambiguity to my attention.

things (copyrights, patents, trademarks). The second sort of argument typically points to some defect in a normative justification – for example, that one of the premises is false, or that the reasoning is faulty. Occasionally the two sorts of arguments can be linked. Thus, someone might contend that certain justifications for property rights in material things like tools do not work for non-material things like copyrights. More generally, conceptual revision can alter our sense of what it is, exactly, that requires justification. Yet the existence of a link does not entail that the two arguments are the same.

From time to time in the balance of this essay I point to passages where a particular author seems to be ambiguous in the way described. The difficulty can generally be corrected by disentangling conceptual from justificatory arguments, and by stressing that revision of the concept of property can affect, but does not end, debate over justification. So it will remain confused to argue simultaneously that, say, property is not really individualistic and property is bad because it is individualistic. Yet it will remain coherent to argue, say, both that property is not the individualistic concept some believe it to be and that individualistic justifications for property fail.

IV. Coercion, Power, and Freedom

Social-relations thinkers often articulate their views on property in terms of either power or coercion and some resulting loss of freedom on the part of those who have little or no property. So many different things are going on in these discussions that it helps to disentangle them. This section tries to separate the following expository and critical points: Hale's position; the defensibility of selecting coercion as the central concept; neutral and nonneutral uses of coercion; *success* versus *effort* readings of such verbs as "coerce"; coercion and the nonneutrality of the state; the shift from coercion to power; and the relation of coercion to freedom.

A. Most philosophers would greet with skepticism the position, central to the Hale–Singer statement of a social-relations view, that even minor differences in economic power involve coercion by the slightly wealthier parties. One sense of "coercion" is the "use of physical or moral force to compel to act or assent."[28] In comparison with the word "force," "coercion" often "suggests unethical, unjust compulsion, as by threat."[29] A commentator who had access to Hale's private papers observes that "Hale long felt that 'coercion' was an infelicitous term and sought an alternative which would convey his limited and neutral intended meaning and nothing more."[30] Hale considered and some-

28 *Webster's Third New International Dictionary* (Springfield, Mass.: G. & C. Merriam Co., 1981), *s.v.* "coercion," p. 439 (sense 1a).
29 Ibid., *s.v.* "force," p. 887 (entry 1, syn.).
30 Warren J. Samuels, "The Economy as a System of Power and Its Legal Bases: The Legal Economics of Robert Lee Hale," *University of Miami Law Review,* 27 (1973): 261–371, at 280.

times used instead such terms as "compulsion," "pressure," "force," "influence," "duress," and "oppression."[31]

B. One problem lies not in Hale's failure to find a better word than "coercion" but in his apparent belief that any single word is the best word. The alternatives that Hale considered pick out different phenomena, and it is misguided to settle on any one of them. A bank teller with a gun to his or her head is under "duress" rather than "influence." A slave ordered to pick cotton under threat of force is under "coercion" rather than "influence." Parents exposed to the marketing techniques of phonics programs or computer makers are perhaps vulnerable to the marketers' "influence," but it would distort ordinary English to describe the situation as one of "coercion," "compulsion," "duress," "force," or "oppression."

C. Although Hale and his contemporary followers may have intended to use the word "coercion" neutrally, they sometimes lapse into using that word in its ordinary sense, which carries a connotation of unjust compulsion due to threat. For example, Kennedy develops an account of social relations by using an approach of Michel Foucault to move beyond Hale. Kennedy accurately points out that Hale is asserting that the distribution of property is central to law and the effects of law[32] and that the law plays a role in "setting the background conditions"[33] of a conflict over distribution.

This accuracy does not, however, prevent Kennedy from using the language of coercion nonneutrally. Thus, Kennedy applauds the "recharacterization" of agreements between labor and capital as the product of mutual coercion and force, because "it punctured the conservative economic rhetoric of the [realists'] time."[34] To the realists "capitalism was as coercive in its way as socialism."[35] But compare two different punctures: a blowout and a slow leak. If the coercion of socialism is preferable to the coercion of capitalism, there is a blowout of the conservative analysis of freedom. To establish the preferability, however, requires normative argument, not merely an unusually broad understanding of coercion. If one shows only that there is a sense in which capitalism is coercive, without addressing socialism at all, then the conservative analysis of freedom has only a slow leak. Of course, Kennedy may be countering the rhetoric of the "free" market with the rhetoric of "coercion." Yet what is needed is something that gets past the rhetorical excess of "freedom" on the one side and "coercion" on the other and attends to the complexity of social and economic life.

D. Now distinguish between two different understandings of coercion. On the one hand, to say that someone employs coercion is to hold that he or she

31 Ibid., at 280.
32 Kennedy, "Hale and Foucault!," at 337–8/pp. 96–7.
33 Ibid., at 340/p. 99.
34 Ibid., at 328/p. 85.
35 Ibid. (citation omitted).

succeeds. On the other, it is to hold that he or she *tries.* Thus, if "coerce" is a success-verb, to say that *A* coerces *B* is to hold that *A* succeeds in getting *B* to do what *A* wants. But if "coerce" is an effort-verb, to say that *A* coerces *B* is to hold that *A* tries to get *B* to do what *A* wants, but leaves open the matter of whether *A* succeeds. *B* could resist *A,* and if *B*'s resistance were strong enough it could defeat *A*'s effort. The same distinction applies to related verbs such as "compel," "force," "oppress," and "influence" and a verb phrase such as "exert duress."

As a matter of ordinary language, these verbs break down uneasily in regard to the distinction between success-verbs and effort-verbs. If the past tense is used, sentences such as "*A* coerced *B*," "*A* compelled *B*," or "*A* forced *B*" usually imply that *A* was successful. Sentences such as "*A* oppressed *B*," "*A* influenced *B*," and "*A* exerted duress against *B*" often do not imply success on *A*'s part. If the present progressive tense is used, quite often success is *not implied,* even if success turns out to occur. Hence, sentences such as "*A* is influencing (or oppressing, or exerting duress against) *B*" may be compatible with *B*'s successfully resisting *A*'s efforts. Still, sentences such as "*A* is coercing (or forcing, or compelling) *B*" can carry the implication that, if *A* persists and *B*'s efforts at resistance do not increase, *A* will ultimately succeed in getting *B* to do what *A* wants.

How does Hale use the word "coercion" and its cognates? Though his texts may not be wholly consistent, almost always he uses "coerce" and related verbs as effort-verbs. As a corollary, his use of "coercion" does not imply success. For example, he writes:

It is the law of property which coerces people into working for factory owners – though, as we shall see shortly, the workers can as a rule exert sufficient counter-coercion to limit materially the governing power of the owners.[36]

Thus, Hale's allowing for "sufficient counter-coercion" suggests that, for him, even past-tense reports of coercion do not carry the implication that whatever or whoever coerces – be it "the law of property" or "factory owners" – succeeds in getting what is wanted. This suggestion intimates in turn that he desires to use the language of coercion in a specialized, technical way.

This analysis, besides elucidating Hale, helps to clarify a further dimension of the nonneutral use of the language of coercion, force, and power. My point is not that the neutral/nonneutral distinction tracks the effort/success distinction. Obviously, the two distinctions come apart. If *A* tries to coerce or force *B* to hand over *B*'s money, *A* has wronged *B* regardless of whether *A* succeeds. Still,

---

36 Hale, "Coercion and Distribution in a Supposedly Non-Coercive State," at 473.

if *A* succeeds, the harm to *B* is greater than it would be had *A* tried but failed. From this argument two conclusions follow. First, even if social-relations thinkers were to adhere to Hale by using *coerce* as an effort-verb, it would not exculpate them from failing to use it neutrally. Second, social-relations thinkers must be specially careful of using the language of coercion, force, power in a way that assumes success. To assume success is to suppose the infliction of greater harm and thus would compound the tendentiousness of a nonneutral use. Furthermore, if offers of employment carry the choice work-or-starve, and if the existence of coercion depends on a baseline, such offers would be coercive on either the effort-reading or the success-reading only if the baseline is that the offerees ought to be able to eat while rejecting all offers of employment.

In one passage, Kennedy extols the realists' insight into the role of legal rules but either misapplies Hale or misanalyzes a problem. "To the extent that these rules affect the outcome, forcing the parties to settle for x rather than y percent of the joint product, the state is implicated in the outcome."[37] Kennedy leaves it unclear whether the state is implicated because it enforces but does not create the rules, or because it both creates and enforces the rules. The latter interpretation tallies better with the radical character of Kennedy's critique, for it involves the state more deeply. Kennedy also leaves it unclear whether the participle "forcing" derives from what I call a success-verb or an effort-verb. If it comes from a success-verb, Kennedy implicates the state in an especially harmful way but departs from Hale's usage. If it comes from an effort-verb, Kennedy conforms to Hale's usage yet implicates the state in a less harmful way, for *both* parties might successfully resist the state.

E. Kennedy's implicating the state points up the need to clarify the seventh proposition listed in Section II: In what senses or respects is the state not a neutral party? If the state *creates* or *specifies* the rules of property law, it is nonneutral if its representatives consciously favor one group (workers) over another (employers). The state is nonneutral in a weaker sense if its representatives try to avoid favoring any group but nevertheless end up favoring employers over workers. If the state only *enforces* rules upon which all groups agree, the state is nonneutral only in a weaker sense still. The state might now seem to be somewhat like an umpire in baseball or tennis, or a referee in boxing or soccer, who enforces the rules but is, ideally, neutral in almost all respects. Differently, one could drop the unrealistic assumption that all groups agree on the rules, and add the realistic assumption that representatives of the state are open to some suasion – think of campaign contributions to or lobbying of legislators. Now the state seems nonneutral in the sense of complicitous with those who seek to shape rules of property law to their advantage.

37 Kennedy, "Hale and Foucault!," at 329/pp. 85–86.

Social-relations thinkers are wise to mine the legal-realist insight that the state is not a neutral party, but much work remains to illuminate the varied nature of its nonneutrality.

F. Later Kennedy links Hale and Foucault[38] but does not establish his desired conclusions pertaining to property under capitalism, socialism, or mixed economies on the basis of a neutral account of either coercion or power. Kennedy points out, accurately, similarities and differences between Hale and Foucault. He analogizes Hale's "coercion" to Foucault's "power."[39]

But a characterization of power cannot, as a piece of analysis, deflate the pretensions of scientific Marxism[40] any more than a supposedly neutral characterization of coercion can blow out economic conservatism. True, both scientific Marxism and economic conservatism might assume that contracts between workers and owners of the means of production have a constant value: always bad to the Marxist and always good to the laissez faire conservative. To show that power relations within these contracts are more complicated than either account assumes is a first step to describing these bargains more accurately. Yet in both cases independent moral and political argument are required. I do not mean to criticize Kennedy unduly; much of interest resides in his article; and he describes it, modestly, as "more a rude appropriation of text-fragments of Hale and Foucault than a study of their thought."[41] Still, I do not see how one can infer normative conclusions regarding property under capitalism, socialism, or various mixed economies on the basis of a neutral account of coercion (or power).

G. So far the path has gone from coercion to power and now leads to the relation between coercion and freedom. Some of the recent philosophical literature approaches this relation through various hypothetical examples, one of which is dubbed the Lecherous Millionaire: B's child will die unless the child receives expensive surgery for which the state will not pay; A, a millionaire, offers to pay for the surgery if B becomes his mistress.[42] Is A's offer coercive? One analysis holds that it is coercive, at least from B's point of view,

---

38 Ibid., at 351–62/pp. 111–25.

39 Kennedy quotes at length from Michel Foucault, *The History of Sexuality, Volume 1: An Introduction,* Robert Hurley trans. (New York: Pantheon Books, 1978), pp. 92–6. In one passage Foucault offers two different characterizations of power – as, first, "the multiplicity of force relations" and, second, "the moving substrate of force relations." Foucault, pp. 92–3, quoted by Kennedy, "Hale and Foucault!," at 352/pp. 112–13. But power cannot be *both* a set of relations *and* the substrate in which those relations inhere. The two characterizations may reflect confusion about power and identity. Even if the relations spring from the substrate, they are not identical with it. And even if the substrate determines the relations, it is not the same as them. The relations may be manifold or various, but the substrate need not be.

40 See Kennedy, "Hale and Foucault!," at 360/p. 122.

41 Ibid., at 327/p. 84.

42 See Joel Feinberg, "Noncoercive Exploitation," in Rolf Sartorius, ed., *Paternalism* (Minneapolis: University of Minnesota Press, 1983), pp. 201–35, at p. 208.

because *A* uses his money to structure *B*'s options so that *B* must choose between becoming *A*'s mistress and her child's dying.[43] Another analysis maintains that *A*'s offer is not coercive, for it gives *B* an option she did not have before and hence amounts to an increase in freedom. This second analysis distinguishes between coercion and exploitation. *A*'s offer is exploitative because *A* opportunistically takes advantage of *B*'s unfortunate situation. There is no coercion because *A* did not create *B*'s situation and has enlarged *B*'s options. "[C]oercing goes beyond exploiting, however morally objectionable the latter may be."[44]

The relevance of these two analyses to social-relations views of property is as follows. In the first place, these analyses as well as most other philosophical discussions view coercion as morally wrong or as in some way objectionable. Coercive offers are a species of threats, and offers and proposals that are coercive differ from those that are noncoercive, even if the line is hard to draw. Hence, the supposedly neutral use of the word "coercion" by Hale and others departs from standard philosophical views as well as from ordinary usage and the dictionary. And so a slide, unawares, by some followers of Hale from a neutral to a nonneutral understanding of coercion is misleading.

Second, although no need exists to choose between these two analyses here, the distinctions on which they rest throw light on property and power. If property does involve what Hale calls coercion and countercoercion, it is vital to focus on who creates a situation of relative vulnerability in the first place. In the event that one can identify such an entity with respect to a particular use of property – United States Steel, perhaps, in the plant-closing case – its actions seem, other things being equal, more objectionable than if the company simply took advantage of the situation of the workers and the town. They are more objectionable because, in terms of the second analysis, this is a case of both coercion and exploitation. Even those who prefer the first analysis might argue that coercion is worse if the coercer creates the situation of vulnerability. Now most social-relations views stress the web of interlocking relationships and the ubiquity of coercion and counter-coercion. Therefore, it may be harder to determine, both as a matter of general policy and in particular situations, which party (if any) created the vulnerability than it would be in many of the hypothetical examples that populate the philosophical literature on coercion. To the extent that a social-relations thinker is more interested in criticizing private property as a whole and suggesting a globally different alternative, and less

---

43 See Joel Feinberg, *Harm to Self* (New York and Oxford: Oxford University Press, 1986), pp. 189–268, especially pp. 229–49.
44 David Zimmerman, "Coercive Wage Offers," *Philosophy & Public Affairs,* 10 (1981): 121–45, at 134. There is a substantial secondary literature on these and other analyses. See especially Alan Wertheimer, *Coercion* (Princeton: Princeton University Press, 1987).

interested in fixing moral, political, or legal responsibility on a particular party, a distinction between coercion and exploitation may seem less important.

V. Kennedy and Nedelsky on Selves and Autonomy

If property is seen as a matter of power, coercion, and social relations, implications flow concerning selves and autonomy. More justice can be done to Singer's view on autonomy and the nature of the self in Section VI, but it helps to get an advance perspective on some connected views now. The context of the discussion is as follows. If property is viewed as social relations, it is crucial to get clear on what social relations are, which social relations are at stake, and among whom these relations exist. Yet the thinkers who have developed social-relations views of property are so varied that it would be foolhardy to suppose that they all share the same position on these matters.

Given that, it makes sense to concentrate on several prominent thinkers and examine their views independently. Felix S. Cohen, as I have remarked, seems to have been among the first to use the phrase "property as social relations."[45] But he treats it as a "vague generality,"[46] and has no special view of those between whom the relations hold — they are just "human beings" or "people."[47] He does not say that property is *all* social relations among them,[48] and counts among the advantages of his "realistic definition of private property" that it "helps us to avoid emotional entanglements."[49] For development of social-relations views, especially as they relate to autonomy and the nature of the self, it is necessary to look to later thinkers. This section explores some of the work of Kennedy and Nedelsky.

Kennedy. Once again taking a cue from Foucault, Kennedy writes:

But another product of the deployment of power in unequal relations is knowledge, meaning particular understandings of the world and how it works.

Knowledge conditions the valuation process, indeed creates valuing subjects, as well as the particular values of valuing subjects.[50]

This passage is important because it espouses a potentially controversial position on the persons among whom social relations hold. These social relations involve power, which leads to a distribution of property.[51] At least two

---

45 Cohen, "Dialogue on Private Property," at 361 (emphasis and initial capitals omitted).
46 Ibid., at 365.
47 Ibid., at 365, 378.
48 Property is "*a set* of social relations among human beings." Ibid., at 365 (emphasis added).
49 Ibid., at 378, 379.
50 Kennedy, "Hale and Foucault!," at 361/p. 124.
51 "Law is one of the things that constitutes the bargaining power of people across the whole domain of private and public life. One of the things this power produces is a distribution of income, understood as a distribution of whatever people value that is scarce."

features of this position merit attention. One is that persons – "valuing subjects" – are entities whose needs, goals, and preferences are in more or less constant flux. This reading is supported by Kennedy's remark that "individuals . . . are themselves reconstituted through exercises of power that seem merely instrumental to preexisting goals. Then they bargain again from the new starting point."[52]

This feature of Kennedy's position may be open to question. True, many thinkers who stand outside critical legal studies and who are uninfluenced by Foucault believe that persons' preferences, and probably also their needs and goals, change over time. Profiles of change vary along many dimensions. For example, in most cultures the preferences of teenagers change more rapidly than those of middle-aged persons. Again, some individuals are rather settled in their preferences, whereas others are flighty or mercurial.

What could make Kennedy's view questionable is the remark that individuals are *reconstituted* through exercises of power. A literal reading of reconstitution suggests that individuals are socially broken down into components and then set up anew in a different form. If this were Kennedy's position, it would make his version of the social relations view of property unstable at the core. Social relations have to exist between particular, identifiable, and reidentifiable entities. The reconstitution of individuals, so understood, would make it difficult to reidentify the individuals – the valuing subjects – among whom social relations hold.

Yet it is charitable to read Kennedy's discussion of reconstitution in a milder way that avoids this objection. He does not contemplate transformations that are so radical as to disable individuals from sustaining social relations to one another. Still, his position is stronger than saying merely that individuals exhibit rather more variation in their goals over time than do most theorists of property. Kennedy seems rather to be saying that exercises of power *bring about* variations in preferences, which makes his position dynamic in the following way. Social relations provide a means not only for understanding property but also for understanding people in relation to property, because the same forces that set values on property also bring about changes in valuing subjects themselves. This position may, however, overemphasize evanescent exercises of power at the expense of long-term patterns of formation of preferences. If fundamental social determinants are often fairly settled and durable, then exercises of power may not so much reconstitute as *maintain* and *reproduce* stable preferences in valuing subjects.[53] This position also raises the

---

Ibid. I believe that in this passage Kennedy uses "income" more or less as he uses "property" elsewhere in the article. Scarcity is often regarded as a presupposition of what can be regarded as a subject of property rights.

52 Ibid. See also the statement that "Foucault adds yet another system of circular causation and stable or unstable equilibrium." Ibid., at 361/p. 123.

53 Perhaps some stable exercises of power affect how valuing subjects view their interests over

question of whether, if exercises of power result in changes in valuing subjects, their apparent choices are just the products of exercises of power.

A different milder reading makes an impression even on my tin ear for Foucault. Perhaps Kennedy's concern is with the reconstitution of the person not as the subject of personal identity but as the locus of experience. Such a concern would shift the focus from philosophy to psychology. This reading, however, fits Kennedy's text ("individuals . . . are themselves reconstituted") less well than the previous milder reading. Moreover, *re*constitution may not be apt unless the subject is individual persons over time. It will suffice to say that, on Foucault's view, institutions and power mold and shape – *constitute* – persons' take on the world. That is, the conceptual categories, meanings, structures of desire, and bodily experiences are constituted by the "discipline" of institutions and power. And were the reader to hold on to *re*constitution all the same, it remains to ask, as with the previous milder reading, whether Kennedy unduly emphasizes evanescent rather than durable exercises of power, and whether the choices of valuing subjects are just the products of exercises of power.

A second, connected feature of Kennedy's position has to do with the freedom of individuals or valuing subjects. He writes:

Power deployed across the whole range of social life shapes the consciousness of people who at any given moment in history pursue what appear to them to be their "freely chosen" or just their "natural" "human" goals through the strategic deployment of that very same power.[54]

It is important to separate what is innocuous in this passage from what is not. It is not a "natural" or (universally) "human" goal to have a Barbie doll or a Seiko watch. Before developing these and many other goals and preferences individuals come under parental influence, peer pressure, or the blandishments of advertising. Nor is it just a matter of brand names. Influences of all kinds have a bearing on individuals' choice of dolls and watches. To that extent Kennedy's position is uncontroversial but innocuous.

If, however, Kennedy puts quotation marks around "freely chosen" because he believes that no goals are freely chosen but only appear to be so, he adopts a controversial position without argument. Given the ubiquity and pervasiveness of Foucauldian power, it seems plausible to ascribe such a belief to Kennedy. Should he have this belief, notice the consequences. Not only is there an absence of free choice in humdrum goals such as saving enough money for a doll or knives and forks. Free choice is also absent in more rarefied goals, such as the goal of writing an article that analyzes "the role of law in the reproduc-

time. See Steven Lukes, *Power: A Radical View* (London: Macmillan, 1974), and the participant-observer study of John Gaventa, *Power and Powerlessness: Quiescence and Rebellion in an Appalachian Valley* (Oxford: Clarendon Press, 1980).

54 Kennedy, "Hale and Foucault!," at 361/p. 123.

tion of social injustice in late capitalist societies."[55] Yet my point is not to saddle Kennedy with a determinist view that excludes moral responsibility for supposedly free choices.[56] Nor is it to suggest that theorists of property are barred from assuming either that not all human actions are determined or that, if they are, determinism does not rule out moral responsibility.[57] My point is rather that because Kennedy uses language that suggests an absence of free choice, his position is not fully clear until he explains whether he believes that all human actions are unfree and, if so, how he believes that affects moral responsibility.

There is one way of looking at my remarks on these two features of Kennedy's position that lessens their critical force but it has the consequence, I believe, of significantly reducing the intellectual interest of his project. This way moves everything to a rhetorical plane. So defenders of Kennedy might concede that he has no developed argument relating to debates about free will and determinism. They might also concede that he hovers between a modest critique (some choices are freer than others) and a radical critique (no choices are free). But, defenders might suggest, Kennedy is trying to disrupt a stable rhetoric of freedom in relation to property, power, and the self. This disruptive attack is a possible academic project. Yet, so far as I can see, the project has modest intellectual interest unless the rhetorical move rests on arguments about free will and determinism.

Nevertheless, another way of looking at my remarks suggests that Kennedy might be on to something of deep interest. This way harkens back to the second of the two milder readings of Kennedy on reconstitution. If the disciplinary structures of Foucauldian power constitute subjective experience, then the issues are more complicated than saying that exercises of power cause preferences and choices. Neither is the only issue that of freedom and determinism. One further issue is whether it is illusory for us to think that we are free agents outside of the social matrix that shapes the way we think. The critical reader may object that the response should be that because under Foucauldian constitution we are all equally unfree, Kennedy's position is only rhetorical. I believe that the objection is overstated. Doubtless his position would command even more interest if he got to the root of free will and determinism. But even as it is Kennedy uses Foucault to underscore the ubiquity of dynamics of power in molding the experience and understanding of ourselves and the world. A

55 Ibid., at 327/p. 84. On this page Kennedy uses the word "motive" rather than "goal."
56 For the view that determinism excludes free will and moral responsibility, see, for example, C. A. Campbell, "Is 'Freewill' a Pseudo-Problem?," *Mind,* 60 (1951): 441–65.
57 Sophisticated statements of the "compatibilist" view that determinism and moral responsibility are mutually consistent positions include Harry G. Frankfurt, "Alternate Possibilities and Moral Responsibility," *Journal of Philosophy,* 66 (1969): 829–39; Harry G. Frankfurt, "Freedom of the Will and the Concept of a Person," *Journal of Philosophy,* 68 (1971): 5–20; John Martin Fischer, *The Metaphysics of Free Will: An Essay on Control* (Oxford and Cambridge, Mass.: Blackwell, 1994).

specific payoff of looking at Kennedy's project in this way is that it suggests how the law of property usually reflects, rather than shapes or curtails, the institutions that are already dominant in a society.

Nedelsky. In a prominent article Nedelsky offers an account of law, property, and the self.[58] Unlike Kennedy, she focuses on the alleged disadvantages of insisting on boundaries between people. In brief outline, her view is that the U.S. Constitution created rights, and especially property rights, that serve as boundaries between the right-holder and other people. The metaphor of a "bounded self" is central to such a view of constitutional law. It gives "a picture of human beings that envisions their freedom and security in terms of bounded spheres."[59] But, Nedelsky believes, this picture and the notion of rights as limits represent a misguided effort to address the "inevitable tension between the individual and the collective."[60] In Nedelsky's view, "boundary is destructive as a central metaphor for addressing the real problems of human autonomy."[61] Hence she begins a search for "a language of law whose metaphoric structure highlights rather than hides the patterns of relationship its constructs foster and reflect."[62]

Thus, Nedelsky takes the social character of the self as fundamental to thinking about law, politics, and property. Her case makes both the descriptive claim that selves are social and the normative claim that the social character of the self is an important constituent of human flourishing. She rejects the idea that autonomy as usually conceived ought to be a primary concern. She suggests, instead, that we shift our concern to the creation and maintenance of rightly ordered relationships, within which some revised conception of autonomy may be constructed. Above all, she suggests, bounded selves are illusory, and the attempt to create bounds is destructive.

Nedelsky offers an intelligent and provocative approach to the self, but reservations are in order on at least three counts. First, I wonder whether, methodologically, she gets the matter backwards. If the issue is how to provide the best account of property rights, selves, and autonomy in social relationships, one should begin with the strongest arguments that one can deploy on this complicated matter. After providing such an account, or within limits during the process of developing it, one can cast about for "new mythic structures, new visions and metaphors"[63] to express it. To seek these structures, visions, and metaphors first confines the search to those that already exist or come to mind. It also runs the risk of giving loose usage and speculative material pride of place over careful argument. If Nedelsky's view is that only

---

58 Nedelsky, "Law, Boundaries, and the Bounded Self."
59 Ibid., at 163.
60 Ibid., at 162.
61 Ibid., at 163.
62 Ibid.
63 Ibid.

through particular metaphors can one grasp any account of property, then some defense is needed of the apparent underlying position that here one can understand metaphors but not nonmetaphorical expression. It may, however, make sense to explore structures, visions, and metaphors concomitantly with the building of strong arguments so that the best account emerges of property rights, selves, and autonomy in social relationships. At all events, to the extent that Nedelsky performs a service by uncovering some implications of the metaphor of boundaries, she undermines this service by launching a search for alternative metaphors, for part of the lesson here is that concentration on metaphors is less helpful than thinking clearly.

Second, Nedelsky seems to go wrong in various ways by trying to get rid of bounded selves and rights as limits. (1) Except for conjoined twins, each person is physically bounded by his or her skin and sometimes has a legitimate interest in repelling attempted invasions. Part of the point of rights in a broad sense is a power to exclude other people and the state. One of the specific functions of property rights is to fence out others and the state in pursuit of legitimate interests. Property rights have important connections with privacy, the exercise of control over one's life, and the development of individuality.[64] (2) Nedelsky's discussion of ownership and sharing[65] seems to confuse two notions of sharing, or at least to move too rapidly from one to the other. The first is sharing in the sense of allowing others to partake of what is mine. The other is sharing in the sense of having co-ownership from the beginning. (3) Setting boundaries, in raising children[66] and in other contexts, often is not inimical to relationships. Only if there are individuals who have some powers to exclude others and some liberty-rights to interact with others can one move on to meaningful interpersonal and social relationships.

Yet Nedelsky is on to something, and it may be possible to adjust her project helpfully. Suppose that rejecting the idea of boundaries altogether would be misguided for at least two reasons. It would obscure the distinguishability of persons and their capacity for agency on which much if not all social protest rests. And it would make it needlessly hard to describe the harms that many people, especially women, suffer in relationships. Even so, boundaries can sometimes be in different respects *both* essential *and* threatening to the creation and maintenance of relationships. Some vulnerability is inevitable in both interpersonal and social relationships. If possible, one should reshape Nedelsky's project so that some personal boundaries survive, with some rights as limits and some modified conception of autonomy, and yet retain an emphasis on social solidarity.

Third, I suspect that something akin to the ambiguity uncovered in Section

---

64 See Stephen R. Munzer, *A Theory of Property* (Cambridge: Cambridge University Press, 1990), Ch. 5.
65 See Nedelsky, "Law, Boundaries, and the Bounded Self," at 172.
66 See ibid., at 171–6.

III is latent in Nedelsky's article. Initially, it might appear that she is criticizing claims relating to autonomy and property on normative grounds. But upon inspection the normative argument turns out to be thin at best. The weight of her critique is conceptually revisionary. The "real problems of human autonomy" do not attach to a concept of property that involves legal rights between bounded selves. They attach instead to a different concept of property – one in which selves are not bounded and the emphasis lies on "patterns of relationship."[67] If this reading of Nedelsky is correct, her critique of property and autonomy pivots mainly on a conceptual maneuver. Her concept of property is vague, because it is unclear what nonbounded selves are and which patterns of relationships are relevant. In the end her critique of property and autonomy, however attractive, rests on few careful normative or conceptual arguments.

VI. Kennedy and Singer on Social Relations

The heart of social-relations views of property lies in their accounts of social relations. It is time to examine the most prominent of these accounts.

Kennedy: From Hale to Foucault. Kennedy suggests that Hale's work, though highly illuminating, is deficient in three respects. First, Hale never applies his account of "the impact of law on bargaining power to the legislative or judicial processes."[68] Second, Hale concentrates on conflicts between workers and owners and between consumers and producers, "to the total neglect of the other 'wide ranging cleavages that run through the social body as a whole', to use Foucault's phrase."[69] Third, Hale assumes that the economic actors who "fight, bargain and cooperate exist independently of those activities as 'subjects' (that is, as autonomous, individual beings) with goals that are just a given of the analysis."[70]

Kennedy believes that Foucault's approach improves on Hale in two ways.

The first is that he [Foucault] sees the play of force as pervading all aspects of social relations, including particularly institutions like the prison, the hospital and the family, and the domain of sexual activity. The second is that he sees the distribution of power as one of the factors that determines the evolution of human knowledge in one direction rather than another.[71]

The first point supplies no definition of "social relations" but it does shed some light on them. It suggests that social relations can exist both inside and outside institutions. Kennedy does not define the word "institution," but for present purposes it will do to say that an institution is an organization con-

67 Ibid., at 163.
68 Kennedy, "Hale and Foucault!," at 360/p. 123.
69 Ibid., at 361/p. 123.
70 Ibid.
71 Ibid.

stituted by rules and practices that serves some purpose or purposes. Prisons, hospitals, and families are all institutions in this sense. To these examples may be added clubs, religious organizations, fraternal orders, chambers of commerce, stock markets, and many others. The quoted passage gives one example of apparently noninstitutional social relations – "the domain of sexual activity." Kennedy is well aware that such activity can occur within an institution, as his later discussion of marriage makes clear.[72] Yet the phrasing of the passage suggests that sexual activity could occur outside any such institution. Two individuals might meet and, under the promptings of passion, engage in sexual intercourse.

If this is a plausible unpacking of the first point that Kennedy extracts from Foucault, at least two questions arise. One is whether all relations are social. I am not interested in captious examples like mathematical relations or relations of distance between planets in our solar system. Nor is the interest in whether all social relations are relations between people; plainly they are not, because people have social relations to their pets, and these relations can even involve institutions, such as the American Kennel Club. Rather, the interest attaches to whether all relations between people are social relations. If Kennedy believes that they are, a very broad understanding of social relations is in play, for it would appear that all interpersonal relations are, or are a proper subset of, social relations. If, however, Kennedy believes that not all relations between people are social relations, some account is needed of how some interpersonal relations fail to be social.

The second question is whether all social relations are property, or at least help to constitute property. Insofar as legal relations are a proper subset of social relations, many legal relations help to constitute property. This proposition is true of legal relations between landlords and tenants, mortgagors and mortgagees, corporations and shareholders, banks and depositors, and many others. Yet it seems implausible to claim that all social relations are, or help to constitute, property. Consider legal relations between judges and bailiffs, prison guards and inmates, the President and Congress. Of course, there are borderline cases, especially in the area of the so-called new property,[73] such as the legal relations between welfare agencies and recipients. If it is not the case that all social relations are or help to constitute property, Kennedy owes the reader an account of which social relations do so and which do not.[74]

Singer on Free Markets and Social Relations. Singer's exposition of property as social relations differs from Kennedy's. Absent is the invocation of Foucault. Much in the foreground is a contrast between the supposed individualism of the free market and the social individuals among whom exists a

---

72 See ibid., at 361–2/p. 124.
73 See Charles Reich, "The New Property," *Yale Law Journal,* 73 (1964): 733–87.
74 A suitable account could allow for borderline cases and distinguish between property relations (or rights) and personal relations (or rights). See Munzer, *A Theory of Property,* pp. 24, 44–56.

network of social relations. In one place Singer writes of various social-relations approaches to property as if they were *schools*.[75] This description is unhelpful insofar as it neglects to clarify the core of all social-relations approaches and the systematic ways in which various "schools" differ from one another. In another place Singer and a coauthor write, on the connected topic of the origins of property, that by "affirming the social origins of property, we mean that property rights do not have a built-in, inherent structure which can be discerned by logical deduction from either the concept of property or the social practices surrounding property use."[76] This statement presupposes a false dichotomy and attacks a figure of straw. Only the most uncautious – or daring! – of contemporary theorists of property would subscribe to the position that this passage opposes.

The best of Singer's writing on property is, however, considerably stronger, and for that reason I concentrate on his well-known article "The Reliance Interest in Property." There he contrasts two approaches to property: "the free market model" and "the social relations approach." The former is said to exhibit these features:

(1) It encourages us to see people as autonomous individuals; (2) It limits the types of social relationships that are relevant to legal analysis by focusing on voluntary agreements and entitlements defined *a priori* by the state; (3) It characterizes rights as fully articulated at specific decision points – when the state allocates property rights and defines personal rights of security initially, and when individuals enter into contracts; (4) It focuses our attention on two questions: (a) who is the owner? and (b) what did the corporation promise?[77]

Although some thinkers may have operated with the model Singer describes, his use of the definite article – *the* free market model – is misplaced, as the following discussion shows. To begin, most individuals are "autonomous" in some sense of that word. Autonomy, as I understand it, is the psychological capacity to be self-governing, which is part of the foundation of a moral right to be treated as self-governing.[78] By contrast, Singer understands autonomous individuals, at least within his articulation of "[t]he free market model," "as fundamentally separate from each other; they are alone in the world. They are basically self-interested, and their interests conflict."[79] It is scarcely conceivable that acute defenders of markets view individuals as "alone in the world." It would also be ironic, for the point of markets is to facilitate voluntary

---

75 Singer, *Property Law: Rules, Policies, and Practices,* p. 21, mentions "a wide variety of schools, including feminist legal theory, critical race theory, law and society, and critical legal studies."
76 Singer and Beermann, "The Social Origins of Property," at 228.
77 Singer, "Reliance Interest," at 655.
78 Munzer, *A Theory of Property,* p. 39.
79 Singer, "Reliance Interest," at 652.

transactions between people. Neither need those who view markets as important regard individuals as "separate" in the sense of isolated or atomic, for individuals live in societies, and it would be a careless mistake to identify markets with societies. Nor must defenders of markets see individuals as "basically self-interested" – whose interests, moreover, "conflict." At least since the early eighteenth century, philosophers have understood that individuals' interests are not necessarily antagonistic to the interests of others, for people sometimes have an interest in the interests of others.[80] Both social conditioning and natural sentiments such as sympathy can lead to interests that are to some extent harmonious. A source of the difficulties in Singer's discussion of individuals is his assimilation of Hobbes and Locke to each other and to neoclassical economists and his uncritical reliance on Macpherson's treatment of possessive individualism.[81]

Next, consider the limits that "the free market model" allegedly places on the types of social relationships that are relevant to legal analysis. Singer is right to say that defenders of markets focus on voluntary agreements. Contracts are unquestionably the hallmark of market transactions. He is also right to suggest that defenders of markets often accept entitlements set by the state, though these entitlements are hardly "defined *a priori*," and it is a mistake to associate this position with Locke, who believed that individuals could acquire property by labor without the consent of others and prior to the existence of society or the state.[82] It is not clear, however, why defenders of markets should be *limited* to voluntary agreements and state-generated entitlements. Conceivably, they could allow for the legal recognition of property rights generated by

80 See, for example, Joseph Butler, *Fifteen Sermons Preached at the Rolls Chapel* [1726], W. R. Matthews, ed. (London: G. Bell & Sons, 1964 [1914]), especially Sermon XI (no opposition necessarily exists between self-love and benevolence); David Hume, *Enquiry Concerning the Principles of Morals* [1751], Sec. IX, Pt. I, Para. 220, in *Enquiries Concerning the Human Understanding and Concerning the Principles of Morals,* L. A. Selby-Bigge, 2nd ed. (Oxford: Clarendon Press, 1966 [1902]), p. 271 (stating that "there is some benevolence, however small, infused into our bosom"); Adam Smith, *The Theory of Moral Sentiments* [1759], Pt. I, Sec. I, Chs. I–II, pp. 9–16, D. D. Raphael and A. L. Macfie, eds. (Indianapolis: Liberty*Classics,* 1982 [1976]) (adopting a position similar to those of Butler and Hume). For comment on these philosophers in relation to property, see Munzer, *A Theory of Property,* pp. 105–7.
81 See Singer, "Reliance Interest," at 652. Macpherson's book *The Political Theory of Possessive Individualism,* though a classic, needs to be reexamined in light of later work on Hobbes and Locke. See, for example, Jean Hampton, *Hobbes and the Social Contract Tradition* (Cambridge: Cambridge University Press, 1986); Matthew H. Kramer, *John Locke and the Origins of Private Property: Philosophical Explorations of Individualism, Community, and Equality* (Cambridge: Cambridge University Press, 1997); James Tully, *A Discourse on Property: John Locke and His Adversaries* (Cambridge: Cambridge University Press, 1980); Jeremy Waldron, *The Right to Private Property* (Oxford: Clarendon Press, 1988), pp. 137–252; and, now, Seana Valentine Shiffrin, "Lockean Arguments for Private Intellectual Property," in this volume.
82 Singer, "Reliance Interest," at 652, 655. Contrast John Locke, *Second Treatise of Government* [1690], Secs. 25–51, in *Two Treatises of Government,* Peter Laslett, 2nd ed. (Cambridge: Cambridge University Press, 1967).

custom. They could also allow that many disputes characterizable as disputes over property could be settled outside the legal system.[83]

Some qualification is also required for the "specific decision points" at which rights are "fully articulated."[84] Doubtless some defenders of markets will emphasize, once again, contracts and state-generated entitlements. But they can also permit custom and quasi-legal orderings of relationships. They can, as does the Uniform Commercial Code, allow course of performance and course of dealing to affect the position of parties to a contract.[85] They can also recognize special legal relationships and concepts, such as that of a holder in due course, whose rights can be greater than any state-generated rights previously allocated to the holder's transferors.[86]

Last, in the context of plant closings, Singer believes that defenders of markets will search for a single owner and focus on what that owner, typically a corporation, promised. Perhaps some judges and thinkers, including some defenders of markets, conduct such a search. Yet many do not. It is a commonplace, among lawyer-economists and academic lawyers of all stripes, that the full bundle of rights called ownership may be split up into smaller bundles held by different entities such that no single "owner" exists. The focus that Singer attributes to defenders of markets also leaves out of account the doctrine of equitable estoppel, which looks at nonpromissory representations made by a party on which others may have reasonably relied to their detriment.

It has been suggested to me that Singer, in presenting "the free market model," is offering an ideal type and is not suggesting that any theorist subscribes to each of the features of the model. Yet the text of his article does not lend itself to this interpretation. And if this interpretation accords what Singer thinks, it is a curious intellectual method to ascribe a welter of vulnerable positions to a certain approach to property without pursuing the exact language employed by those who might be seen as proponents of the free market approach. In this essay I have tried to employ a different method in examining social-relations views: to summarize in Section II these views, and then to examine in later sections the texts of various figures, including Singer, who would be seen as expositors of social-relations views of property.

If Singer caricatures "the free market model" to some extent, "the social relations approach" he favors is, surprisingly, presented in a partly vulnerable way:

(1) It encourages us to see people as situated in various relationships with others that continue over time; (2) It describes social relations as comprising a spectrum from short-lived relations among strangers to continuing relations in the market to intimate

83 See, for example, Robert C. Ellickson, *Order Without Law: How Neighbors Settle Disputes* (Cambridge, Mass. and London: Harvard University Press, 1991).
84 Singer, "Reliance Interest," at 655.
85 See U.C.C. Sec. 2–208.
86 See U.C.C. Secs. 3–302, 3–305.

relations in the family; (3) It comprehends rights as emerging out of understandings that develop over the course of relationships rather than as being fully articulated at clear decision points; (4) It encourages us to ask various questions about the relationship between the parties.[87]

This passage furnishes as tidy and lucid a statement by a proponent of property as social relations as is currently available, even though it raises new issues. For a start, though in litigation it pays for courts to think of the parties in fully contextualized relations, and though contract law contains relational doctrines such as course of dealing and course of performance, Singer does not explain the metes and bounds of the social-relations approach. Furthermore, while Singer is right to point out that there are many types of relations of varying duration, he does not, any more than Kennedy, explain which social relations are, or help to constitute, property. To illustrate, an intriguing article by David Friedman uses Schelling points as a key to explaining property.[88] It portrays property as a characteristic of a set of interacting commitment strategies. In this portrayal the "social relations" are networks of mutual threats and responses. It is scarcely imaginable that Singer would share Friedman's way of understanding social relations (and certainly not Friedman's libertarian payoff). But Singer's treatment of social relations is so amorphous that it is not obvious *how* he would exclude Friedman's portrayal on analytical grounds. It is obvious, though, that Singer would disagree with Friedman on normative grounds. A different point is that Singer, like Macpherson before him, no doubt believes that there are bad as well as good social relations. He hardly wants to import oppressive relations between conquerors and indigenous peoples, or between slumlords and poor tenants, into the law of property. But then he needs some way to identify which social relations are good and, among them, which should make their way into the law of property. Moreover, though rights can grow out of relationships, not all rights do so (consider the right not to be tortured), and some that do are moral rather than legal rights.

These new issues are not merely academic talking points but practical problems. Consider the plant-closing case discussed by Singer.[89] His main conclusion is that the "relational idea" allows us "to take seriously Judge Lambros's intuition that *property rights* should be recognized from the long-standing relation between U.S. Steel, its workers, and the town."[90] Singer's lengthy discussion does not, however, provide helpful guidelines on which

87 Singer, "Reliance Interest," at 655.

88 David Friedman, "A Positive Account of Property Rights," *Social Philosophy & Policy,* 11, no. 2 (Summer 1994): 1–16. A Schelling point is a possible outcome of strategic conflict that is a good candidate for resolving the conflict because of its perceived uniqueness. See Thomas C. Schelling, *The Strategy of Conflict* (Oxford: Oxford University Press, 1960), Ch. 3.

89 See *Local 1330, United Steel Workers of America v. United States Steel Corp.,* 631 F.2d 1264 (6th Cir. 1980).

90 Singer, "Reliance Interest," at 657 (emphasis added).

social relations suffice to justify legal property rights. The practical significance of this point is that it promotes stability to have relatively clear legal
rules, and the amorphous character of Singer's version of the social relations
approach makes clear legal rules much harder to achieve.

There is a deeper difficulty: How can one squeeze a legal, or a moral,
justification out of the fact of a relation of mutual dependence? Suppose that I
have you over for dinner every day for a week because you are a witty and
charming conversationalist. You come to expect food from me, and I come to
expect excellent conversation from you. If, on the first day of the next week, I
decide to invite someone else, or you decide to have dinner alone, one of us
may have disappointed expectations. Yet the fact of these expectations grown
out of our week-long dining relations does not establish that you have a moral
or legal right to dinner from me, or that I have a moral or legal right to your fine
talk. As a point of etiquette, it would certainly be polite for each of us to
mention being unavailable on the next day. But to justify any moral or legal
right it would appear that some moral or legal premise is needed. By parity of
reasoning, one needs a defense of whatever moral or legal premise grounds the
asserted rights of employees and a town in the wake of a corporation's decision
to close a plant. Without such a premise, the fact of relations of mutual dependence does not appear to justify any such rights.[91] One might suggest, as a
friendly amendment, that Singer investigate whether the plant-closing case, as
well as the dining example, can be described as a relationship of moral reciprocity (especially return for good sought or welcomed from others) rather
than of mutual dependence, for that might make a relevant moral or legal
premise easier to defend. There are of course reasons for opposing Hume's
Law (no "ought" from an "is").[92] Should Singer wish to oppose this principle
in convincing fashion, he will need to set out these reasons and grapple with a
substantial philosophical literature.[93]

To prevent misunderstanding, I should clarify the point of the dinner example. I am not saying that that example and *United Steel Workers* are on all fours.
The dinner example involves a much shorter duration and is far less developed
than the plant-closing case. It has only two participants, whereas the legal case
has many participants of different sorts (workers, their families, unions, the
town and its inhabitants, and a large corporation). There would be a vast
difference in detrimental reliance if the workers can show that had it not been
for their and the town's investment in a long-term relationship with U.S. Steel,

91 Munzer, *A Theory of Property*, p. 347, expresses appreciation for Singer's article but suggests
   that, rather than just the fact of mutual dependence, what is needed is a moral and political
   theory of property with special attention to moral reciprocity.
92 See David Hume, *A Treatise of Human Nature* [1739], Bk. III, Pt. I, Sec. I, L. A. Selby-Bigge,
   ed. (Oxford: Clarendon Press, 1960 [1888]), p. 469.
93 Classics include John R. Searle, "How to Derive 'Ought' from 'Is'," *Philosophical Review*, 73
   (1964): 43–58; R. M. Hare, "The Promising Game," *Revue Internationale de Philosophie*, no.
   70 (1964): 398–412.

they would have developed human and social capital with other firms or industries. The point of the dinner example is to present a simple, stripped-down case on the basis of which one can isolate the further features of complicated cases in real life. In addition to the features implicit in the contrasts just drawn, one can list whether mutual dependence is knowing, solicited, and even (not lopsided), whether some relations besides mutual dependence are involved, and how these various relations evolve and change over time. I suspect that a full analysis of the differences between the dinner example and *United Steel Workers* would show, first, that still more factors are involved, and second, that it is perilous to try to generalize from anything so fully contextualized as the plant-closing case.

Behind this deeper difficulty in Singer's work lies another problem: how to keep a professedly neutral concept or method of analysis from sliding into something with a substantial normative commitment. Some pages after the passages examined here, Singer writes: "So far, I have *described* the social relations approach as a way to understand and *describe* social life better."[94] Only then, more than fifty-five pages into his article, does he add: "I now shift to a more explicitly *normative* argument."[95] This sentence signals a need for normative premises, and Singer gives them as "goals" or "policies." One is "allowing market participants real freedom to fashion their relationships within joint enterprises." The other is "protecting vulnerable persons in times of crisis."[96] Though these are humane and even laudable normative premises, Singer offers no independent or clear arguments for them.[97] What is clear is that he cannot have it both ways. If his social-relations approach is descriptive and, apparently, as neutral as possible, then he needs to argue for the relevant normative premises. If that approach is not wholly descriptive or neutral, as the later qualifier "more explicitly" normative argument suggests, then he should from the outset make clear which normative commitments his social relations approach makes.

Nevertheless, it is possible to develop helpfully Singer's version of property as social relations in at least two ways. One is to adapt a suggestion rejected earlier in regard to his discussion of "the free market model." The suggestion is to see Singer's "social relations approach" as an ideal type. It is not so much that current property law *is* in accordance with this approach. Rather, it is that it *could become* so. We could aspire to a system of property law that emphasizes the variety of fully situated social relationships. We could encourage judges to be sensitive to these manifold relationships in rendering decisions. How far this sensitivity should extend without disrupting a desirable stability of property law is itself a matter for judicial decision.

94 Singer, "Reliance Interest," at 659 (emphasis added).
95 Ibid. (emphasis added).
96 Ibid.
97 See ibid., at 659–63 (citing the work of others).

Another way is to reintroduce autonomy. The sort of autonomy that Singer ascribes to "the free market model" is both implausible and, to many (including Singer and me), unattractive. But I do not think that Singer need be hostile to autonomy as I understand it – namely, as the psychological capacity to be self-governing, which is part of the foundation of a moral right to be treated as self-governing. Singer, unlike Kennedy, does not use language that intimates doubt about a capacity for free choice. One can read Singer as favoring the development of a capacity for free choice and free action – or at least choices and actions that are consonant with moral responsibility. This capacity should be exercised in a fashion that is sensitive to fully contextualized relationships with others. Autonomy so articulated does not, for Singer, imply that any person is entitled to ride roughshod over others.

My aim is to interpret Singer's approach sympathetically but not to elide differences. Singer mentions allowing people "real freedom to fashion their relationships within joint enterprises."[98] I am sympathetic to employee ownership of and control over some business enterprises, though in the light of empirical evidence I suspect that in many circumstances traditional manager-controlled firms are more efficient.[99] Singer also stresses the importance of shielding "vulnerable persons in times of crisis."[100] I share such a view, but at the same time have doubts about some forms of poor relief and some social welfare programs.[101] So, due to different normative premises and to different understandings of social situations, Singer and I may part company on some points, but that fact does not preclude my interpreting irenically some features of his larger position on property.

I come, finally, to the remedial dimension of Singer's social-relations view. The reader will recall from Section II the general proposition that the reform of institutions sometimes requires changing basic rules of property law. An example is Singer's call for a decision in the plant-closing case that would have given the workers not money damages but property rights in the plant. Other social-relations views give such examples as homesteads[102] and articulate reasons for more radical redistributions of property.[103]

I agree in principle but may disagree with particular changes. I accept the general proposition. Elsewhere, I have argued that sometimes land reform is preferable to tax-and-transfer redistribution.[104] There are, for instance, strong

---

98 Ibid., at 659.
99 See Munzer, *A Theory of Property,* pp. 290, 317–79.
100 Singer, "Reliance Interest," at 659.
101 See Munzer, *A Theory of Property,* pp. 98–119, 142, 191–3, 216, 241–53, 267, 274–6, 313–14.
102 See Note, "Distributive Liberty: A Relational Model of Freedom, Coercion, and Property Law," at 868–75.
103 See Kennedy, "Law-and-Economics from the Perspective of Critical Legal Studies," at 472–3.
104 See Munzer, *A Theory of Property,* pp. 314, 422, 460–64; Munzer, "Special Case," at 564–5.

arguments of both policy and constitutional law for the Hawaii Land Reform Act of 1967.[105] Likewise, I support most homestead legislation. However, promissory estoppel and equitable estoppel are more plausible legal arguments in cases like *United Steel Workers*.[106] And if one is to offer a policy argument sounding in property rather than in contract, moral reciprocity seems more promising than Singer's reliance interest in plant-closing cases.

VII. Property, Liberalism, and Communitarianism

It would be a boring trick to show that an avowedly pluralist theory of property like mine can accommodate some insights of social-relations approaches. Pluralists are known for their slack morals and receptivity to intellectual compromise. So it will be more interesting to show that social-relations thinkers may be closer to Rawlsian political liberals than either of these groups has imagined. By turning the analysis in this direction, I can also partly tie off some loose ends regarding autonomy and the nature of the self. This section presupposes a modest acquaintance with liberal political theory in the last three decades of the twentieth century.

To define terms: *Liberalism* is a theory of the state that tolerates different moral values and is open to challenges to tradition and established institutions. *Kantian liberalism* is a species of liberalism that holds itself out as a comprehensive doctrine. Rawls's Kantian liberalism holds that the state must remain neutral with respect to competing moral values because even if some moral values are objectively better than others, consensus is lacking on which are better. *Rawlsian political liberalism* is a species of liberalism that rests the state on reasonable foundations that are publicly acceptable and involve no commitment to a particular conception of the good. Rawls himself provides two different versions of liberalism.

In *A Theory of Justice* (1971), Rawls offers a variety of Kantian liberalism. There he cashes out "moral values" as "conceptions of the good." He rests the state on principles that "free and rational persons . . . would accept," behind a veil of ignorance, "in an initial position of equality" to have a just "basic structure of society."[107] This work provides a Kantian liberalism that Rawls later calls a *metaphysical* conception of justice as fairness.

---

105 Hawaii Rev. Stat. ch. 516 (1985), upheld in *Hawaii Housing Authority v. Midkiff,* 467 U.S. 229 (1984). I defend the decision in *A Theory of Property,* pp. 460–64.

106 I do not mean that these arguments are winners, only that they state accepted causes of action rather than a novel cause of action sounding in property. Compare *Charter Township of Ypsilanti v. General Motors Corp.,* 506 N.W.2d 556 (Mich. App. 1993) (rejecting theories of breach of contract, promissory estoppel, unjust enrichment, and misrepresentation in a plant-closing case) (General Motors later settled on terms favorable to Ypsilanti), with *Mazer v. Jackson Insurance Agency,* 340 So. 2d 770 (Ala. 1976) (accepting theories of promissory and equitable estoppel in a land-development case).

107 John Rawls, *A Theory of Justice* (Cambridge, Mass.: Harvard University Press, 1971), pp. 11–12. In terms of subsequent literature, Rawls's Kantian liberalism, not only Rawlsian political liberalism as defined later, is *political* rather than *comprehensive* liberalism and is

This first version of Rawlsian liberalism, insofar as it bears on property, contains various features that might be taken to be sympathetic to a social-relations view of property. For Rawls, no property exists prior to social institutions; justifiable property rights and distributions of property must be tied to self-respect; and the products of natural talents are social assets.[108] Furthermore, the concept of autonomous individuals is to some extent a social construction.[109] Under Rawls's Kantian liberalism, moreover, the value of individual autonomy is one competing conception of the good among others. The state may not promote autonomy as a particular substantive value (first-order autonomy), but it can support whatever ways of life individuals adopt by autonomous choice (second-order autonomy).[110]

The situation of private property under Rawls's Kantian liberalism is weakly similar to its situation under a social-relations theory. Points of affinity include the social character of property and the socially constructed nature of the idea of autonomous individuals. Yet differences remain. One difference concerns the origins of property. For Rawls, the principles that govern the narrow system of property that is part of the basic structure of society are determined by what people would choose in the original position. But social-relations theorists like Singer hold that property rights are created by historically situated actual people. Another difference has to do with autonomous choice. Each of the people in Rawls's original position rationally chooses principles of justice – including principles relating to property – without taking into account the interests of others. In social-relations views that make room for autonomy, such as those of Nedelsky and Singer, autonomy rests partly on social relations. It would thus appear that these autonomous individuals have a moral obligation to make choices regarding both principles of property and their own property that are moral, not merely rationally self-interested, choices.

The situation of private property under Rawlsian political liberalism, however, is more similar to its situation under a social-relations theory. In *Political Liberalism* (1993), Rawls does not use a social contract theory. His project is no longer metaphysical but *political.* He now believes that reasonable but incompatible moral views imperil the stability of a well-ordered society of

---

based on the *fact* of competing moral values rather than on the supposed *truth* that these values are incommensurable. See, respectively, Stephen Gardbaum, "Liberalism, Autonomy, and Moral Conflict," *Stanford Law Review,* 48 (1996): 385–417; Stephen A. Gardbaum, "Why the Liberal State Can Promote Moral Ideals After All," *Harvard Law Review,* 104 (1991): 1350–71.

108 For a critical discussion see Munzer, *A Theory of Property,* pp. 233–41.

109 See Allen E. Buchanan, "Assessing the Communitarian Critique of Liberalism," *Ethics,* 99 (1989): 852–82, and Will Kymlicka, *Liberalism, Community, and Culture* (Oxford: Clarendon Press, 1989), Ch. 4, who discuss pertinent passages in Rawls with reference to communitarian criticisms.

110 See Gardbaum, "Liberalism, Autonomy, and Moral Conflict," at 394–5.

justice as fairness. For present purposes, key features of Rawls's revised theory are the idea of public reason and the need to build an overlapping consensus.

Rawlsian political liberalism retains as a basic liberty the right to hold and have the exclusive use of personal property. Rawls rejects two wider conceptions of a right of property. One is a powerful conception that includes rights of bequest and the ownership of means of production. The other is a conception that includes "the equal right to participate in the control of means of production and natural resources, which are to be socially owned."[111] Neither of these conceptions is needed for the development and exercise of the moral powers, and hence cannot be part of a basic liberty. However, a society might adopt either conception later when more is known about the society's history and circumstances.[112] To the extent that property relates to autonomy, notice that Rawls's views on autonomy have changed. Earlier Rawls had emphasized moral agency and espoused a roughly Kantian idea of autonomy as a capacity to act on self-acknowledged principles of justice.[113] This value Rawls now calls "moral autonomy."[114] He believes that it cannot be part of a political conception of justice precisely because many citizens reject it. The relevant value now is "political autonomy," which is "the legal independence and assured political integrity of citizens and their sharing with other citizens equally in the exercise of political power."[115]

Rawlsian political liberalism, I suggest irenically, can be compatible with some social-relations views of property, for two reasons. First, the existence of a specifically political form of autonomy, as Rawls defines it, brings with it equal sharing in the exercise of political power. Of course, the *concept* of political autonomy does not generate political power any more than does the *concept* of moral autonomy. The point is rather if political autonomy in Rawls's sense exists, it brings with it political power – including the power to seek arrangements of property that attend to persons as politically situated individuals. Second, deferring the selection of any "wider" conception of property until more social and historical knowledge is available makes it easier to accommodate actual social relations among persons. I do not suggest that Rawlsian political liberalism and social-relations views are congruent in this respect. Some social-relations thinkers may resist the privileging of political contexts over property contexts when it comes to specifying principles of justice. They may urge that principles relating to justice in property arrangements are vital at early stages of the constitution of civil society. I do suggest,

---

111 John Rawls, *Political Liberalism* (New York: Columbia University Press, 1996 [1993]) (paperback ed. with new introduction), p. 298.
112 See ibid., pp. 298, 338–9. Compare Rawls, *A Theory of Justice*, pp. 270–74, 280–82.
113 See Rawls, *A Theory of Justice*, pp. 252–6, 515–16.
114 Rawls, *Political Liberalism*, p. xliv.
115 Ibid.

however, that some principles regarding property cannot be formulated, and certainly not wisely formulated, until some social and historical knowledge is at hand. For instance, whatever principles Singer would support in plant-closing contexts could hardly have been formulated prior to the industrial revolution and the advent of labor unions.

It may be objected that no social-relations theorist can accept a Rawlsian hand extended in peace because its political liberalism is not communitarian.[116] I do not know that all social-relations thinkers must be, or even are, communitarians in any sense. Yet likely some are in some sense of communitarianism. But which sense? Stephen A. Gardbaum usefully separates three positions.[117] Antiatomist communitarianism holds that an individual's identity is constituted in part by the community to which he or she belongs. Metaethical communitarianism maintains that moral values are engendered by the social practices of historically situated communities. Strong communitarianism asserts that a life lived within a particular (nonliberal) political community is intrinsically good and in particular is better than a life lived under a liberal state. Plainly, the last of these is incompatible with Rawlsian political liberalism. But the first two seem compatible with it. In particular, an emphasis on social relations and a nonindividualistic conception of autonomy seems especially characteristic of Singer's work. So if Singer is a communitarian at all, it seems sensible to place him in the antiatomist camp, which seems compatible with Rawlsian political liberalism.

It is possible to develop this line of thought in the following way. Suppose that autonomy is understood as the psychological capacity to be self-governing. Suppose also that autonomy in this sense is part of the foundation of a moral right to be treated as self-governing. Suppose finally that autonomy in this sense represents, within Rawlsian political liberalism, an ideal to which individuals may aspire, even though a neutral state may not promote this ideal. Even so, autonomous choosers of ends may be seen antiatomistically. They may also be seen as individuals who can freely bind themselves to others in a community, and indeed bind themselves in a way in which they are not free to repudiate their commitments. If this line of thought is sound, then autonomous individuals within Rawlsian political liberalism can choose to participate in and sustain community life. In particular, they can do so in regard to property

---

116 Representative communitarian thinkers include Alasdair MacIntyre, *After Virtue: A Study in Moral Theory,* 2nd ed. (Notre Dame, Ind.: University of Notre Dame Press, 1984); Michael J. Sandel, *Liberalism and the Limits of Justice,* 2nd ed. (Cambridge: Cambridge University Press, 1998); Charles Taylor, *Philosophy and the Human Sciences: Philosophical Papers,* vol. 2 (Cambridge: Cambridge University Press, 1985), especially the chapters on "Atomism" and "The Nature and Scope of Distributive Justice," pp. 187–210, 289–317; Charles Taylor, "Cross-Purposes: The Liberal-Communitarian Debate," in his *Philosophical Arguments* (Cambridge, Mass. and London: Harvard University Press, 1995), pp. 181–203.

117 See Stephen A. Gardbaum, "Law, Politics, and the Claims of Community," *Michigan Law Review,* 90 (1992): 685–760.

by, for example, entering marriage, assisting family members, and giving to churches and charitable organizations.[118]

This line of thought must, however, be qualified for at least two reasons. First, Rawlsian political liberalism is only *partly* compatible with antiatomist communitarianism. Antiatomist views do not hold merely that individuals can choose their communal commitments, but that *some* communal commitments are both unchosen and constitutive of the self. Some thinkers may suggest that quintessential antiatomist communitarians (for example, Michael Sandel) take themselves to disagree with Rawls, as does the leading defender (Will Kymlicka) of specifically liberal approaches to community. This suggestion contains much truth in regard to Rawls's earlier Kantian liberalism. Yet it is overdrawn with respect to the later position here called Rawlsian political liberalism. Second, to say that Rawls's later liberalism is partly compatible with *some* social-relations views is not to say that they are closely related. Sharp differences in method and substantive values remain. The degree of compatibility is greater for a system builder like Singer than for a more radical and less systematic thinker like Kennedy. And even Singer is not trying to provide a philosophical theory of justice in the manner of Rawls.

These reflections help to tie off some loose ends concerning autonomy and the self in relation to property. Even if some lawyer-economists think of autonomy as Singer says they do, Rawlsian political liberals do not. The latter view political autonomy as an idea of legal independence and political integrity as they relate to citizens' sharing equally in the exercise of political power. Rawlsian political liberals can respond positively to the modified conceptions of autonomy I developed for Nedelsky and Singer in Sections V and VI. So far as the nature of the self is concerned, Rawlsian political liberals are unlikely to share Kennedy's musings about valuing subjects or Nedelsky's worries about rights as limits. Yet they can share Singer's concern that in the end whatever wider conception of property a society adopts it must take account of the fully situated social relations among persons.

VIII. Retrospect and Prospect

If one looks back over this examination of social-relations views of property, one sees in these views a mixture of flaws and insights. The Introduction telegraphs the mix; a précis here would spill ink to little use. Far more useful, I think, is a conspectus of the problems that social-relations thinkers face in the future development of their views. Setting forth these problems can aid two more or less distinct groups of legal and political theorists. On the one side stand those with intellectual reservations about property as social relations.

---

118 Here I build on an insightful discussion in Buchanan, "Assessing the Communitarian Critique of Liberalism," at 866–71.

They may not share all of my criticisms of or endorse my partial sympathy with social-relations views. But their sense that such views should be taken seriously would increase if criticisms were met and problems were solved. On the other side stand social-relations thinkers themselves. Perhaps some in this group are content to write for those who are already disposed to agree with them. Yet, I doubt that most are or should be. To the extent that they have an intellectual or an ideological interest in convincing others, they should meet criticisms, dissolve apparent problems, and solve real problems. In this final section, I attempt to promote the future mutual engagement of those interested in the theory of property.

Conceptual Revisions, Social Descriptions, and Normative Claims. One problem for social-relations thinkers is to separate conceptual revisions, social descriptions, and normative claims in their views – or to show why such separations are misguided or impossible. This problem underlies, *inter alia,* an ambiguity between revising the concept of property and attacking familiar justifications of property (Section III), neutral and nonneutral uses of "coercion" (Section IV), and Singer's apparent slide from descriptive to normative claims (Section VI). To some degree, this problem is a matter of exposition: At times, social-relations thinkers are not clear on what they are doing, or think they are doing. But to a greater extent the problem is methodological: Some social-relations thinkers might protest the philosophical methods that I employ. They might, for example, challenge the coherence of any distinction between the descriptive and the normative. Nevertheless, for progress on methodological issues to occur it is vital that social-relations thinkers take account of the nuances in positions with which they disagree. To illustrate, though I use Hume's Law (no "ought" from an "is") in setting out a possible criticism of Singer, I am careful to say that there are reasons for opposing it (Section VI). Elsewhere, I recognize that social or legal commitments can be built into the language that people use, and I am agnostic on whether the evaluative content of some words and concepts can be squeezed out so as to leave conditions for applying these words and concepts that are wholly nonevaluative.[119]

Coercion, Power, and Freedom. Two quite different problems arise here for social-relations approaches to property. One problem is what account of coercion or power best serves their purposes. I submit that social-relations thinkers would do well to drop coercion and to cast their net more widely in constructing an account of power. Despite Hale's best intentions in proposing a technical, neutral use of the term "coercion," he and his followers have lapsed into using that word in its ordinary sense, which carries a connotation of unjust compulsion due to threat. In the bargain they have fallen into a briar patch of philosophical difficulties that almost anyone would find daunting (Section IV). Power seems a better concept for exploring the social dimensions of property.

119 See Munzer, *A Theory of Property,* p. 78; Munzer, "Special Case," p. 562.

In Foucault, Kennedy finds an undeniably insightful analyst of power relations. I suggest, though, that social-relations thinkers look beyond Hale and Foucault.[120] Work on durable influences on preferences might correct an undue emphasis on evanescent exercises of power and the reconstitution of the self (Section V). I do not assume that Kennedy would be averse to looking elsewhere, for he evidently regards his article on Hale and Foucault as a rough appropriation of bits of their work (Section IV.F) and not necessarily as the entire truth about power.

The other problem concerns the relations between coercion and power on the one hand and freedom on the other. To deal with this problem social-relations thinkers need to say either a good deal less or a great deal more. At present, social-relations writing on coercion seems largely oblivious to sophisticated debates on the connections between coercion, exploitation, and freedom (Section IV). And, again at present, some social-relations writing on power and freedom flirts with grand issues of free will and determinism but supplies little argument to back up a stand on these issues (Section V). The easier course would be to issue a promissory note on these issues or forswear them altogether. If, however, social-relations thinkers wish to disrupt a stable rhetoric of freedom in relation to property, power, and the self, and if they intend to procure this disruption by honest toil, then they must take up the great issues of free will and determinism.

Autonomy and the Nature of the Self. A central problem is to show what account of autonomy is most useful for thinking about property. Among the accounts, or gestures in the direction of an account, that have surfaced in the course of this essay are the following: the psychological capacity to be self-governing (my basic understanding); a capacity for agency in which some rights and some personal boundaries remain (Nedelsky revised); a capacity for free choice and action that is consonant with moral responsibility and sensitive to fully contextualized relationships with others (Singer reformulated); a Kantian capacity to act on self-acknowledged principles of justice (Rawls's "moral autonomy"); and the legal independence and assured political integrity of citizens and their sharing with other citizens equally in the exercise of political power (Rawls's "political autonomy").

To make progress with any of these accounts, or others that might be offered, several steps need to be taken. First, one must explain how unequal property holdings impinge on the exercise of autonomy. Second, one has to clarify which personal relations are important and how those relations are

---

120 In a vast literature, see in addition to the works of Lukes and Gaventa (note 53) the different Marxist views in Ralph Miliband, *The State in Capitalist Society* (London: Weidenfeld and Nicholson, 1969), and Nicos Poulantzas, *Political Power and Social Classes,* trans. and ed. Timothy O'Hagan (London: NLB and Sheed & Ward, 1973), the sociological discussion in Dennis H. Wrong, *Power: Its Forms, Bases and Uses* (Oxford: Basil Blackwell, 1979), and Peter Morriss, *Power: A Philosophical Analysis* (Manchester: Manchester University Press, 1987).

compatible with some rights and some boundaries.[121] Third, one must display the connections between moral and political autonomy and justify the treatment of morally autonomous noncitizens in relation to autonomy.

A related problem is to show how the self should be understood in relation to property. It is clear what falls short. On the one hand, the stripped-down rational choosers in Rawls's original position will not suffice, because the only actual phenomenon for investigation is property in social situations. One the other hand, Kennedy's highly plastic valuing subjects that are perpetually reconstituted through exercises of power, as well as Nedelsky's selves with a plethora of relations and a paucity of boundaries, yield a much too amorphous view of the self (Section V). Plainly more work needs to be done both by political liberals and by social-relations thinkers. The former must do more than they have to explain how property, and especially unequal property holdings, affect the self.[122] The latter have to be much clearer and more specific. A potentially useful start would be to develop the remarks in the final paragraph on Kennedy in Section V. The remarks point to his use of Foucault on power to show how property helps mold our experience of ourselves and property and to explain how property usually reflects, rather than shapes, socially dominant institutions.

Social Relations. The most serious problem is to demonstrate what is novel, illuminating, and right in speaking about *property as social relations.* Felix S. Cohen apparently originated the phrase. But he considered it a vague generality. Some will agree: Property and property rights are a matter of law; they involve legal relations, which are among other things social relations – indeed, what else could they be? At present, nowhere are social-relations thinkers less successful than in their treatments of social relations themselves (Section VI).

Providing answers to questions like the following would help. Do the relations that are, or help to constitute, property belong to an independently identifiable class? An answer might show how to exclude David Friedman's networks of mutual threats and responses (Section VI). Is there a moral or political litmus test for social relations that are, or help to constitute, property? An answer could clarify whether a social-relations view is descriptive or normative or both and, if it is normative at least in part, which "good" social relations should make their way into the law of property. How do social relations help judges to solve real-world problems? An answer could explain whether a

---

121 See, for example, Catriona Mackenzie and Natalie Stoljar, eds., *Relational Autonomy: Feminist Perspectives on Autonomy, Agency, and the Social Self* (New York and Oxford: Oxford University Press, 2000).

122 Munzer, *A Theory of Property,* pp. 37–187, 317–418, does a little but not nearly enough. One anonymous reader described me as a liberal. I have never so described myself, in part because I have no developed views on many of the issues that separate liberals from other political thinkers. It is accurate to say that I am a moderate egalitarian and a pluralist so far as the theory of property is concerned.

Catholic or Mormon landlord may refuse to accept a cohabiting couple as tenants, and whether a Zionist Jewish landlord may refuse to accept a Palestinian activist as a tenant.

Political Commitments. Another, and for the present final, problem concerns the defense of political commitments. Most present-day exponents of social-relations views belong to critical legal studies or to the political left in English-speaking countries. It is difficult, however, to descry in their views carefully articulated defenses of their political commitments.[123] One point of bringing up the libertarian perspective of David Friedman is to inquire whether a quite different political commitment could nevertheless be a social-relations view. Similarly, one point of the extended treatment of Rawlsian political liberalism in Section VII is to ask whether political commitments that are to the left of the political center in the United States, but do not go so far to the left as critical legal studies, could still be closer to social-relations views than most have imagined. If social-relations thinkers were to take this final problem seriously, their future work, I suggest, could clarify methodological differences between them and other thinkers, and could provide a stronger defense of their political commitments than is currently available.

Whatever the merits of this suggestion, it is possible to develop social-relations views sympathetically and to diminish needless conflict with other views. Current statements of social-relations theorists' views on property may be more nearly exaggerations of what they see as neglected features of law and society than cool or detached propositions of legal theory. The language employed in some passages may reflect loose usage rather than carefully considered claims to which the authors would cling to the end. Moreover, Singer's social-relations approach can be seen as an ideal type – not so much the way that property law *is* as what it *could become.* One can interpret, or perhaps recast, his views on autonomy so as to leave room for free choices that are sensitive to fully contextualized relationships with others. Perhaps most interestingly, it is possible to effect some rapprochement between Rawlsian political liberalism and social-relations views. I have no interest in papering over genuine intellectual disputes. Yet I believe that if debate about the legal and political theory of property settles down to a cooler temperature of engagement, those who study these debates will be rewarded by an increase in light.

---

123 Cf. Matthew H. Kramer, *In the Realm of Legal and Moral Philosophy: Critical Encounters* (London: Macmillan Press Ltd., 1999), pp. 122–32. He argues, convincingly in my opinion, that the critique of the public/private distinction by Hale and Morris R. Cohen is "politically neutral in the abstract" (p. 124) and can be used by thinkers of quite different political persuasions.

3

Must We Have the Right to Waste?

EDWARD J. MCCAFFERY

I. Introduction

Anglo-American law has long since gotten to the point where an owner can pretty much do whatever she wants with her property, right down to the limiting case of using it all up. Indeed, even if there are things an owner cannot do with her property – "absolute" ownership never really having meant "absolute"[1] – she probably *can* waste it. The *jus abutendi,* or the "right of destroying or injuring [one's property] if one likes," as Roscoe Pound put the matter in 1939, or, equivalently, the affirmative right "to consume, waste or destroy the whole or part of [one's property]," as A. M. Honoré phrased it in 1961, has long been recognized as one of the basic rights in property's "bundle of rights."[2] William Blackstone stated the case bluntly two centuries ago: "[I]f a man be the absolute tenant in fee-simple . . . he may commit whatever waste his own indiscretion may prompt him to, without being impeachable or accountable for it to anyone."[3]

I thank Scott Altman, Robert Ellickson, Richard Epstein, Terry Fisher, Jim Krier, Steve Munzer, Seana Shriffin, and many anonymous readers for helpful advice, and Negin Mirmirani and Tim Lan for excellent research assistance. Many of the ideas in this chapter are developed in greater length in my manuscript currently titled *A New Understanding of Property* (Chicago: University of Chicago Press, forthcoming).

1 See Carol M. Rose, "Canons of Property Talk, or, Blackstone's Anxiety," *Yale Law Journal,* 108 (1998): 601–32. See also Duncan Kennedy, "The Structure of Blackstone's Commentaries," *Buffalo Law Review,* 28 (1979): 205–382; Albert W. Alschuler, "Rediscovering Blackstone," *University of Pennsylvania Law Review,* 145 (1996): 1–56; Robert P. Burns, "Blackstone's Theory of the 'Absolute' Rights of Property," *University of Cincinnati Law Review,* 54 (1985): 67–86.

2 Roscoe Pound, "The Law of Property and Recent Juristic Thought," *American Bar Association Journal,* 25 (1939): 993–8, at 997; A. M. Honoré, "Ownership" in A. G. Guest, ed., *Oxford Essays in Jurisprudence* (Oxford: Clarendon University Press, 1961). See also J. E. Penner, "The 'Bundle of Rights' Picture of Property," *UCLA Law Review,* 43 (1996): 711–820.

3 William Blackstone, *Commentaries on the Laws of England,* at Book III, Chapter 14; see also Book III, Chapter 18.

On even a moment's reflection, however, this right to waste is as puzzling – or ought to be – as it is entrenched. Anglo-American society has never liked waste, in moral or in consequential terms, as Blackstone's language in announcing the right to waste ("his own indiscretion") itself suggests. There are good reasons, sounding in a reasonable social contractarian moral and political theory, for this disdain: Private waste imposes social harms. Where then did the right to waste come from? Why do we still have it to this day – indeed, why is it so taken for granted that we never seem to question it? More important, must we have it, as a descriptive matter? Should we continue to have it, as a normative one?

I explore these typically unexplored questions in this chapter and argue against the continuance of the *jus abutendi*. The argument proceeds in four basic steps.

One, the right to waste emerged as part of an absolute conception of ownership developed largely in the context of an agrarian economy, where waste referred to the dissipation or destruction of a permanent physical asset, paradigmatically land. The right was seen as both a necessary and a nonproblematic, because self-limiting, aspect of the absolute conception of ownership, which was itself desired for other reasons, such as wealth-maximization.

Two, there is another conception of "waste" besides the dissipatory one, a conception long present in ordinary moral language and intuition. This is the idea of waste as the relatively nonurgent expenditure of scarce resources, paradigmatically time or money.

Three, as fungible capital has replaced land as the chief carrier of social value, waste in this second sense has become the more important threat to the collective welfare of a reasonable society. Nonurgent waste is socially harmful from a political liberal point of view, and is not as constrained by self-interest as dissipatory waste is.

Four, it is possible to use the tax system, specifically a progressive cash-flow consumption tax, to affect a revised conception of ownership modeled after a life estate form of ownership. Under this new conception, property owners no longer have an unequivocal right to waste; the tax system exerts a general levy on high-end, nonurgent expenditures.

My principal aim in this intellectual journey is to get readers to rethink conceptions of property ownership and in particular the wisdom and necessity of having a general, affirmative right to "consume, waste, or destroy" all of what one owns. I also aim at an important but long neglected intellectual synthesis: the joining together of our normative theories about tax and property.

II. Two Conceptions of Ownership

A. The *jus abutendi* is a byproduct of an absolute conception of property ownership that was itself desired – as the right to private property was itself initially desired – in large part to *prevent* waste. Aristotle saw early on in the Western political tradition, in direct response to Plato, that private property was needed to ensure that property be cared for properly, or at least not wasted.[4] A similar movement repeated itself when forms of property ownership moved from diverse and often limited term interests, in the period of feudal tenancies, toward absolute ownership, a move clarified by Blackstone and confirmed by Honoré.

Time is a necessary element in conceptions of ownership. Without some sense of time, a claim of ownership means little. The child who insists that a toy she is grasping is "mine" is right, up to a point. An early step in developing a conception of property is to establish that there is anything at all that can endure through time; a necessary later step is to address the question of for how long. Much of Anglo-American property law concerns the question of ownership in time: what the "terms" of various possible "estates" are.

The fee simple absolute is the largest possible estate; its holder owns the property indefinitely. A fee simple absolute stands in contrast to a life estate, which terminates on the death of the measuring life, typically belonging to the beneficial owner or user of the property. (A life estate is a paradigm for a limited term interest, but it is by no means the only or even the most common one. A mortgagee or leaseholder, for two very important examples, also has a limited term and is thus constrained not to waste the underlying property.) Property held under a life estate passes over to the successor or future interest, typically a "remainder," on the death of the measuring life.

I shall use this vocabulary to compare and contrast two conceptions of ownership, an absolute and a life estate one. The absolute conception, though long checked in some of its present-oriented powers, has also long dominated our thinking about the concept of ownership through time.[5] There is, in contrast, no generally invoked life estate conception of ownership. I aim to establish that such an understanding of ownership is in fact an attractive one.

B. Consider the six incidents of ownership as listed, in somewhat typical fashion, by Pound:

(1) the *jus possidendi* or right of possessing;
(2) the *jus prohibendi* or right of excluding others;
(3) the *jus disponendi* or right of disposition or alienation;
(4) the *jus utendi* or right of using;
(5) the *jus fruendi* or right of enjoying the fruits or profits; and
(6) the *jus abutendi* or right of destroying or injuring if one likes.[6]

---

4 Aristotle, *Politics,* Book II, Sections 5–6.
5 Rose, "Canons of Property Talk."
6 Pound, "The Law of Property."

These rights are a modern distillation of ones brought down from Roman law – although where, exactly, the *jus abutendi* came from is a matter of some dispute.[7] Most of the six rights readily extend to a life estate owner, or to any other present interest of limited duration. A life estate holder can possess the property (1), exclude others from it (2), dispose of her life estate (3), use the property (4), and enjoy its fruits or profits (5). One can think of these as the present-oriented rights of ownership, for they use or affect the present interest.

A fee simple absolute adds but two powers to the life estate. One is the power to direct where the property is to go on the termination of the life estate: that is, a *jus disponendi* (3) as to the remainder, or future, interest. Two is the *jus abutendi* or right of waste (6). We could add a third difference – the right to sell or alienate the entire estate in fee simple absolute. But although the ability to sell the whole property is of immense practical importance, it is entailed in the rights set out above. One can sell what one has. A life estate owner already has the *jus disponendi* as to her life estate.[8] What she lacks is the right of disposition as to the remainder, which, when combined with what it is that she does have, would give her a right of disposing of the whole.

This all follows from the fact that the fee simple absolute owner owns the remainder interest, but the life estate holder does not. The *jus disponendi* as to the whole and the *jus abutendi* are rights that affect the remainder interest as well as the present one – one can think of them as the future-oriented rights of ownership. Under a life estate conception of ownership, the property holder cannot waste the property or direct where the remainder is to go. Later, in Section II.E, we shall see that it is possible to engraft a power to direct the disposition of the remainder onto a life estate conception. This is equivalent to subtracting the right to waste from an absolute conception of ownership.

C. These same ideas come into play in the language of trusts, as a simple example illustrates. Imagine that a benefactor, Ann, has placed a stock of valuable property into a testamentary trust, with a life estate to her surviving husband, Bob, remainder to her daughter Cynthia. Bob has the right to the "fruits" or income of the trust – he has the *jus fruendi* – but not to the *res* or capital itself.

To tie the trust discussion together with Pound's vocabulary, what this should mean is that the right to capital generates the same rights as owning the

---

7 See generally Barry Nicholas, *An Introduction to Roman Law* (Oxford: Clarendon University Press 1962), p. 154 ("[t]hus, the commentators adapted the definition of usufruct by adding to the rights of use and enjoyment the right of abuse – *ius utendi fruendi abutendi.* The adaptation is a little forced, since 'abuse' has to include alienation, but it is also, in its emphasis on the plenitude of enjoyment conferred by ownership, misleading.").

8 See, for example, *White v. Brown*, 559 S.W.2d 938 (Tenn. 1977). See also cases such as *Kendall v. Ernest Pestana, Inc.*, 709 P.2d 837 (Cal. 1985) (tenants must have reasonable right to assign their term interest in a lease).

remainder interest. This right is precisely what Bob does not have; it belongs to Cynthia. Honoré describes the "right to capital," which he sees as one of the incidents of "ownership," as follows:

The right to the capital consists in the power to alienate the thing and the liberty to consume, waste or destroy the whole or part of it; clearly it has an important economic aspect. The latter liberty need not be regarded as unrestricted; but a general provision requiring things to be conserved in the public interest, so far as not consumed by use in the ordinary way, would perhaps be inconsistent with the liberal idea of ownership.[9]

Honoré's general right to capital consists of two more specific rights or powers: the "power to alienate the thing," precisely analogous to Pound's *jus disponendi* as to the whole, and the "liberty to consume, waste or destroy the whole or part of it," precisely analogous to Pound's *jus abutendi.*

Pound's and Honoré's formulations thus lead to the same place. An absolute owner has both a full *jus disponendi* and the *jus abutendi,* meaning that she can transfer or destroy the capital of the trust, whereas a life estate owner has neither right. Honoré's phrasing of the right to capital is especially helpful, however, because it focuses further attention on the puzzling right to waste. Honoré notes that the liberty to "consume, waste or destroy . . . need not be regarded as unrestricted." He also comments that a general provision limiting the *jus abutendi* by a public interest requirement "would *perhaps* be inconsistent with the liberal idea of ownership" (emphasis supplied). Honoré senses that the *jus abutendi* stands on very different ethical footing from the *jus disponendi,* and his language in supporting a right to waste is tentative and equivocal. But he puzzles over the impracticability of any "general provision requiring things to be conserved in the public interest, so far as not consumed by use in the ordinary way. . . ."

Honoré does not dwell on this puzzle for long, however, because he sees an easy way out. In the next words after the above-quoted language, Honoré makes clear that he sees the *jus abutendi* as being fairly inconsequential:

Most people do not wilfully destroy permanent assets; hence the power of alienation is the more important aspect of the owner's right to the capital of the thing owned. This comprises the power to alienate during life or on death, by way of sale, mortgage, gift or other mode, to alienate part of the thing and partially to alienate it.[10]

This is the predominant view of the right to waste: it's not important, because the *fact* of waste is not important. The contemporary libertarian legal scholar Richard Epstein has recently used much the same line of reasoning. Epstein argues in a naturalistic way, pointing out, as Honoré did before him, that most people do not destroy assets:

9 Honoré, "Ownership," at 107.
10 *Ibid.*

[L]and is necessarily permanent, and the improvements on it generally have an expected life beyond the present owner. These assets will be passed on, unless we think it likely that persons in the present will take great pleasure in destroying what they have created. This last risk seems quite small. . . . Regulatory intervention at common law has never been concerned with people who want to destroy what they own; rather it has been to restrict the period of time during which assets could be tied up in trust.[11]

The *jus abutendi* stands as an embarrassment in Anglo-American law. Blackstone condemns it in moral terms; Honoré finesses it, because he sees the right to waste as an inconsequential, perhaps difficult to remove, and in any event inevitable ancillary of the important *jus disponendi;* and Epstein essentially follows suit – he sees no problem of waste, because he denies the prevalence of it.

D. An absolute conception of ownership differs from a life estate conception in its *jus disponendi* as to the remainder and its *jus abutendi.* The latter is an unattractive feature of a social property regime. The attraction of an absolute conception can thus be expected to lie in its unfettered *jus disponendi.*

There are indeed good collective reasons for having a full *jus disponendi,* lying in what Honoré saw as "the economic aspect." As economists since at least Adam Smith have noted, the right to alienate property is efficient. There are two aspects to this greater efficiency. The first is allocative or asset-specific. Free alienability furthers the flow of resources to their highest and best use and users. Under limited term interests, selling is hazardous and complicated and so less selling occurs: imagine purchasing a life estate from its holder and wondering about the condition of his health, centrally relevant to the value of the term interest. This *de facto* restraint on trade is more or less per se inefficient.

The second aspect of the greater efficiency of a full *jus disponendi* involves time. As Harold Demsetz noted in an oft-cited 1967 article, a property owner who owns property indefinitely will optimally maximize its value over and in time, rather than exploit it for short-term gain.[12] If a farmer only owned land until her death, in contrast, she would have a perverse incentive to maximize its produce over the course of her lifetime alone, ignoring longer term provision for the quality of the soil and so forth. This sets the tragedy of the commons in temporal terms: The absence of absolute private property rights can lead to a destructive tyranny of the present. Granting the farmer a *jus disponendi* as to the whole not only allows her to sell the farm more readily (allocative

---

11 Richard Epstein, "Justice Across the Generations," in Peter Laslett and James S. Fishkin, eds., *Justice Between Age Groups and Generations* (New Haven: Yale University Press, 1992), p. 102 (footnotes omitted).

12 Harold Demsetz, "Toward a Theory of Property Rights," *American Economic Review, Papers and Proceedings,* 57 (1967): 347–59. Rose, "Canons of Property Talk," comments critically on Demsetz's "just-so story," but also notes its significant influence.

efficiency), it also gives her the right incentive to care for the property used in the best way, even if this way entails some near term sense of restraint (temporal efficiency).

The temporal efficiency of the *jus disponendi* takes into account a human tendency to be concerned with one's heirs – to have what David Hume described as "confined generosity."[13] With the brilliant simplicity of free market mechanisms, this intergenerational altruism need not be complete or even especially pervasive. If a particular farm owner cared only about her own or her own generation's consumption, for example, her best course of action is to sell the farm to someone prepared to optimize over time. Even if she did not value the remainder for itself, as long as she could sell the entire estate she could do so to someone else who did value the remainder – and so indirectly act for the long term. The spendthrift farmer would receive the greater value generated by someone else's intergenerational altruism, and still get to maximize her own lifetime pleasure. The general effect of optimizing over time depends on some, but not total, concern for future generations, in addition to free alienability.[14]

The movement towards an unfettered *jus disponendi* – as, indeed, the movement towards private property itself – was therefore *antiwaste*. "Waste" in the classical legal sense was precisely concerned with temporal inefficiency. Absent effective monitoring mechanisms, limited term owners could be expected to try to favor the present over the future by wasting the property. An attractive solution to the problem of waste was to avoid competition between limited term owners by moving to an absolute conception of ownership, *jus abutendi* and all, and trust in the basic rational self interest of human nature to prevent the fact of waste. In giving owners an absolute right of disposition, the law curtailed any compelling reason to exercise the concomitant right to waste.

E. Is it possible to start with a life estate, add in the attractive features of a fee simple absolute, but stop short of granting a *jus abutendi?* It turns out that by granting a life estate three doctrinal mechanisms, all widely used in modern trust practice, we get close to just this goal.

One, we can give the life estate holder broad managerial powers over the specific assets of the trust. This is akin to making Bob the trustee of Ann's testamentary trust, as is in fact common for surviving spouses. This first modification deals with the problem of allocative or asset-specific inefficiency. Suppose the trust corpus consisted of a farm. Bob doesn't know much about farming and has little interest in learning. Under modern trust practice, Bob, as trustee, could sell the farm and reinvest its value in whatever he deems appro-

---

13 David Hume, *A Treatise of Human Nature* (L.A. Selby-Bigge ed., 2nd ed. Oxford: Clarendon University Press 1978 (1740)) p. 499.
14 See generally Robert J. Barro, "Are Government Bonds Net Wealth?," *Journal of Political Economy*, 82 (1974): 1095–117 (seminal paper using "overlapping generations model").

priate: a mix of stocks and bonds, say. Bob is limited by fiduciary duty to invest in a way that doesn't "cheat" on the remainder interest – he couldn't buy exclusively "junk bonds," for example, risking principal to increase interest, a rule that actually implements an antiwaste norm.[15] But Bob is free to make broad decisions over the best allocation of resources, provided that he acts with some solicitude for the future – that he respects the absence of his right to waste, that is.

Two, we can give the life estate holder limited powers of invasion into the corpus or principal of the trust. Once again, current trust law and practice sanctions just such devices.[16] Rights to get at value otherwise belonging to the remainder would be limited to certain specified purposes, like the reasonable needs of health, education, support, or maintenance of the income beneficiary. The limited power to invade corpus can be seen as a refinement of what is meant by "waste": Using the trust *res* for serious medical needs is not necessarily an exercise of the *jus abutendi,* as opposed to *utendi.* Spelling out in greater detail the terms and conditions of the power of invasion would lead into a consideration of objective urgency: One would have to somehow come to distinguish needs from wants and so forth, topics I shall touch on only briefly here.

Three, we can add a "power of appointment" to the life estate.[17] A power of appointment gives its holder the right to designate the heirs – a sort of *jus disponendi* as to the remainder. The right of disposition isn't unlimited, however, for there is no effective way to sell or transfer the remainder in the present tense – a person holding a life estate with a power of appointment is constrained to maintain the existence of a remainder. The power is only a testamentary one. Such powers of appointment are often used, in practice, to preserve flexibility as to where the remainder passes on the life estate holder's death. If Ann insisted on the remainder going to her children, but left the terms, proportions, and conditions up to Bob, this would be a "limited" power of appointment; if the power were fully open, it would be a "general" one. The power of appointment allows Bob to make prudent decisions about the varying needs of the children at a later date than Ann's death, while giving Ann assurance, at the moment of trust creation, that Bob will not squander the entire trust on his own selfish wants. It thus addresses some of the concerns over temporal inefficiency, while accommodating a human desire to choose or direct one's own heirs.

Consider now what Bob has. He has a life estate with full managerial powers to direct the sale and investment of the trust *res;* he can enjoy the "fruits" or income of the trust and he also has a limited power to invade the

---

15 See Uniform Principal and Income Act (Revised 1961) 2; Simon Gardner, *An Introduction to the Law of Trusts* (New York: Oxford University Press, 1990) pp. 113–27.
16 See, for example, 26 U.S.C.A. ("I.R.C.") 2041(b)(1)(A).
17 See generally I.R.C. 2041.

corpus for urgent personal needs; he has a power of appointment to direct where the remainder is to go on his death. This all moves us to a conception of a property owner as a general fiduciary as to part of his property – the capital part. Bob has the use of the property during his life and most of the other rights of full ownership. He can use the capital and thus deplete the remainder for urgent needs. What he does not have – just about all that he does not now have – is the *jus abutendi*. He cannot waste the property. While he retains the power to direct where the remainder is to go, he must reasonably insure that there *is* a remainder to go somewhere, absent extraordinary circumstances.

These collective powers are what I mean as the life estate conception of ownership. They consist of all of the rights of the absolute conception save the *jus abutendi;* the life estate holder cannot "consume, waste or destroy" all of "his" property, because he is constrained to leave a remainder. Later we will come to see that a properly designed tax system can make just such a conception of ownership practicable.

III. Waste

A. I have argued that in the evolution of the common law of property, an absolute conception of ownership with an unfettered *jus disponendi* appeared to be a better constraint on temporal inefficiency or "waste" than any direct legal restriction on the *jus abutendi*. This becomes more evident when one considers the historical problems with laws against waste.

The common law doctrine of waste – more properly a doctrine against waste – strictly concerns the temporally inefficient situation of a present owner's neglecting the interests of some future owner.[18] The doctrine can only come into play under a life estate or other limited term interest where there is a specific, named future interest to assert it. A life estate holder is constrained not to – whereas an absolute holder has an unequivocal right to – commit waste. Under the ancient and particular legal doctrine of waste, however, only certain forms of future interest holders could assert the right.[19] Other limitations plagued the doctrine, as the law was unable or unwilling to engage in frequent, particular disputes between "neighbors in time" over the proper management of property. The legal literature for example draws distinctions between "permissive" and "affirmative" waste, that tend to turn on the form of wasteful action taken.[20] These distinctions are not germane to an objective, reasonable social concern about waste. Nor, for that matter, and relatedly, are they of much interest to future interest holders: a person inheriting a dilapidated farm is apt

18 See Richard A. Posner, *Economic Analysis of Law,* 3rd ed. (Boston: Little, Brown, 1986), pp. 64–5.
19 Blackstone, *Commentaries* at Book III, Chapter 14 and Book II, Chapter 18.
20 Ibid. at Book II, Chapter 18; see also Jesse Dukeminier and James E. Krier, *Property, Fourth Edition* (New York: Aspen Law & Business, 1998), pp. 224–5.

to be unconcerned with whether or not acts of omission or commission have led to its state.

The common law against waste was asset specific, nearly exclusively concerned with land. The general matter of squandering wealth could in theory be met with a more general law against waste, one that would apply without a specific party in interest to assert it. But herein lay a rub. A general social doctrine of waste was virtually incomprehensible to Blackstone and his peers. Blackstone clearly thought it was a *moral* problem to waste property. "Though the waste is undoubtedly *damnum*," Blackstone wrote, referring to waste that a fee simple absolute holder might commit, "it is *damnum absque injuria*"[21] – a moral wrong without legal redress. Honoré likewise had paused over the practicalities of a general law against waste. Society was prepared to concede an unlimited *jus abutendi* both because it considered the factual problem of waste limited and any direct theoretical solution to it impracticable.

B. It is time to mark more clearly a distinction between two conceptions of waste. One is the idea of waste as dissipation: the pure loss of value, with none but some possibly perverse – to an Anglo-American at least – pleasure in the loss. Think of letting the farm go to seed or burning down the house. Such "dissipatory" waste represents no tangible good to anyone; the value disappears into the ether.

The legal and property scholars who have discussed waste – and tolerated the general right to it – have meant it in this dissipatory sense. Blackstone first defines waste in Book II of his *Commentaries* as follows:

Waste, *vastum,* is a spoil or destruction in houses, gardens, trees or other corporeal hereditaments, to the disherison of him that hath the remainder or reversion in fee-simple or fee-tail.[22]

When Blackstone picks up the topic of waste again in Book III, dealing with real property, he first mentions that waste is "destruction in lands and tenements" and goes on to elaborate:

[W]aste is a spoil and destruction of the estate, either in houses, woods, or lands; by demolishing not the temporary profits only, but the very substance of the thing; thereby rendering it wild and desolate; which the common law expresses very significantly by the word *vastum* . . .[23]

The focus on dissipatory waste led legal scholars to conclude that the problem of waste is a self-limiting one, at least once absolute ownership was established. Why would anyone literally throw value away? It is not necessarily

---

21 Blackstone, *Commentaries* at Book II, Chapter 14.
22 *Ibid.* at Book II, Chapter 18.
23 *Ibid.* at Book II, Chapter 14.

so — the fact that dissipatory waste is not common in our culture is more a matter of social and economic institutions, including, importantly, custom and mores, than any kind of necessity — but we can nonetheless concur with Honoré's view that "most people do not wilfully destroy permanent assets."

A second conception of waste refers to nonurgent, frivolous, or excessive consumption: poor choices of how to spend time or value.[24] Such nonurgent waste does not destroy property but rather moves it into other hands — think of selling the farm for a sack of beans. We might therefore expect that a capitalist society be more concerned with dissipatory than with nonurgent waste, and would even use different terms for the two; this might indeed explain the law's exclusive concern with the former conception of waste. Yet ordinary moral discourse and etymological senses of the word "waste" from medieval times down forward have *not* drawn this sharp distinction.[25] The two senses often blend together in ordinary discourse; we talk of foolish choices of how to spend value as if the spendthrift were indeed "throwing money away." Whereas dissipatory waste might be seen as only a metaphor for nonurgent waste — foolishly spending money is *like* throwing it away — the two senses have become much more closely linked than that.[26]

I wish to be clear about what is intended from these matters of definition. Legal theory invariably refers to dissipatory waste. Life estate holders, tenants, mortgagees, and others have legal duties not to waste specific assets in this dissipatory sense. But dissipatory waste is rare in practice, constrained in large part by an absolute conception of ownership and self-interest. Only if one would rather destroy a thing than sell it and consume its value would an absolute owner willingly commit dissipatory waste. Nonurgent waste, however, presents much different challenges and concerns. Most important, the very absolute conception of ownership that makes dissipatory waste less likely

---

24 Money presents an interesting case. One could, of course, literally burn money, thus engaging in dissipatory waste. In a complete monetary equilibrium, an absolute destruction of money would have a deflationary effect on the remaining money supply — other money would increase in its relative value. Whether this would completely offset the loss of value associated with the initial destruction of cash is a complex question of practical economics not considered here. All dissipatory waste will have pricing effects as well, that lessen — but would not normally eliminate — the loss of value to society. The issue of greater concern to the essay in regard to money is nonurgent waste.

25 I discuss the etymology and related points in my book manuscript. I am much indebted to Ruth L. Harris, "The Meanings of 'Waste' in Old English and Middle English," unpublished Ph.D. dissertation, University of Washington, 1989.

26 Thorstein Veblen uses the term "waste" to describe the conspicuous consumption of the "pecuniary class," choosing the term precisely because ordinary moral discourse uses it: "It is here called 'waste' because the expenditure does not serve human life or human well-being on the whole." Thorstein Veblen, *The Theory of the Leisure Class* (New York: Funk & Wagnalls, 1899) p. 76. See also J. Peter Grace, *War on Waste: President's Private Sector Survey on Cost Control* (New York: MacMillan, 1984).

makes nonurgent waste *more* so. If one can do whatever she wants with "her" property, then many individuals will indeed be irresistibly tempted to spend it all on their own wants, however nonurgent these be from a collective perspective. In sum, the two conceptions of waste are connected because each is enabled *de jure* under a *jus abutendi*. But the two conceptions stand apart because the right to waste is *de facto* rare relative to dissipatory waste, but not rare relative to nonurgent waste. People most certainly do "consume, waste or destroy" all or large portions of their capital.

Ultimately, the argument for bringing this second conception of waste into the legal and philosophical analyses of property rights is a normative, not an analytic one. I believe that ordinary moral discourse is right when it comes to "waste": A reasonable society *should* be concerned with nonurgent waste. We also can and should develop legal constraints against it. This is not a matter of definitions. The argument must rise or fall on the strength of the normative concerns motivating it, as set out in the balance of this essay.

C. The conception of waste as nonurgent expenditure relates to a philosophic vocabulary developed by Thomas Scanlon and used in a related fashion by John Rawls.[27] To a thorough-going utilitarian, value is simply and strictly a matter of subjective preferences, perhaps corrected for factual errors. Comprehensive ethical utilitarians have little use for a conception of waste as nonurgent consumption; one man's waste is another's need.[28]

Scanlon points out that in ordinary moral discourse, however, we do not act as simple utilitarians: we do not, that is, accept at face value a person's subjective statement of worth. Rather, we make reference to some objective measure of interpersonal value, which Scanlon calls "urgency." We classify different sorts of desires: preferences for medical expenditures, for example, strike us as more urgent – up to at least a fairly high quantum – than preferences for different types of gourmet cuisines, regardless of the subjective intensity of the preference in the soul of its holder. Scanlon does not mean "objective" here to relate to some foundational truth claim; he means merely to get outside of the language of subjective preferences and hedonic utility. He explicitly leaves open the grounding for the objectivity – either in some "naturalist" or "conventional" understanding.[29]

---

27 See Veblen, *The Theory of the Leisure Class.* I discuss Veblen's conception of waste in Edward J. McCaffery, "The Tyranny of Money (Book Review)," *Michigan Law Review,* 98 (2000: 2126–53). See also T. M. Scanlon, "Preference and Urgency," *Journal of Philosophy,* 82 (1975): 655–69; John Rawls, *A Theory of Justice* (Cambridge, Massachusetts: The Belknap Press of Harvard University Press, 1971).

28 Veblen, *The Theory of the Leisure Class,* explicitly makes this point but proceeds to use the term "waste" to get at ordinary moral understandings in any event.

29 Scanlon, "Preference and Urgency."

Rawls uses a similar understanding of objective values to develop the important concept of "primary goods," which stands at the core of his social contractarian response to utilitarianism:

The thought behind the introduction of primary goods is to find a practicable public basis of interpersonal comparisons based on objective features of citizens' social circumstances open to view, all this given the background of reasonable pluralism.[30]

There is no reason to engage here in any complex project of political philosophic taxonomy. We need not specify precisely what goods are or are not "urgent." The ultimate practical instantiation of a law against waste in the tax system can – and I believe should – rest on rather crude classifications of urgency, turning more on the level or degree of private use than on the kind. Scanlon after all begs off the task of defining what, exactly, is "urgent," and Rawls similarly leaves the precise content of primary goods to be spelled out by others acting within fair epistemic procedures.

The important point is that we have a way to – and do – talk about things in a vocabulary of urgency. This is both a matter of kind and of degree. We see some goods – food, clothing, minimal shelter and medical supplies, education – as being basic and essential. Others we see as less important, and even – at some quantum or point – not urgent at all. We have long used the word "waste" in ordinary moral discourse to get at this latter category. It is a waste, say, to spend money on a lesser urgent need while allowing more pressing matters to wait, or to buy one more luxury car or fur coat when one has garages and closets full enough as is.

D. A third conception of waste involves nonuse – the failure beneficially to use one's time, talents, or resources. This conception of waste is especially salient in regard to human capital, an increasingly important repository of value: a mind is a terrible thing to waste, as the saying goes.

I do not here draw on this idea of waste as nonuse. The nonuse of a material resource is constrained in much the same way as dissipatory waste is, namely by its being self-harming. Consider money. Burning cash or stashing it under one's mattress are both self-harming acts; spending it all on a grand binge, in acts of nonurgent waste, may not be. This is the essence of the social, objective problem with nonurgent waste: one cannot count on the invisible hand of subjective self-interested action to serve the collective good, as one plausibly can, on balance, when it comes to the dissipation or nonuse of potentially productive physical assets or money. The subjective and reasonable objective interests diverge when it comes to nonurgent waste.

---

30 John Rawls, *Political Liberalism* (New York: Columbia University Press, 1993, 1996 [paperback ed. with new introduction]), p. 181.

Insofar as human capital is concerned, a doctrine against wasteful nonuse would also push the theory to violate norms of political liberty. Taken to a certain limit, after all, an antiwaste norm becomes a wealth-maximizing one: any failure to optimize value is a waste, in some sense. But it is important not to push the theory this far. In particular as to human capital, compelling an individual to devote her talents to the accumulation of social value sets material wealth as a kind of *summum bonum* and is an illegitimate intrusion of the state into individual pursuits of different comprehensive conceptions of the good. (This is not to say that some requirement that able-bodied adult citizens must work if at all possible as a condition of receiving state support – workfare, in short – is illegitimate; I express no opinion here on this difficult set of questions.[31]) But once an individual has exercised her talents in a social market, and has received money or some other carrier of social value in recompense, it is within the legitimate powers of society to determine what it is she can or cannot do with her property or, equivalently, what of the material is "her" property in the first instance. A doctrine against the nonurgent use of social resources does this, as part of the social delineation of property rights.

E. The chief repository of property value has moved since the eighteenth century from real to intangible property, paradigmatically money. The capital stock writ large is now the most important carrier of social value, at least putting aside human capital, which presents its own distinct difficulties alluded to above. The concern with dissipatory waste has remained subdued – people don't generally burn money any more than they destroy land. But a social concern with nonurgent waste has, or should have, increased. People *do* waste money, even as they do not generally misuse land, in this nonurgent sense.

There have been periodic attempts throughout Anglo-American history to curb excessive luxury spending by so-called sumptuary taxes and laws.[32] These laws have been specific ones that face the problems of identifying particular offensive goods, item by item; they do not address the more general problem of nonurgent expenditure. Such sumptuary laws have invariably failed and been repealed.

It is therefore not surprising that, with an affirmative *jus abutendi* and without effective legal sanctions against nonurgent waste, we find moral condemnations against luxurious living and excessive consumption, as in the writings of Smith, Hume, and Benjamin Franklin in the eighteenth century, and

---

31 See Edward J. McCaffery, "The Burdens of Benefits," *Villanova Law Review,* 44 (1999): 445–93, and sources cited therein for some relevant considerations.
32 See Alan Hunt, *Governance of the Consuming Passions: A History of Sumptuary Law* (New York: St. Martin's, 1996); Robert H. Frank, *Luxury Fever: Why Money Fails to Satisfy in an Era of Excess* (New York: The Free Press, 1999), pp. 199–201.

Thorstein Veblen in the nineteenth.[33] A concern with opposing excessive consumption is understandable and pragmatic. Since savings is nonconsumption, society can only have a capital stock if some of its members do not consume all that they can. In particular, there has to be some way to keep the rich from spending all that they might on themselves – from not wasting "their" capital.

There is reason to believe that cultural values or social norms have helped matters in capitalist democracies. Keynes, in a passage cited with approval by Rawls, saw that a frugal aristocracy was critical to England's power and success throughout the nineteenth century. In Rawls's text:

Keynes remarks, for example, that the immense accumulations of capital built up before the First World War could never have come about in a society in which wealth was equally divided. Society in the nineteenth century, he says, was arranged so as to place the increased income in the hands of those least likely to consume it. The new rich were not brought up to large expenditures and preferred to the enjoyments of immediate consumption the power which investment gave.[34]

Rawls is troubled by this state of affairs, understandably enough, although he does not deny the facts of the matter. This is as we would expect of a political liberal theorist – at least one who has not seen the possibilities of a general social law against waste. Rawls proceeds:

If the rich had spent their new wealth on themselves, such a regime would have been rejected as intolerable. Certainly there are more efficient and just ways of raising the level of well-being and culture than that Keynes describes. It is only in special circumstances, including the frugality of the capitalist class as opposed to the self-indulgence of the aristocracy, that a society should obtain investment funds by endowing the rich with more than they feel they can decently spend on themselves.[35]

Rawls here sees the "frugality of the capitalist class" as a fortuity. He is reluctant to grant the "rich more than they can decently spend on themselves" out of the obvious fear that this frugality will soon turn into the "self-indulgence of the aristocracy." These comments presume a *jus abutendi* – the absence of a law against waste. Such a law would and will ensure that the capitalist class remain frugal.

---

33 I discuss many of the sources in my book manuscript. See generally Stephen Innes, *Creating the Commonwealth: The Economic Culture of Puritan New England* (New York: W. W. Norton, 1995); Barry Shain, *The Myth of Individualism: The Protestant Origins of American Political Thought* (Princeton: Princeton University Press, 1994); Albert O. Hirschman, *The Passions and the Interests: Political Arguments for Capitalism Before its Triumph* (Princeton: Princeton University Press, 1977, 1997 [paper]).

34 John Rawls, *A Theory of Justice,* pp. 298–99, citing John Maynard Keynes, *The Economic Consequences of the Peace* (London: Macmillan, 1919).

35 John Rawls, *A Theory of Justice,* p. 299.

This is a central paradox of capitalist society. The common law of property grants absolute ownership, in part to give individuals the incentive to amass and care for large stores of capital, which in turn serve the collective good. But in giving individuals this absolute power, society has also given the wealthy the *right* to waste that capital, which would not generally serve the public good. The result is a delicate and fragile balance. Society must continue to hope for the frugality and not the self-indulgence of its affluent members, with none but the tools of moral approbation to help realize the hope.

How might a reasonable society better encourage the accumulation of capital on the one hand while discouraging its waste on the other? We shall soon see that society can respond with a general law against waste by using the tax system. But first let us canvass why this task is so important.

IV. The Political Liberal Problems of Waste

A. Waste in both its dissipatory and nonurgent senses has been frowned on throughout Anglo-American history. But what, exactly, is wrong with waste from a political or moral point of view?

There is something obvious and irreducible in ordinary moral discourse's condemnation of waste – everybody knows that waste is bad; this is, in fact, largely what the word means. But in moving this ordinary moral insight into legal and political contexts, we encounter certain conceptual difficulties. On closer inspection, however, many of these difficulties turn out to be artifacts of the way we have grown accustomed to thinking about property rights.

If we begin with the premise that private property is absolute, there seems to be nothing politically wrong with waste in either of its senses. Indeed, it is the very question – What's wrong with waste? – that seems odd. Waste might be a bad thing, of course – prudence counsels against it, and we try to dissuade our friends and loved ones from engaging in it – but it would, ultimately, be none of our official public business. A social concern with waste would be meddlesome, paternalistic, envious. It's your property, after all, and you can do whatever you want with it, "without being impeachable or accountable for it to anyone," as Blackstone had put it.

But why should we begin with the premise that the private-ness of property is absolute? This only begs all of the most important questions. It is after all part of the task of a reasonable society to come up with fair conceptions of property rights in the first instance. Indeed, a compelling argument for the absoluteness of private property is that this is wealth-maximizing or – in my preferred vocabulary – antiwaste. The "absoluteness" of private property derives its justice from other, independent goals – the social, collective good justifies and grounds the private right, not vice versa.

We have grown accustomed to a certain priority of thought in thinking about property. We first determine what property is private, up-front. Then – and only then – do we feel compelled by conceptions of liberty to leave private parties alone, at least absent some strong, overriding public interest. We must in these lights first justify specific, particular social intrusions or limitations on property, for these forever threaten to be "takings" of private property, as opposed to refinements of what private property means in the first place, or society's enforcing the terms of its tacit agreement that property can only stay private, provided, say, that it is not wasted.[36]

We do not have to decide matters this way. We can change the time at which decisions over what is public and private are made – we can effect a fundamental shift in the timing of our thinking of property. Rather than decide up-front what is private, we can hold back and keep our judgments in abeyance until the moment of ultimate private preclusive use. Here the parallel to environmental regulation or common law nuisance is strong: The law has long imposed reasonable restrictions on the use of nominally private property in the name of the greater public good. We can understand these restrictions as holding that the property ceases to be private – or the rights of the private owner are no longer "absolute" – when, as, and if a proscribed use is attempted. In this light, curtailing the right to waste is tantamount to maintaining that the nonurgent waste of capital is a harmful public use: Squandering money on baubles is like failing to replenish the soil, or polluting waterways. It is only at the moment of the attempted conversion of capital into private preclusive use that we can distinguish between *utendi et abutendi,* use and abuse. Until then, we can view one's claim on "private" wealth, accumulated from work or savings, provisionally, as held in a kind of trust, part public, part private.

Having seen that the question of what's wrong with waste cannot be finessed from the start – we do not lack the right or ability to ask it – we need to get a better handle on what is indeed wrong with waste in its nonurgent sense. There are at least four problems that a reasonable, pluralist, political liberal society might see with such waste.

B. One, nonurgent waste distorts the allocation of resources. Capital is directed towards the social production of less important goods, viewed objectively. Now someone might object at this point that consumption *per se* is

---

36 See generally the work of Richard Epstein, perhaps especially his book *Takings: Private Property and the Power of Eminent Domain* (Cambridge, Mass.: Harvard University Press, 1985). On the idea that property rights assume a certain baseline of what is and is not "private," "property," or a "right" in the first place, see Duncan Kennedy and Frank Michelman, "Are Property and Contract Efficient?," *Hofstra Law Review,* 8 (1980): 711–80. See also Honoré, "Ownership," at 144–5.

good – and so it is, as Keynes, among others, taught us.[37] But savings is good, too. And savings is nonconsumption. All wealth is either spent, which spending we can call consumption, or not, which nonspending we can call savings. Once we have made a social determination over the appropriate social level of capital – as economists and political theorists constantly press us to do – we have, axiomatically, made a decision about the appropriate social level of nonconsumption.

This way of putting the matter underscores that there is a posterior question of what nonconsumption we want. All consumption stimulates the economy, but we need some nonconsumption as well. We might reasonably conclude that the consumption of sports cars and fur coats is less important a stimulation than, say, the manufacture of middle-class coats and cars; conversely, we might conclude that the best consumption not to happen in order to fund the common capital stock is the consumption of the wealthy, and not that of the lower economic classes. A revised conception of property would look to the distribution of goods and resources in the consumption or use "space" of social resources, to employ a metaphor used by Amartya Sen and others.[38]

One might also object at this point that a social determination over the relative urgency of consumer expenditures is moralistic. This vocabulary, however, turns out to be unhelpful and misplaced, especially when the tax system is put into play – as modern life has definitely put it. Decisions over what, whom, and when to tax are unavoidably moral. This does not mean that we should invoke particular comprehensive moral doctrines, such as the religious ones that have typically condemned luxurious living in the past; indeed, the general norms of political liberalism preclude us from doing precisely that.[39] But we cannot escape the fact of the matter that decisions over the boundaries of private property are moral ones, and tax is the principal social instrument for marking these boundaries.

An income tax maps up with an absolute conception in the timing of its decisions over ownership. The moral judgments involved in setting tax rates under the current income tax structure occur up-front, by and large, as money is earned, rather than on the back-end, as money is used. This choice of timing does not make these decisions any more or less "moralistic" – they simply involve moral judgments of entitlement based on work and savings. I believe that this is mistaken. In any event it is arbitrary. An income tax makes

---

37 John Maynard Keynes, *A General Theory of Employment, Interest, and Money* (San Diego: Harcourt, 1936).

38 Amartya Sen, *On Economic Inequality* (New York: Oxford University Press, 1997).

39 See John Rawls, *Political Liberalism,* Lecture VI; John Rawls, "The Idea of Public Reason Revisited," *University of Chicago Law Review,* 64 (1997): 765–807, reprinted in Samuel Freeman, ed., *John Rawls, Collected Papers,* (Cambridge, Mass.: Harvard University Press, 1999). See also Edward J. McCaffery, "The Tyranny of Money."

judgments about how much an individual ought to share with the public – on what is private and what is public – based on in-flows. A more sensible tax system, I shall argue, makes such decisions at the time of use or spending. But the structure of the argument – its inherent "moralism" – need not be fundamentally different.[40]

There is also some reason to believe that the rich are too few, and spend too little, seriously to affect the distribution of resources. A thorough-going consequentialism would look askance at this first argument against waste as nonurgent consumption. The contemporary economic historian Stanley Lebergott makes this argument,[41] and there are fairly compelling reasons to believe that, in the aggregate, it is correct as a description of the status quo. There are nonetheless several reasons that a concern about the allocation of resources is not idle.

A major reason according to Lebergott that the wealthy do not significantly distort the allocation of resources by their consumption is that they save a great deal – both in terms of a percentage of their available wealth and in terms of the aggregate capital stock. But this savings behavior of the wealthy is a good thing, and one that a reasonable society will want to preserve. It is not so much that the rich do or do not distort the allocation of resources as that they *could*, under an absolute conception of ownership with its right to waste. A reasonable society will want to take steps to ensure that its wealthiest citizens not suddenly disgorge all of their wealth and engage in high-end consumption – that they do not, that is, exercise a right to waste.

There are also some reasons to fear that inequalities of wealth are growing worse, more acute, with at least the possibility of greater disparities in spending leading to a greater distortion in the allocation of resources than any we have yet witnessed. There is thus reason to fear that a social consensus against highend consumption and in favor of thrift and intergenerational altruism is – or could be – breaking down.[42] These gloomy predictions may not come true: Historic fears of outbreaks of "luxury fever" have generally not come to pass. But a reasonable society will want to stand its guard against the very possibility.

C. The second problem with waste is that it depletes the capital stock. This point is of course connected to the first – all four arguments against nonurgent waste are integrally connected. The capital stock can be seen

---

40 I have repeatedly attempted to make this point, most forcefully in Edward J. McCaffery, "Being the Best We Can Be (A Reply to My Critics)," *Tax Law Review,* 51 (1996): 615–37, at 631–2.
41 Stanley Lebergott, *Pursuing Happiness* (Princeton: Princeton University Press, 1993).
42 Robert Frank argues for this trend in *Luxury Fever,* though nothing of any great import in my argument turns on whether or not luxurious spending is increasing.

as a public good – it helps the entire society, in a nonrival, nonexclusive fashion.[43] Capital has important intergenerational effects, which is the way that Rawls and other political theorists have tended to view the matter. But there is more to it than that. Capital also keeps down interest rates, which under typical economic conditions inures to the benefits of laborers, students, and middle-class consumers. A reasonable society will want to have some capital stock, which means, necessarily, that it must have some non-consumption.

This second point against nonurgent waste is thus the flip-side of the first. Spending by the rich might be relatively frowned on because it directly distorts the allocation of resources. But it also, at the same time, represents the failure to not-consume – a failure to save – that affects the body politic through its impact on the common pool of capital. A revised conception of ownership would hold that those fortunate few who can produce more than they can prudently use on their own needs have an obligation to save for others – either directly, on their own, or in the form of paying a toll to society for their greater, and less urgent, private expenditures. That toll is the price for waste or non-urgent consumption. It shall be collected by the tax system.

D. Three, nonurgent waste, by stipulation, lacks urgency in Scanlon's vocabulary. In and of itself, this might be of no concern to the state. There is no reason to care about the urgency of private actions, as a general matter; liberalism gives us the freedom to make our own even foolish choices with what to do with our lives. But modern states have very large tax requirements. Since society must tax something, it is perfectly reasonable to look to the least urgent expenditures to bear the greatest weight.

This may, again, strike some as illiberal. But this objection is simply a habit of mind. Looking to the relative urgency of consumption is no less liberal, and considerably more sensible, than looking to the relative "entitlement" of earnings as a metric for deciding on the appropriate degrees of progressivity in the tax system. Indeed, many of the arguments typically made at the moment of earnings sound in conceptions of urgency – "equal sacrifice" or "diminishing marginal utility of money income," for two quick examples.[44] These matters are better raised at the moment of ultimate spending.

---

43 See Hal Varian, *Microeconomic Analysis,* 3rd ed. (New York: W. W. Norton & Co, 1992), pp. 414–31 (discussion of "public goods.").

44 For representative arguments in favor of progressivity in income tax rates, see, for example, Walter J. Blum and Harry Kalven, Jr., "The Uneasy Case for Progressive Taxation," *University of Chicago Law Review,* 19 (1952): 417–520; Joseph Bankman and Thomas Griffith, "Social Welfare and the Rate Structure: A New Look at Progressive Taxation," *California Law Review,* 75 (1987): 1905–67; Marjorie E. Kornhauser, "The Rhetoric of the Anti-Progressive Income Tax Movement: A Typical Male Reaction," *Michigan Law Review,* 86 (1987): 465–523.

E. Four, and finally, nonurgent expenditure incites envy and, left unchecked, can represent an offense to the important primary good of the social bases of self-respect. Excessive spending by the wealthy raises the cost of "appearing in public without shame," as Adam Smith put the matter.[45] High-end consumption validates a system of values that has the rich and powerful set the tone for society – it shows material goods to be a kind of *summum bonum*.

A reasonable political liberal society cannot take a stand on whether or not the acquisition and public display of material goods represents part of the best conception of the good. But a political liberal theory will also not be neutral as to its effects on conceptions of the good, and in particular it cannot ignore the effects that some behaviors have on all or most members of society. The problem with nonurgent waste in this light is that it sets a value system that is unattainable for most, who cannot afford waste in any of its senses, and trivializes their own accomplishments. If we allow luxuries to set the measure of success, we let disappointment and a lack of self-respect run rampant throughout society.

The general argument against nonurgent waste, and the particular tax system proposal that implements it, extend beyond what Veblen referred to as "conspicuous consumption." Public displays of wealth, against which sumptuary laws have been enacted in the past, do indeed pose distinct harms from less conspicuous forms of high-end consumption. Nonetheless, the case against nonurgent waste is cumulative, and the harms in terms of resource allocation, depletion of the capital stock, and inurgency extend beyond the more particular case of the ostentatious display of wealth. Furthermore, there is a social harm in knowing that private wealth can buy better goods, however removed from social view these may be. These harms plausibly go to the social bases of self-respect as well.

These concerns with nonurgent expenditure are not narrowly consequential ones. In particular, they do not turn on the size of the capital stock *per se*. The general law against waste effected through the tax system is actually agnostic as to the overall level of social capital accumulation; the greater concern is with what persons in society ought to be doing the social saving. Holding the level of the aggregate capital stock constant, if we allow the wealthy to deplete this stock by their high-end consumption, then we must expect the less wealthy classes to save more. The question is not one of how much savings, but of from where the savings should come. The answer given by the general approach outlined here is that it is the wealthy who should be held accountable for society's capital stock needs.

---

45 Amartya K. Sen, *Inequality Reexamined* (Cambridge, Mass.: Harvard University Press, 1992), pp. 114–16.

V. Tax as a General Law Against Waste

A. The modern legal attitude toward a law against waste, from Blackstone through Honoré and Epstein, has revolved around two thoughts: one, that a liberal society does not need such a law because the problem of waste is self-limiting, and, two, that it would be impossibly difficult to design such a law in any event. The first prong collapses once the problem shifts from dissipatory to nonurgent waste. Nonurgent waste is not nearly as self-limiting as dissipatory waste, and, especially as property has moved towards intangible, fungible capital, poses potentially severe problems to a reasonable society. We must face head on the practical question not faced by the earlier view.

Here we face another puzzle of property theory. Legal and political theory of property, at least since John Stuart Mill, has rarely taken on questions of the tax system, with the limited exception of libertarian arguments against tax *in toto*.[46] This is no doubt due in no small part to the dizzying complexity of modern tax systems. But the neglect, while understandable, cannot be excused. Tax is large and coercive. It has far more of a say in what is "public" and what "private" than any laws regarding regulatory takings or rent control, say. Tax is fundamentally connected to our conceptions of property, whether we like it or not. It also turns out that a readily available tax system provides a rather simple mechanism for effecting a general law of waste.

B. This is not the occasion to get too technical. I have written extensively on progressive consumption taxation elsewhere, drawing on a literature begun in modern times by Nicholas Kaldor and carried on by many economists and legal academics. I shall only sketch ideas here.[47]

Suppose that we adopted a postpaid consumption tax and a progressive rate structure. This is analogous to proposals actually advanced in the United States and elsewhere, of which there are important precursors in the scholarly literature.[48] My preferred plan would make some modifications, particularly in the treatment of debt and in the abolition of the estate tax. It thus calls for a progressive consumption-without-estate tax. This calls for some amplification.

---

46 Robert Nozick, *Anarchy, State & Utopia* (New York: Basic Books, 1974, 1977 [paper]).

47 For fuller discussion, see Nicholas Kaldor, *An Expenditure Tax* (London: George Allen & Unwin, 1955); William D. Andrews, "A Consumption-Type or Cash-Flow Personal Income Tax," *Harvard Law Review,* 87 (1974): 1113–88; U.S. Department of the Treasury, *Blueprints for Basic Tax Reform* (Washington, D.C.: Government Printing Office, 1977). For my own views see Edward J. McCaffery, "The Uneasy Case for Wealth Transfer Taxation," *Yale Law Journal,* 104 (1994): 283–365; "The Political Liberal Case Against the Estate Tax," *Philosophy & Public Affairs,* 23 (1994): 281–312; "Being the Best We Can Be (A Reply to my Critics)"; "The Missing Links in Tax Reform," *Chapman University Law Review,* 2 (1999): 233–52; "Real Tax Reform: The Case for a Progressive Consumption Tax," *The Boston Review,* December 1999/January 2000, 46–8.

48 See generally Laurence S. Seidman, *The USA Tax: A Progressive Consumption Tax* (Cambridge, Mass.: MIT Press, 1997) (describing and critiquing the USA Tax Plan). See also Joel

A postpaid consumption tax differs from an income tax principally in allowing unlimited deductions for savings. Under the celebrated Haig-Simons definition, simplified:

Income equals Consumption plus Savings.[49]

This is no more than an accounting identity or tautology; it tells us simply enough that all material resources (Income) are either spent (Consumption) or not (Savings). Rearranging terms, we see that:

Consumption equals Income minus Savings.

Any "income" tax system that systematically exempts savings is in fact a consumption tax. This is because savings is nonconsumption; consumption, nonsavings. Tax all but savings and we tax consumption, all consumption, and only consumption.

The proposal for a consistent consumption tax is not, in fact, a major doctrinal departure from the status quo; current law already exempts most forms of savings.[50] To implement a more consistent consumption tax, we need take only three major steps:

- Allow unlimited deductions for contributions to savings accounts, such as qualified pension plans under current tax law, while continuing to tax withdrawals from such accounts;
- Include net borrowing as taxable "income"; and
- Repeal the gift and estate tax.

That's it. Taxpayers would list all of their sources of income and borrowing on a tax form, much like the dreaded 1040 now filled out every April 15 in the United States. They would then subtract any amounts contributed into their savings accounts, which I shall call here – to make points clearer – "Trust Accounts." Taxpayers then add in any withdrawals from their Trust Accounts. Following the basic logic of the Haig–Simons definition, these simple steps isolate out money available for and in fact used on consumption for tax.

Slemrod and Jon Bakija, *Taxing Ourselves: A Citizen's Guide to the Great Debate over Tax Reform* (Cambridge, Mass.: MIT Press, 1996), pp. 203–8; Alvin C. Warren Jr., "The Proposal for an 'Unlimited Savings Allowance'," *Tax Notes* (August 28, 1995), reprinted in *Selected Readings on Tax Policy: 25 Years of Tax Notes,* Charles Davenport, ed. (Arlington, Va.: Tax Analysts, 1997), pp. 114–19. See also U.S. Treasury Department, *Blueprints.*

49 Henry Simons, *Personal Income Taxation* (Chicago: University of Chicago Press, 1938).
50 See Edward J. McCaffery, "Tax Policy Under a Hybrid Income-Consumption Tax," *Texas Law Review,* 70 (1992): 1145–218; "Real Tax Reform: The Case for a Progressive Consumption Tax."

C. Let us call this plan the Modest Proposal. It includes all cash available for spending as Income, and then subtracts out net Savings to arrive at actual Consumption.

For those not familiar with tax policy, the Modest Proposal may sound strange. It is not. To understand it better, compare it to a sales tax, the most commonly considered form of postpaid consumption tax. The Modest Proposal is in essence a progressive national sales tax. Under a sales tax, savings are not taxed. Withdrawals from a savings account used to fund current consumption are taxed. So, too, borrowing used to fund consumption is taxed. When you buy store goods on a credit card, you don't get out of paying the sales tax on account of the fact that you are spending someone else's money. Borrowing used to fund savings is not taxed. Under a consistent sales tax, there is also no tax on gifts or bequests – heirs are taxed, just like anyone else, when and as they spend their money in commercial transactions.

All of these points obtain as well under the Modest Proposal. Money contributed into Trust Accounts would not yet have been taxed, and would thus have no tax "basis."[51] These accounts would be treated just as current U.S. law treats qualified pension plans or individual retirement accounts (IRAs), only without any contribution limits. Under the Modest Proposal, a donor can transfer these amounts at any time, on life or on death, without tax. Such transfers maintain value in the common stock of social resources and so do no harm, in and of themselves, to the reasonable society – they do not waste capital. The heir takes her part of the Trust Account with no basis. She pays tax, when, if, and as she withdraws money and consumes it, all under a progressive rate schedule. It is the spending by the heir – and not her mere receipt of capital – that warrants the collection of the public's share.

The Modest Proposal rests on the simple, consistent principle of taxing people as they spend, not as they earn or save. The tax rate depends on the general level of spending. All this fits into a revised conception of ownership, one shorn of the right to waste. As long as a wealthholder does not deplete "her" capital, she is preserving a remainder and so is not engaging in waste. If, when, and as she spends, questions arise. At this point, the tax system implements a general law against waste by its progressive levy on expenditures.

D. To be sure, this is not a precise matter – the law against waste effected through the Modest Proposal is not as Draconian as the actual, particular doctrine of waste that obtained in Blackstone's time. But this particular and *ad hoc* doctrine proved limited and unattractive for a variety of reasons, including

---

51 "Basis" refers to already-taxed dollars. If, for example, a taxpayer purchases corporate stock for $100 that she has left after tax on her earnings, she has a basis of $100 in the stock. In contrast, pension plans or other tax-deferred savings accounts have no basis in them, because this value has never been taxed.

that the severity of its penalties – among them forfeiture of the property plus potential treble damages[52] – made courts reluctant to trigger it. The Modest Proposal more simply exerts a greater "toll" in the form of a tax for the less urgent use of property. It does not confiscate, in part because it is necessary, as under all real world tax systems, to make reasonable concessions to private incentives. But still the Modest Proposal represents a far more consistent, pervasive law against waste than any Anglo-American law has ever had or even imagined possible.

A different social logic obtains under a postpaid consumption tax from that under an income tax. Taxes fall on spenders, not workers or savers. The rates can thus both be higher and society can continue to differentiate among levels of the wealthy, without fear of any direct deterrent falling on work or savings.[53] There is no need to be precise here; mine is not a task in economic modeling. But a sensible rate structure under the Modest Proposal for a family of four might look something like the following:

Table 1. *Modest Proposal Tax Rates*

Consumption	Tax Rate
$0–20,000	*0%*
$20,000–100,000	*15%*
$100,000–200,000	*30%*
$200,000–500,000	*40%*
$500,000–1,000,000	*50%*
$1,000,000–5,000,000	*60%*
over $5,000,000	*70%*

This hypothetical rate structure is more progressive than the one that obtains under present law. It is roughly revenue-neutral: The expansion of the lower tax brackets and the elimination of gift and estate taxes should be offset by the higher rates at higher brackets, the repeal of any preference for "capital" gains (which is not needed under a consistent postpaid consumption tax), and by the important inclusion of debt financed consumption in the tax base.[54] The plan allows for higher rates to take effect at higher levels without the argument that the law directly deters the socially productive activities of work and savings. It

---

52 Blackstone, *Commentaries* at Book III, Chapter 14.
53 All taxes create disincentives. The Modest Proposal will deter from working those whose only motive for additional labor is the ability to engage in high-end consumption. There are good reasons to believe that this concern will not amount to much – and that, to the extent the disincentive binds, it is a normatively appropriate one. See Edward J. McCaffery, "The Uneasy Case for Wealth Transfer Taxation," at 353–6.
54 See Edward J. McCaffery, "The Tyranny of Money."

is spending in excess of five million dollars a year – not earnings – that justifies and receives the highest tax rate. This is a different matter altogether, and one that a reasonable society can support.

E. The tax rates of the Modest Proposal implement objective social judgments over urgency as a matter of degree. But there is nothing inconsistent with further modifying the plan by allowing deductions, exclusions, or credits for certain expenditures as a matter of kind. There is no reason, for example, not to consider medical, educational, and charitable use deductions from the tax. The question for the reasonable society is whether such uses reflect a different degree of urgency than other uses, and thus should be subject to a lower, or no, social charge. There are complicated questions here, of distinguishing needs from wants and so forth, and of considering the impact on the wider society of allowing and perhaps even encouraging private expenditures for medical and educational luxuries. Various ceilings or limitations may be called for in the name of fairness. I do not mean to minimize the difficulties or importance of these discussions over the classification of uses. My point is simply the more limited one that these are questions for political liberal reason, nicely framed by the structure of the proposal. There is nothing wrong – and a good deal right – with asking them.

The Modest Proposal is not a classic sumptuary tax. There are several reasons, of an economic, consequential, and a moral sort, for this. Sumptuary taxes are specific taxes, and thus distort the price system. The Modest Proposal is a general tax. It is concerned with the general level and not the particular type of private consumption. It preserves a liberal commitment to neutrality. It is not overly intrusive or judgmental.[55]

F. What is it that the Modest Proposal has in connection with a life estate conception of property and the right to waste?

Consider again what a life estate owner such as Bob has under the modified life estate form of ownership set out in Section II.E above. The wealthy citizen under the Modest Proposal has all of these rights. She can direct the investments of assets within her Trust Account, subject to reasonable social regulations designed to prevent either the waste or the political abuse of the power of capital. She can enjoy the fruit or income of the Trust Account under the lower tax rates available for moderate levels of spending. Given an appropriate scheme of deductions, credits, and so forth, she can invade the corpus of the Trust Account at lower tax rates for urgent needs, such as medical, educational, or charitable uses. She can also direct, through a form of universal general power, where the Trust Account is to go on her death. The only right she does not have is the *jus abutendi;* she cannot "consume,

---

55 See also Robert Frank, *Luxury Fever* (criticizing sumptuary taxes).

waste or destroy" all of her Account, or she will face a large tax bill. She is constrained, in other words, either to leave a remainder to her designated heirs or to pay over a large portion of "her" capital to society for its collective preservation.

To put this into numbers, suppose, for example, that a taxpayer were fortunate enough to amass a Trust Account of $100 million. If she were to attempt to spend this all at once, on her own nonurgent wants, the government would claim nearly $70 million as the public's share. We can understand that large levy as a charge for nonurgent waste. Large stores of nominally private capital became like a farm in which society has a remainder interest.

VI. Some Objections

A. Questions of course arise. One set of objections to the general law against waste and its Modest Proposal is that it ignores or inadequately deals with the power of money. Capitalists will be able to build up large stocks of value tax-free in their Trust Accounts. Such concentrated wealth brings pleasure and power, critics contend, that a reasonable society must take steps to control. This logic has led most proponents of a consumption tax, including Rawls, to tack on a wealth or wealth transfer tax in their recommended comprehensive tax systems.

These objections from concentrated wealth cling to the idea of an absolute conception of ownership – they rest, that is, on a view of property as absolutely owned by private parties with the right to waste it. The objectors fear the misuse of the vast sums of wealth that can be stored up within the Trust Accounts. But under a revised conception of ownership – one without the right to waste – the Trust Accounts are not, in any narrow or complete sense, "private." A trust holder acts as a trustee of the capital component of "his" wealth. The Modest Proposal checks what he can do with his money. If he tries to use it too quickly, in too large amounts, the government will step forth to claim its share, which will be larger on account of the nonurgency of the intended use. The excessive private use of capital is waste and we tax it accordingly.

The ability to curtail the large-scale private expenditure of resources creates a considerable advantage for the Modest Proposal. Objections to the proposal on the grounds that it ignores the power or pleasure of the rich tend to come from defenders of the status quo. But it is the current tax system, with its porous income-plus-estate tax, that ought to disappoint political liberal theory. Under present conditions, wealthy people can and indeed do spend large sums of money on themselves in short periods of time with utter impunity from tax. One noticeable and disturbing trend lies in individuals spending vast sums of money to finance their own personal political campaigns. H. Ross Perot, for example, spent $60 million of his own money running for President of the United States in 1992. Under the income-plus-estate tax, Perot paid no taxes on account of this largesse; indeed, he saved his estate more than $30 million in taxes – present consumption being the surest way to avoid an estate tax. Under the Modest Proposal, in order to spend $60 million on himself, Perot would have had to pay nearly $140 million to the collective fisc.

B. A parallel objection looks to the power that wealth-holders might have by virtue of investment decisions and control over the Trust Accounts. Once again, however, the objection sits poorly with a revised conception of ownership, one without a right to waste. Under the Modest Proposal, savers will be hemmed in by a general fiduciary duty much like the prudent investor rule that any trustee must follow. Society need not micro-manage or engage in overly specific regulation of Trust Account holders. A sensible diversification rule – the kinds of policies already in place for regulating large endowments, banks, and mutual funds, as well as pension plan and IRA investments – is quite sufficient. This further implements an antiwaste norm.

The reasonable society can control and contain the power of the capitalist class to influence policy and politics via its expenditure decisions – in fact, the Modest Proposal gives us a means of serving this reasonable political end that modern institutional theory otherwise altogether lacks. At a minimum, the law can prohibit lobbying or running for office out of Trust Account funds, as it does now for nonprofit sector monies. Once again, we can understand this feature as following from the systematic decision to monitor the use of resources – to abrogate the private right to waste. Under the Modest Proposal and a life estate conception of ownership, the wealthy cannot be motivated by narrow decadent pleasures nor by a quest for excessive power. They must be motivated, instead, by a sense of "natural duty," a pride in their accomplishments, a desire to provide a fund for the urgent needs of their family and their posterity, and to do well by us all. They must, that is, serve as allies, not enemies, to the reasonably pluralist society of which they are members.

C. A final version of the standard liberal objection relates to the social problem of iteration over time.

A plausible interpretation of the relevant aspects of Rawls's theory and the political liberal project is this: The task of justice as fairness – of the reasonable society – is to set up the fair terms and conditions of background justice. Once these are in place, in part to avoid the problems of placing an overly restrictive moral psychology or sense of individual duty on its citizens, a reasonable society will sit back and allow citizens to engage in trade, transactions, and the voluntary contributions to cooperative enterprises. But the net result of these voluntary transactions, when repeated over time, can easily undermine the original fairness of the basic structure.[56] Thus the reasonable society must somehow, sometime, step in to address the problem of iteration. This logic forms the core of the social contractarian response to libertarian or "patterned" arguments for the justice of a minimal government state with little or no redistribution.[57]

Accepting all of that, the precise question is when and how to address the problem of iteration. Although there is some equivocation over this point in Rawls,[58] it would appear as if his preferred answer is to do so once a generation, following a certain "lifetime" approach also found in the tax policy literature.[59] The idea is to allow intragenerational wealth inequalities to build up under the general scheme of things but to check the intergenerational transmission of these inequalities by means of some progressive inheritance or accessions tax.[60] This reasoning is compelling as an *a priori* manner.

In practice, however, the idea of leaving the correction of the problem of iteration in the hands of some intergenerational tax is flawed for several reasons. First, the current astonishing degrees of private one-generation wealth accumulation suggest that there is indeed a need to address the problem of iteration within lifetimes as well. Second, the holding of capital, in and of itself, is not and need not be the central harm to be addressed by a corrective to the problem of iteration. Rather, it is the private consumption – and not the mere possession – of wealth that is the relevant harm.[61] Any estate or inheritance tax, in contrast, falls on unspent wealth – on capital, that is.

These two points lead to a third, namely that the revised conception of ownership with its Modest Proposal is the best practical alternative for addressing the problem of iteration, both intra- and intergenerationally. Within lifetimes, unlike the flawed status quo, the Modest Proposal stands ready to charge a toll for large amounts of private consumption, now identified as the relevant social harm. Across generations, the Modest Proposal stands ready to allow capital to remain "private" albeit regulated, but it continues to monitor private preclusive use – once again, much better than the flawed status quo does. Put in other but equivalent terms, the revised conception of ownership and the Mod-

---

56 John Rawls, *Political Liberalism,* Lecture VII.
57 *Ibid.*
58 Cf. Rawls, *A Theory of Justice,* pp. 277–80 (advocating proportionate consumption plus accessions tax) with *Political Liberalism,* pp. 268, 283 (suggesting the possibility of progressive income taxation).
59 See, for example, Henry J. Aaron and Harvey Galper, "A Tax on Consumption, Gifts, and Bequests," in Joseph A. Pechman, ed., *Options for Tax Reform* (Washington D.C.: Brookings Institute Press, 1984), p. 106 (advocating once-per-lifetime model for taxation).
60 See Rawls, *A Theory of Justice,* pp. 279–80.
61 This is an idea I have frequently tried to communicate. See, for example, "Political Liberal Case"; "Being the Best We Can Be." Deborah Weiss seems to be one of the first authors fully to understand and appreciate this idea, and I am grateful for her comments. See Deborah M. Weiss, "Liberal Estate Tax Policy," *Tax Law Review,* 51 (1996) 403–17 (1996).

est Proposal allow the "problem" of iteration to persist, within or across generations, until and unless there is some actual harm inflicted on the wider society, in the form of the mismanagement or excessive private preclusive use of capital. The problem of iteration, far from militating against the Modest Proposal and life estate conception of ownership, thus argues for them.

D. So much can be said for the Modest Proposal as a normative tax system. But we have also seen that the Modest Proposal can be understood as implementing a revised conception of ownership, which we have seen differs from an absolute conception only in curtailing the *jus abutendi*. What's illiberal about that? Society has long attempted to rein in the possibility of waste; it has simply lacked a coherent theoretical and practical legal apparatus to do so.

Put in simple terms, the response to the objection that the Modest Proposal is illiberal can come down to the simple question: Must we have the right to waste? The revised conception of ownership answers this question decisively in the negative. We can be a perfectly reasonable society without giving any of our members the right to consume, waste, or destroy everything they can with any claim of legitimacy whatsoever get their hands on.

4

Inheritance and the Justice Tribunal

J. W. HARRIS

I. Introduction

Individual owners of property, like the rest of us, must die some day. The question then arises, as it was put in St. Luke's gospel to the rich man who sought contentment from amassing wealth: "Then whose shall those things be, which thou hast provided?"[1]

Across cultures and across time, legal systems and social conventions have provided a variety of answers to the question. Within modern property institutions we find combinations of (unlimited or circumscribed) testamentary power with rules of intestate succession. In England legal estates in land could not be devised until the sixteenth century and early and medieval customary law restricted the power to bequeath even personal property where a testator was survived by dependants.[2] Civil law systems exclude the *legitima portio* (fixed share) of certain heirs from the deceased's testamentary power.[3] In modern English law there has, since 1938, been vested in courts a discretionary jurisdiction to override a testator's dispositions (or the effect of intestacy rules) if it is concluded that the deceased has failed to make reasonable provision for certain classes of dependants.[4]

I am grateful for helpful comments on earlier drafts of this essay by Stephen Munzer, Seana Shiffrin, Edward McCaffery, and Joshua Getzler.

1 Luke 12:20 (Authorized Version).
2 See W. S. Holdsworth, *A History of English Law* (3rd ed.) (London, Methuen and Co., 1923), vol. 2, pp. 93–95; vol. 3, pp. 550–56. George W. Keeton and L. C. B. Gower, "Freedom of Testation in English Law," *Iowa Law Review,* 20 (1935): 326–40 at 331–9.
3 See A. G. Guest, "Family Provision and the Legitima Portio," *Law Quarterly Review,* 73 (1957): 74–88, at 75–80, comparing the positions under Roman, Scots, and French law.
4 Inheritance (Family Provision) Act 1938 [1938 c. 72], GB: Parliament, London: HMSO. For a survey of the legislative history, see Joseph Dainow, "Limits on Testamentary Freedom in England," *Cornell Law Quarterly,* 25 (1940): 337–60, at 344–57. The legislation is now contained in the Inheritance (Provision for Family and Dependants) Act 1975 [1975 c. 63], GB: Parliament, London: HMSO, as amended by the Law Reform (Succession) Act 1995 [1995 c. 41], GB: Parliament, London: HMSO, 2.

So far as political philosophers are concerned, John Locke supposed that the natural right to support enjoyed by children entails a prima facie right to inherit, but he did not make clear whether this right constitutes a restraint on unfettered testation.[5] In Adam Smith's opinion, "[t]here is no point more difficult to account for than the right we conceive men to have to dispose of their goods after their deaths."[6] He concluded that testamentary power could only be explained on the basis of a sentiment of "piety to the dead," one which emerges only in advanced cultures, and which ought not to hold sway save in respect of dispositions made to persons known to the deceased.[7]

Nevertheless, the concept of ownership has evolved in such a way that it is generally assumed to carry, at least prima facie, a power to dictate what is to happen to that which is owned after the owner has died. John Stuart Mill wrote:

Unlike inheritance *ab intestato,* bequest is one of the attributes of property: the ownership of a thing cannot be looked upon as complete without the power of bestowing it, at death or during life, at the owner's pleasure: and all the reasons, which recommend that private property should exist, recommend *pro tanto* this extension of it.[8]

Mill went on to recommend that an owner should not be at liberty to bequeath, to any single individual, wealth greater than that which would be needed to afford the donee "the means of comfortable independence."[9] Hegel had also concluded that testamentary power was a prima facie attribute of ownership, but one that ought to be carefully circumscribed to prevent its arbitrary exercise within the family. "In England, where all kinds of eccentricity are endemic, innumerable foolish notions are associated with wills."[10]

In my *Property and Justice,* I argued that all questions of property-institutional design must be addressed in terms of what I called the "mix of property-specific justice reasons" and that the core component of a property institution consists, not in a singular concept of ownership, but rather in a "spectrum of ownership interests" protected by "trespassory rules."[11] I rejected theories that adopt a single-track stance toward both the nature and the normative foundations of property. In support of that general approach to property theory, I shall in this essay explore the consequences of single-track

5 For discussion of the ambiguities on this point in Locke, see A. John Simmons, *The Lockean Theory of Rights* (Princeton: Princeton University Press, 1992), pp. 204–12; Gopal Sreenivasan, *The Limits of Lockean Rights in Property* (Oxford: Oxford University Press, 1995), pp. 104–6.
6 Adam Smith, *Lectures on Jurisprudence* (R. L. Meek, D. D. Raphael, and P. G. Stein eds.) (Oxford: Oxford University Press, 1978), p. 63.
7 Smith, *Lectures on Jurisprudence,* pp. 63–71.
8 John Stuart Mill, *Principles of Political Economy: With Some of Their Applications to Social Philosophy,* in J. M. Robson (ed.), *Collected Works of John Stuart Mill* (Toronto: University of Toronto Press, 1965), vol. 2, p. 223.
9 Mill, *Principles of Political Economy,* p. 225.
10 G. W. F. Hegel, *Elements of the Philosophy of Right* (trans. H. B. Nisbet) (Cambridge: Cambridge University Press, 1991), p. 218 (para. 180 addition).
11 See J. W. Harris, *Property and Justice* (Oxford: Clarendon Press, 1996).

visions of the inheritance problem. I shall argue that such visions are unaccept-able, but that their errors illuminate sensitive questions about which there is no political or philosophical consensus.

I suggest that we distinguish three stereotypical positions. One view – which we may call "libertarian" – views resources as discrete parcels, each assigned to an owner. Opposed to this is the starting-point of the "egalitarian," who portrays resources as a wealth-pie, capable of being sliced many ways. Between these lies a position that I here call "communitarian." It shares the libertarian ownership-parcel perspective, but then attaches obligations to disgorge or share some of what is owned. In the following section, I seek to tease out the implications of these different perspectives for the problem of inheritance. Instead of confronting incompatible positions at a high level of abstraction, I offer a thought-experiment in which their implications have to be brought to bear on a particular context.

The thought-experiment asks the reader to envisage a modern property institution in which there is no intestacy law and in which testamentary power is altogether excluded whilst power to make *inter vivos* dispositions is not. That requires an imaginative leap away from the familiar. It is, nevertheless, as we shall see, precisely the position advocated by at least one contemporary political philosopher.[12] Mill supposed that ownership "cannot be looked upon as complete" without testamentary power. One way of testing whether he was right is to ask how a society might deal with the assets of dead people if it adopted a conception of ownership from which that power was hived off. Anyone might give away his property at any time while life was in him, but ownership transmission powers would expire with his last breath.

A variety of arrangements can be envisaged. Social norms might dictate a specified distribution amongst close family members, or distant kin, on the assumption that their relationship to the deceased afforded them some "natu-ral" claim to be owners of what he had once owned. Or distribution might be ordered in such a way as to implement obligations which it was supposed the deceased had undertaken while he lived. Alternatively, some resources might be distributed to those whose life-chances had developed in such a way that their need for the particular assets in question ought to be respected. Or again, it might be thought that the state, as representative of the entire society, should take everything. Or, perhaps, no person or agency would be thought to have a better right to be considered owner than any other, and the assets should stay ownerless until someone had established a claim in the way that the society's property institution allowed to happen with other ownerless things.

These are competing candidates for a solution to the problem that would arise were ownership shorn of testamentary power. Suppose it were concluded that none of them would represent a just outcome were it applied to all cases.

12 See the views of Hillel Steiner discussed in text accompanying notes 56–72 below.

Instead, on any death, the *ad hoc* merits of each solution would be investigated. That is the awesome task that, in the next section, is imposed upon the imaginary Justice Tribunal.

As we shall see, the members of the tribunal engage in an unusually double-focused discourse. They invoke holistic conceptions of the normative bases of resource-holdings, as political philosophers do. But then they also make discriminatory comparisons between individual claimants and between itemized assets, as courts must. We expect more of the latter than of the former from real-world judges. True, courts are sometimes vested with explicit authority to make such distributive choices as they consider reasonable, fair, or just – for example, in matrimonial causes, or (as in England and other jurisdictions with comparable legislation) where they are given a discretion to re-allocate the property of deceased persons; and, of course, doctrinal developments within common law or equity are often guided by a judge's perception of the just outcome. However, excursions into grand theory are not normally to be anticipated in such contexts.

Indeed, property theory suffers from a characteristic dissonance between philosophers' and lawyers' concerns. As Andrew Reeve has pointed out, when the political theorist asks his lawyer-colleague to explain what property is, he is likely to be informed that the only way to understand the matter is to immerse oneself in the technicalities of "seisin," "remainderman," and "estate *pur autre vie.*"[13] I can record comparable frustrations the other way. Lawyers who would like to know how to tackle the multifarious value judgments thrown up within modern property institutions, and who look to political philosophy for guidance, ask why they are invited to speculate about persons with seemingly strong digestions (known to John Locke) who appear to go about collecting and boiling acorns.

The members of the Justice Tribunal embody three stereotypical philosophical stances. However, the problem they have been set requires them to instantiate these abstract positions in the context of a heterogeneous set of claimants and in relation to very different kinds of resource-holdings. Let us see how they get on.

II. The Justice Tribunal

The Justice Tribunal sits in an imaginary country that resembles contemporary Western societies, except that there is no law of testation or of intestate succession. Disputes about what should happen to a person's resources on her death are submitted to the tribunal. Jurisdiction is conferred on the tribunal by a statute that embodies no preconceptions about the proper destination of such resources. Anyone may apply to become their owner.

13 Andrew Reeve, "Convention and Justification," *Oxford Journal of Legal Studies,* 19 (1999): 323–35, at 327–8.

The tribunal is directed to consider any principled argument. It may assume that the justifications it gives would support decisions in a class of disputes similar to the present one. Beyond that, no kind of argument is ruled out by statute or precedent. Applications must be made to the tribunal within six months of a death. If no applications are made within that time limit, or if all those that are made are rejected by a final judgment of the tribunal in relation to all or any assets of the deceased, such assets are deemed to be abandoned and therefore ownerless. Pending such final determination, ownership is suspended.

(A) In Re Jones decd

Mrs. Jones, a rich widow, has recently died. Her assets were a house, furniture and other chattels, a small factory, cash, bank accounts, shares of stock, patents, and copyrights. The following claimants present themselves before the Justice Tribunal and establish the factual bases of their claims by appropriate evidence:

1. Mrs. Jennifer Brown is Mrs. Jones's only child. She is a childless married woman aged thirty years. Her husband is rich and she leads a luxurious lifestyle. She claims that all Mrs. Jones's resources should be made over to her on the ground that she is Mrs. Jones's natural successor.
2. Septimus Tucker is a penniless artist. There is no public demand for his paintings. Mrs. Jones believed that he had great talent and she took him into her house twenty years ago. Since then she provided him with free board and lodging and paid for all his wants. He is now aged fifty. He claims that there should be set aside from Mrs. Jones's estate a sufficient sum to enable him to continue his artistic work without earning his living for the rest of his life.
3. William Jackson is an acquaintance of Mrs. Jones. A year before her death, Mrs. Jones promised to give him all her property before she died. He claims that he should now receive it.
4. Able Handiman is Mrs. Jones's neighbor and friend. For many years he has come round whenever needed to undertake repairs to Mrs. Jones's house. He renewed the electrical wiring, mended burst water pipes, and rehung defective doors. He was never offered payment for these services. He claims that some recompense should be made to him out of the estate.
5. John Green is the elected spokesman for the workers in the factory owned by Mrs. Jones. The factory has recently been losing money, but Mrs. Jones had decided not to close it down because she did not want the employees to lose their jobs. He claims that the factory should be handed over to a cooperative formed by the workers.
6. Paul Taxman represents the Treasury. He claims that all Mrs. Jones's assets should be made over to the state.

No other claims have been made and the time limit of six months has expired.

(B) Opinion of Libertarian, C.J.

In this society most resources, material and immaterial, are held by individuals, groups, or corporations as "owners." That was so as regards the assets now before the tribunal, prior to the death of Mrs. Jones. We have to decide whether any of the claimants should be substituted as owners of all or any of the assets.

We are directed to make a just allocation of property. It behooves us, therefore, to reflect on the normative bases of property institutions. In my view, such institutions have arisen to subserve the untramelled autonomy of human beings. An individual who appropriates an unowned object may use or dispose of it as he pleases. His ownership freedoms ought not to be curtailed by the state. I refer, in support of this approach, to those contemporary writers who propound "historical entitlement" theories.[14] They differ among themselves in their accounts of the occupancy which, justly, triggers ownership of that which was previously unowned – whether the object must be a member of a class of objects that is relatively abundant, whether the occupying act must be accompanied by meritorious work or must in some other way contribute to the welfare of others, and so on. But they are at one in recognizing that the autonomy of owners includes power, at pleasure, to transfer that which is owned to others. No one may challenge titles derived by successive transfers from a first occupant.

These libertarian considerations are, in principle, all that we need to guide us in making just allocations of resources. I note also that there are consequentialist arguments that indicate that the institution of private property has instrumental merits.[15] One of the freedoms of transmission inherent within ownership consists of the power to strike bargains in a market, and markets augment total wealth. In addition, holdings of private wealth – the fruits of the exercise of ownership freedoms – facilitate the promotion of projects that are independent of centralized governmental control.

In the light of these reflections I turn to consider who ought now to be considered the owners of these assets. The crucial question is: Did Mrs. Jones, at any time up to the moment of her death, exercise her limitless autonomy over any of the resources she owned in such a way that another has become owner of them? If the answer to that question is no, and if we conclude that none of the

---

14 See, for example, Robert Nozick, *Anarchy, State, and Utopia* (Oxford: Basil Blackwell, 1974), pp. 150–83; Murray N. Rothbard, "Justice and Property Rights," in Samuel L. Blumenfeld, ed., *Property in a Humane Economy* (La Salle, Ill.: Open Court, 1974), pp. 101–20; Richard A. Epstein, "Possession as the Root of Title," *Georgia Law Review,* 3 (1979): 1221–43; Richard A. Epstein, *Takings: Private Property and the Power of Eminent Domain* (Cambridge Mass.: Harvard University Press, 1985), passim; Hillel Steiner, *An Essay on Rights* (Oxford: Basil Blackwell, 1994), Chapters 3 and 7.
15 See Harris, *Property and Justice,* pp. 289–305.

present claimants should be awarded ownership, these assets are deemed to be abandoned. In that event, like other ownerless things, they would be available for occupancy to the first-comer. None of the present claimants could assert priority to any of the others, in advance of whatever counts as effective occupation.

Consider the position of Paul Taxman, the representative of the Treasury. Our property institution recognizes that resources may be vested in agencies of the state. Such agencies do not "own" resources in the classical sense, for they are not accorded that autonomy which is characteristic of private owners. Although some of the powers of control and disposition granted to them are modelled on private ownership powers, they are universally constrained by conceptions of public function. They cannot do what they like with their own.[16]

In the arena of public international law, where rules relating to acquisition of territory have to some extent been modelled on those applicable within private law, first occupancy by states has a role to play.[17] In the context of our municipal property institution, however, the state, *qua* state, cannot be viewed as a competitor with private persons for initial acquisition of ownerless things. The significance of first occupancy within a property institution is that it confers full ownership freedoms upon some private individual, group, or corporation. Once a resource is occupied, the individual, group, or corporation may act, in relation to it, as it sees fit. That is what property institutions are for. Public agencies may properly have some resources vested in them that are thereby excluded from private appropriation, but that can only be in order to serve some appropriate public function. A state agency holds what it holds ministerially for others. Thus, if we dismiss all claims now before the tribunal so that the late Mrs. Jones's property becomes ownerless, it is, in my judgment, not open to Paul Taxman to seize it on the basis, merely, of first occupancy.

Is there any other ground on which the state, acting within the municipal sphere, ought to be accorded ownership of ownerless things? I think not. If there were, the whole basis of historical entitlements would be undermined. If one supposed that ownerless resources are justly to be vested in the state sometimes, why not always? If always, how could any just private holdings have arisen? If one subscribes to the underlying libertarian values of property institutions at all, one cannot accept that ownerless resources automatically accrue to the state. The enhancement of human freedom that property confers cannot co-exist with such an idea.

It is true that the community plays an indispensable role in the operation of property institutions. No one could own anything if there were not "trespassory

---

16 See ibid., pp. 104–09.
17 See Ian Brownlie, *Principles of Public International Law* (4th ed.) (Oxford: Clarendon Press, 1990), pp. 123–4, 138–41.

rules" prohibiting others from intermeddling with that which is owned,[18] and the role of policing infractions of such rules falls to the state. As Robert Nozick has shown, no agency other than the "minimal state" can enforce those rules that protect the private domain of each citizen, comprising both his body and the external resources he owns.[19] The enforcement of these rules necessitates the expenditure of resources by agencies of the state and hence justifies compulsory levies on owners. Taxation was rightly exacted from Mrs. Jones while she was alive for this purpose. But I can see no basis on which this protective state function can rightly be financed by appropriation of assets of deceased persons. The contrary view would be neither fair nor proportionate. Public sequestration of just those ownerless things that formerly belonged to persons now deceased would unfairly discriminate against first occupants of that particular category of ownerless things. As to proportionality, there could be no guarantee that the assets thus acquired would not greatly exceed that which is required for the proper protective role of state agencies.

It might be argued that the state should take over these assets in a ministerial capacity, so as to hold the ring pending first occupancy by private persons. In a sense, that is what it does in the international arena. It asserts sovereignty over territory and thereby excludes foreign appropriation so that its citizens, as between themselves, may have the opportunity to acquire ownership. There can, however, be no parallel in this intra-citizen context. Just appropriation of that which is unowned can arise only from first occupancy. Temporary sequestration by the state would either distort that process by increasing or diminishing opportunities to appropriate that would otherwise have existed, or it would have no influence over the process and the problems that I discuss later will remain.

I turn now to the other claimants. It might be urged on behalf of Mrs. Brown (Mrs. Jones's daughter), Mr. Tucker (her protege), Mr. Handiman (her benevolent neighbor), and Mr. Green (who represents the workers at her factory) that, had Mrs. Jones foreseen her death and the circumstances surrounding it, she would have wanted some or all of her assets to go to them. However, we do not respect the autonomy of property-owners by substituting our guesses about their choices for evidence of the choices they actually made.

As I say, if these assets are now ownerless, they are subject to first occupancy. We are familiar with occasional instances in which the true owner of material objects (land or chattels) has disappeared, when the law accords title to the first person to take possession. Unlike the quite different context where the law allows "adverse possession" to displace the title of a known owner, first possession of that which appears to have no owner gives to the possessor a title which is good against the rest of the world without the necessity for effluxion of time. By our statute, if we now reject all the claims brought before us, all the

18 See Harris, *Property and Justice*, pp. 24–7.
19 See Nozick, *Anarchy, State, and Utopia*, pp. 10–18, 88–90, 96–118.

resources once owned by Mrs. Jones will be subject to the same regime. The first person to occupy them, in the assumed character of owner, will be recognized as owner. Mr. Tucker will probably win the race as regards Mrs. Jones's house, since he is living there. Mr. Green and his fellow workers are well placed to appropriate the factory.

Concerning the rest of Mrs. Jones's property, what can we predict? The chattels and cash would be up for seizure by anyone who knows of their whereabouts and of their ownerless condition. I have to say that I do not view the ensuing scramble with equanimity. What about those "cashable rights"[20] that she owned – the bank accounts and company shares? How could such rights be "occupied"? We have little guidance from classical property theorists about what counts as occupancy of such resources. Should we countenance that anyone who can successfully forge Mrs. Jones's signature on a bank deposit book or a share certificate has thereby "taken possession" of these items? How could that happen if the banks and companies know that Mrs. Jones is dead?

I would suggest that the nearest analogy to first occupancy of material objects would be a cancellation by the banks at which Mrs. Jones held accounts, and by the companies in which she owned shares, of all liability to pay out on these cashable rights. The banks and the companies would be the beneficiaries of a first occupancy regime. That would represent a windfall for them of a kind that is not envisaged by standard historical-entitlement theories. Such theories deal in first occupancy of material objects. An ownerless material object, before it is occupied, is the subject of a jural void. Rights and duties relating to it are created by first occupancy. In the case of cashable rights, in contrast, there are subsisting contractual relations that, on the assumptions I have made, would be unilaterally cancelled. First occupancy always brings about a windfall; but if it enables a contractor to escape obligations he has undertaken it is, in my judgment, an unmerited windfall.

So far as the patents and copyrights are concerned, the solution would, I think, be simple. These are not objects that are naturally "scarce," in the sense that competing uses of them must, one way or another, be channeled and policed. Unlike scarce material objects, first occupancy cannot be the basis of title for items within the domain of intellectual property. Exclusive control over them is reserved by special trespassory rules, largely for economic-instrumental reasons. If they are abandoned, they cease to exist as property items. Such ideational entities can be created by human endeavor, but there is no non-artificial sense in which they are out there awaiting occupation. If they are ownerless, they rejoin the public domain, which encompasses all such entities not made artificially scarce by the trespassory rules of a property institution.[21] If the patents and copyrights are not now owned by anyone then,

20 See Harris, *Property and Justice,* pp. 50–55.
21 See ibid., pp. 42–7.

just as would happen when the time for which they are held runs out, they have become "common property," that is, no one's property.

The other assets, in contrast, if not now owned must be the subject of a first occupancy regime. For the reasons I have given, it would be inconsistent with the libertarian underpinnings of a property institution that the state should seize them. I have suggested that the windfalls to the banks and the companies would be unmerited and that the scramble to grab the chattels and the cash is unattractive. These consequences are nevertheless unavoidable if these assets are now ownerless, but they should give us pause before concluding that such really is their state. In the case of an owner now deceased, where there is doubt whether something done by her constituted a dispositive exercise of her ownership powers we should lean in favor of understanding it to have been such. On this basis, I read the firm promise in favor of William Jackson as sufficient. That promise amounts to an intimation that Mrs. Jones's will-to-own is to be withdrawn in favor of his will-to-own, at latest, at the last moment when her autonomy as a person subsists – namely, the instant preceding her death. True, a unilateral promise is not a contract or a transfer. Hence, if it could be shown that Mrs. Jones retracted her promise before she died, then the conditional withdrawal of her will in favor of his would not be operative at the last moment at which she was owner. There is, however, no evidence of this. In particular, none of her dealings with the other claimants amounts to a setting aside of any of her still-owned assets in their favor. Her promise to Jackson encompassed "all my property." We best respect the normative bases of property institutions if we implement that clear expression of ownership autonomy.

Accordingly, I find that William Jackson is now owner of all the assets before the tribunal and I dismiss all the other claims.

(C) Opinion of Communitarian, J.

I agree with Libertarian, C.J. that, in order to discharge our extraordinary responsibility, we must reflect on the nature of our property institution. But, with respect, I cannot follow the path his reflections have taken. The autonomy of owners is important, but it is not the only value fostered by property institutions. Consider Hegel's articulation of the abstract idea of property.[22] The free will of a human subject is confronted with a universe of material objects that have no will. The subject asserts its freedom by infusing its will into some of these objects, to the exclusion of other human wills. By becoming owner in this way, the subject realizes and asserts his or her identity. Ownership persists for so long as the infusion of the will is maintained. It ends when the will is withdrawn either unconditionally (abandonment), or conditionally in favor of another human will which displaces it (conveyance or contract). However, this analysis, as Hegel makes plain, holds only at the "moment" of abstract right.

22 See Hegel, *Elements of the Philosophy of Right,* pp. 73–103 (Part 1, Section 1 *Property*).

The working out of the idea of property must also take account of the moments of "morality" (*Moralität*) and "ethical life" (*Sittlichkeit*).[23]

The historically evolved concept of a property institution includes owner-ship freedoms, certainly. But it also encompasses those ties that bind one individual or group to another as part of a community, so far as they involve the use or allocation of resources. In company with contemporary communitarian theorists,[24] I contend that we should not view individual property owners as isolated monads dealing with each other merely as parties to contracts, or as transferors and transferees. If we are to do justice between these claimants, we must take account of those bonds of fellowship, mutual support, desert, and gratitude that underpin the self-perception of the individual as a member of a community. In performing our task, we should not aspire to unearth timeless, supra-conventional values. Rather, we should take judicial notice of those conventionally recognized virtues, claims, and obligations that make the asso-ciation of our citizens, one with another, specifically communal in character.

Mrs. Jones was a wealthy property owner, but she was much else besides. She had, or had undertaken, relationships that were inherent to the kind of life she led and to the sort of person she was. We have to decide whether, in the case of any of these claimants, there had arisen obligations on her part that bound her to deploy any of her resources in their favor. Ownership cannot survive death, but the obligations integral to a relationship may do so. Libertarian, C.J. would, I am sure, recognize that to be so in the case of a strictly contractual relationship. If a man owes me money for goods I have supplied and he dies, I can look to his assets for payment. The same must be true of other un-discharged obligations.

Able Handiman. Mrs. Jones never offered him payment for the valuable services he rendered when he repaired her house and, before her death, he sought none. It might be said that, because he did not ask for payment, he must be taken to have bargained for something else as consideration for his work – the satisfaction of being an altruist. That, however, would be to force the notion of contract where it has no place. The truth is that they struck no bargain of any kind. They were not isolated individuals swapping quid pro quos. They acted spontaneously against a background of community-shared conventional

---

23 See Hegel, ibid., pp. 133–380 (Parts 2 and 3).

24 See, for example, Alasdair MacIntyre, *After Virtue: A Study in Moral Theory* (London: Gerald Duckworth, 1981), Chapters 15 and 17; Michael J. Sandel, *Liberalism and the Limits of Justice* (Cambridge: Cambridge University Press, 1982), Chapter 2; Michael Walzer, *Spheres of Justice: A Defense of Pluralism and Equality* (New York: Basic Books, 1982), Chapters 2 and 3; Charles Taylor, *Sources of the Self: The Making of the Modern Identity* (Cambridge: Cambridge University Press, 1989), Part 1; Richard Dagger, *Civic Virtues* (Oxford: Oxford University Press, 1997), Chapter 4. For criticisms of communitarian positions, see Allen E. Buchanan, "Assessing the Communitarian Critique of Liberalism," *Ethics,* 94 (1989): 852–82. Stephen A. Gardbaum, "Law, Politics, and the Claims of Community," *Michigan Law Review,* 94 (1992): 685–760.

values. These include the assumption that neighborliness is praiseworthy, but also the assumption that wealthy persons should not take advantage of others' good nature by accepting substantial services without an appropriate display of gratitude.

The conventions of our community, and the underlying values on which they build, allow for a wide variety of transactional arrangements between persons who initially come together as strangers. At one extreme there are pure-gift relationships. Nothing I say here denies the possibility that one person may confer gratuitous benefits on another in a context in which he makes it clear throughout that he neither expects, nor would welcome, anything by way of recompense or indeed any kind of thanks. At the other extreme, people make explicit bargains. In between there lies a wide spectrum of instances where, although there is no bargain, our conventions suppose that some form of reciprocal gesture is due from the recipient of benefit, whether it has been asked for or not. In my judgment, what Mr. Handiman did falls within this middle range. It may be argued that gratitude is sufficiently displayed by verbal thanks – and no doubt these were forthcoming from Mrs. Jones. That would suffice for trifling services, but not, in my judgment, for the extensive operations undertaken by Mr. Handiman.

Property theorists have often supported the view that claims to resources may be sustained on the basis of "labor-desert." I accept this qualification: There is nothing in labor-desert which gives a timeless, natural right to own any particular resource; the content of that which is deserved can be settled only by social convention.[25] However, I take judicial notice of the fact that our society's conventions suppose that someone in Mrs. Jones's position ought to pay for the kind of work performed by her neighbor.

Accordingly, I find that at her death Mrs. Jones owed Able Handiman financial recompense and I uphold his claim for payment out of her assets of an amount to be assessed.

Septimus Tucker. Mr. Tucker seeks provision out of the resources once owned by Mrs. Jones to enable him to continue his artistic work without earning a living. There is no doubt that our conventions include obligations of maintenance *vis-à-vis* dependent members of families. Recognized communal ties carry obligations by virtue of the fact that those who enter into them are presumed to have undertaken the obligations which go with the ties. The category of such ties is not closed. Obligations may be assumed as part of relationships that, by comparison with traditional relationships of dependancy, may appear to be novel. Have we such an instance here?

As in the case of Handiman, we ought not to force the relationship between Mrs. Jones and Tucker into the artificial mold of a surrogate bargain. The importance of the relationship for both parties is not to be expressed in implied

25 See Harris, *Property and Justice,* pp. 204–13.

contractual terms. Mr. Tucker would have been obliged to pursue some other career but for the patronage of Mrs. Jones. She valued his work, as others do not, and expressed its importance to her view of the world by, *inter alia,* expending resources on his support for twenty years. In my judgment, she had thereby entered into a relationship with him that entailed an obligation to support his work for the rest of his career. The strength and the duration of the commitment yield nothing less. If, after so long, she had terminated the support she had been supplying without a good reason – such as a failure to carry on the work which for both of them was of such consequence – she would have treated him unjustly. It may be said that he ought to have foreseen that, were she to die, he would be turned adrift. But that is to beg the question as to whether the obligation she had undertaken was one that would survive her decease. As I have said, ownership perishes with the person but obligations do not. In my judgment, this obligation did not.

Accordingly, I find that Mrs. Jones had assumed an obligation for Septimus Tucker's maintenance in his artistic career and I uphold his claim, in an amount to be assessed.

John Green. I find this claim more difficult. Contrary to the bleak portrayal of unfettered ownership freedoms presented by Libertarian, C.J., I hold that there do exist community-recognized relationships between factory-owners and their workers, restricting what the former may do with their assets. But even if it can be said that Mrs. Jones had assumed an obligation to delay the factory's demise, there is no basis for finding an obligation to make a gift of it to the workers. Suppose that, before her death, she had reluctantly determined that losses could no longer be sustained so that operations at the factory must cease. If the workers had then been able and willing to mount a buy-out at a fair market price, I would have concluded that she had an obligation to sell to them. But they could not justly require her to make them a gift of the factory.

Accordingly, with regret, I dismiss John Green's claim.

The Residue. Once appropriate deductions have been made to meet the just claims of Handiman and Tucker, how should the remainder of the assets before the tribunal be distributed? There are three claimants: Paul Taxman, William Jackson, and Jennifer Brown.

Libertarian, C.J. suggested that, if a first occupancy regime is applied to the assets of deceased persons, there will be unmerited windfalls in some cases. I would go further, for I do not accept the normative assumptions he makes about property institutions and the role that first occupancy is supposed to play in their light. Ownerless things are never "out there" waiting to be gobbled up by the first-comer. There are resources and there are community ties and the interplay between them depends on how conventions of mutual fellowship should be worked out. Every appropriator of an ownerless resource achieves an unmerited windfall. With abandoned ownerless things, we tolerate such wind-falls with a "finders-keepers" rule as a prudential measure against unregulated scrambles. We should certainly do all we can to avoid a first-occupancy regime arising in relation to the goods of deceased persons. In their case it would promote, rather than prevent, a jostle to grab.

I accept that Mrs. Jones had discharged all her obligations to the state during her lifetime. Nevertheless, if she had no outstanding obligations regarding the residue of her resources, they should all go to Paul Taxman. They would constitute wealth to which no one has any claim and which therefore every member of the community should share in equally. There is no mechanism open to us for directing equal division between all citizens. The best that could be done would be for us to direct that the state should take such *bona vacantia* with distributive decisions being made according to normal democratic processes. No one can guarantee that publicly held resources will be deployed or expended equally for the good of all citizens, but democratic accountability is the best method we know for ensuring that they are.

However, I set aside Taxman's claim because I think there were obligations, covering the residue, owed both to William Jackson and to Jennifer Brown. What I have to decide is how the community conventions under which we live rank the obligations owed to these two claimants *inter se*. That may not be an easy question, but it is one that I feel bound to settle in order that there be a principled disposition of their respective claims. I would, for example, reject any suggestion that, since an obligation (of some sort) arises in both cases, we should "split the difference" by awarding some of the property to one and some to the other. When our law is faced with competing claims to property each of which has some merit, for example, where a rogue has disposed of X's goods in favor of an innocent purchaser, Y, we do not adopt such an approach. We decide – and it may often be a difficult decision – that either X or Y has the stronger claim to the whole property.

Mrs. Jones promised to give Jackson all her property before she died. I accept that our society recognizes some sort of convention of promise-making in accordance with which persons who choose to invoke promissory language thereby subject themselves to obligations. However, the scope and strength of this convention depends on the particular kind of relationship and the circumstances in which the promise is given. This promise was unilateral, made to a mere acquaintance, and, from all that appears, gave rise to no reliance on the part of the promisee. Nevertheless it did, in my judgment, institute a (weak) obligation and, had Mrs. Jones been childless, I would have preferred Jackson's claim to Taxman's.

Our society also accepts that blood tie is a source of distributive obligations. It is to blood tie alone that Mrs. Brown appeals. She does not suggest, for instance, that, by virtue of any previous residence in Mrs. Jones's house or any work on the property that she may have undertaken while living in it, there has arisen any specific connection between her and that property of which community conventions might take account. She has for years lived with her husband and pursued a luxurious life-style in which none of the assets of her late mother played any part. However, blood tie in and of itself ranks high among the values underlying our community conventions. Mrs. Brown has spoken of a "natural" right to inherit. I would avoid that description. There is no question of any supra-temporal, convention-independent right.[26] It may be that, in time, we shall come to regard property owners as owing nothing, by way of allocation upon death, to their adult children. That is not now our social attitude. If Mrs. Brown had asked her mother to make a *donatio mortis causa*[27] in her favor, Mrs. Jones would have been expected to give some reason why she should not and, to my mind, the fact that she had made this unilateral promise to a mere acquaintance would not have been a sufficient reason. Conversely, she could properly have declined any demand from Mr. Jackson for such a gift (in fulfilment of her promise), on the ground that, apart from what she owed to Handiman and Tucker, the right thing for her to do was to give the rest of her property to her daughter.

I conclude that, after deducting the assessed claims of Able Handiman and Septimus Tucker, all the late Mrs. Jones's assets should be vested in Jennifer Brown.

(D) Opinion of Egalitarian, J.

I respectfully differ from my colleagues about where we should start. For them the point of departure is the fact that, prior to her death, Mrs. Jones was the owner of these resources. Libertarian, C.J. then asks whether Mrs. Jones had made any effective exercise of her ownership transmission powers. Communitarian, J. asks whether Mrs. Jones had incurred any private obligations the discharge of which required allocation of the resources she had owned. They look backward, where I would look forward. I see these assets as "ownerless" in just the same way that a shower of golden meteorites, or the blessings of uncultivated nature, are ownerless. We must reach a judgment about how they should be distributed that has absolutely nothing to do with the late Mrs. Jones.

My colleagues' approach is guided by axiomatic assumptions about the character and normative status of property institutions. Such institutions award ring-fenced portions of social wealth (plus increments thereto) to individuals. That was the vision of property exploded a century and a half ago by Pierre

---

26 See Mill, *Principles of Political Economy*, Book 2, Chapter 2, 3, pp. 218–23; Henry Sidgwick, *The Elements of Politics* (2nd ed., London: Macmillan, 1897), pp. 100–01, 105–6; Harris, *Property and Justice*, pp. 249–52.

27 According to the doctrine of *donatio mortis causa*, a gift will be effective if it is made (1) in contemplation of death (2) to become absolute only upon the donor's death and (3) by delivery of the subject matter of the gift or the essential indicia of title, amounting to a parting with dominion. See the judgment in *Sen v. Hedley*, [1991] 2 All E.R. 736 (Court of Appeal), which surveys the origins of the doctrine in Roman Law and its introduction into, and development within, the common law.

Joseph Proudhon and satirized by him with his celebrated maxim — "Property is theft."[28]

We do not know how Mrs. Jones came to own the wealth associated with her name. Perhaps it all accrued to her as the result of her productive and entrepreneurial skills. But, as Proudhon demonstrated, augmentation by labor arises (differences in talent and capacity notwithstanding) only from social cooperation. Accordingly, it ought to be divided in arithmetically equal shares among all who work.[29] "Property," in the sense of full-blooded individual ownership, is theft because it sets aside the just claim of all to share equally in what society alone makes possible.

Mrs. Jones was not the just owner of her wealth, whether she worked for it or not. Therefore, if we had the power, I would set aside gifts she made in her lifetime. There have been many writers since Proudhon's time who have not accepted his social analysis of productive labor and have consequently not carried through the requirements of equality in resources; but have, nevertheless, recognized the inegalitarian consequences of inheritance and hence recommended its elimination or drastic modification.[30] The views of such redistribution-upon-death theorists lend support to what I am about to propose. Our power to set right the unjust distribution of wealth resulting from the operation of our property institution is very limited; but, so far as we can, it is for us to redress present inequalities.

Jennifer Brown. It is true, as Communitarian, J. has pointed out, that there are deeply entrenched social attitudes according to which a person's private wealth should, on her death, prima facie pass to her children. That pernicious custom is a major source of wealth disparity.[31] Nothing could be more unjust than that this tribunal should foster it. Even if Mrs. Jones's daughter had been a dependent child, I would have seen no reason why she should look to the wealth of her mother for her maintenance. Society, as a whole, is the only begetter of social wealth, and it is for social agencies to make provision for needy children. We should take note of the unequal access to such things as education and leisure that comes about when wealthy parents buy them for

---

28 Pierre Joseph Proudhon, *What Is Property?*, trans. Donald R. Kelley and Bonnie F. Smith (Cambridge: Cambridge University Press, 1994), pp. 13, 14, 16, 33.

29 See *ibid.*, pp. 94–116.

30 See, for example, Mill, *Principles of Political Economy*, book 2, chapter 2, 4, pp. 223–6; Harold J. Laski, *A Grammar of Politics* (3rd ed., London: George Allen and Unwin, 1934), pp. 526–33; Bruce A. Ackerman, *Social Justice in the Liberal State* (New Haven and London: Yale University Press, 1980), pp. 204–5, 208; D. W. Haslett, *Capitalism with Morality* (Oxford: Clarendon Press, 1994), pp. 235–61.

31 See, for example, Josiah Wedgewood, *The Economics of Inheritance* (London: Routledge, 1929), Part 1; A. B. Atkinson, *Unequal Shares: Wealth in Britain* (London: Penguin Books, 1974); C. D. Harbury and D. M. W. N. Hitchens, *Inheritance and Wealth Inequality in Britain* (London: George Allen and Unwin, 1979). For similar evidence from the United States, see Haslett, *Capitalism with Morality*, pp. 236–7.

their children. Much less should the assets of a deceased person be handed over to an adult child who already enjoys more than her fair share of resources.

William Jackson. Within the framework of the property institution that flourishes in our society, Mrs. Jones could have given all her property to Jackson before her death. Such arbitrary transmission powers are, alas, a feature of that thievish concept of ownership that has developed here. However, for whatever reason, Mrs. Jones never fulfilled her promise. That is something to be welcomed, for it places her resources at the disposal of this tribunal. Disagreeing as I do with Libertarian, C.J.'s normative premises, I am firmly of the view that we should not treat Mrs. Jones's promise as if it had been an outright transfer of property.

Paul Taxman. What can be done to achieve equality between all citizens as regards the resources now before the tribunal? So far as the patents and copyrights are concerned, Libertarian, C.J.'s analysis of the nature of intellectual property provides the clue. If we award these things to no one, they will cease to exist as property items. The special trespassory rules that have rendered these ideational entities artificially scarce will simply drop away. They will rejoin the common stock of all such entities within the public domain. Anyone will be able to make use of them. With intellectual property, equality is achieved through abolition.

As regards the material assets and the shares and bank accounts, the matter is not so simple. This tribunal possesses no mechanism for supervising an arithmetically equal distribution of these things between all members of our large citizen body. The practical implementation of the principle of equality of resources must be left to public agencies, and these Taxman represents. These resources can be liquidated and the proceeds devoted to communal goods, such as roads, hospitals, or schools; or they may be deployed to meet the special needs of the young, the disabled, or the aged. These are choices for the appropriate agency.

I take Communitarian J.'s point that there is no guarantee that democratic processes will yield any particular outcome. For that reason I make an exception, later in my opinion, in the case of the factory. Paul Taxman's claim should undoubtedly prevail over that of Mrs. Brown and Mr. Jackson, as regards the bulk of the assets before the tribunal. All that remains for me to consider is whether some part of those assets should be set aside to meet the other three claims.

Septimus Tucker. He wishes to pursue his artistic career without the distraction of any other kind of work. Distributive choices about which self-styled "artistic" enterprises should be promoted must be made by agencies with the appropriate expertise. Mrs. Jones, when she was an owner, was able to distort this judgment. No further distortion should be perpetuated by virtue of a deceased owner's supposed obligations. Let Tucker apply to the appropriate state arts council for a grant. If he is refused one, he may exercise the right of any citizen to criticize that agency's judgment within the public arena of politics.

Able Handiman. Handiman's work on Mrs. Jones's house was undoubtedly useful and productive. However, there are many others who perform useful services of one kind or another without payment. Perhaps a pool of resources should be set aside for distribution by a public agency among all productive workers who have fallen through the arbitrary net of formal contractual relations. However, as with Tucker's claim, that process should not be governed by the supposed obligations of a deceased owner. Handiman's claim to remuneration out of the assets before the tribunal must be dismissed.

John Green. Should we pass on the factory, along with all the other assets, to Paul Taxman? It is for public agencies, it might be said, to decide which factors of production should be kept in operation, just as it is for them to determine what kinds of artistic work are to be subsidized or whether any kind of reward is to be given to those engaged in meritorious labor. Why should we, in the case of the factory, second-guess any such community choices?

I see the force of that argument, but I find it out-weighed by the following consideration. To hand over a factor of production to the state is not to add some item of fungible wealth to a pot of resources available for any and all public purposes. The factory where Mr. Green and his colleagues work is a specific asset performing an essential role in their lives. One of the grossest injustices of private ownership of productive enterprises is that it empowers owners to dominate the life-chances of workers, and the power of closure is perhaps the greatest source of such domination-potential. Mrs. Jones was unusually benevolent. If the state becomes "owner" of the factory, it will, prima facie, slot into the position of any private owner.

True, state agencies cannot simply ward off criticisms of uses they make of things they own by announcing: "The thing is mine to do with as I please!" Public "ownership" necessarily entails discharge of public functions. On the other hand, we cannot ignore the experience of recent history. That experience shows that many powers modelled on those traditionally supposed to be inherent in private ownership are taken to accompany ownership by public agencies. There can be no guarantee that the state, as owner, might not decide to close down this "unprofitable" enterprise.[32]

We can ensure that the workers are spared the misery of uncertainty that springs from their place of work being owned by someone else only by making them the owners. That might have had the consequence that each of them thereby receives more than his equal share of social wealth, if the factory had been flourishing. Taking a rough-and-ready guide to what equality of resources requires, I hold that handing the factory over to the workers would achieve approximate justice.

32 See Harris, *Property and Justice*, pp. 266–70.

Accordingly, I uphold Mr. Green's claim, and I award the remaining assets (apart from the patents and copyrights) to Paul Taxman. So far as the patents and copyrights are concerned, I dismiss all claims.

(E) Adjournment

Libertarian, C.J.

The result of the three opinions delivered at this hearing is as follows. Each one of the six claimants is supported by one of our number, whilst his or her claim is rejected by the other two. No majority exists in favor of any claimant. I accordingly adjourn the hearing to be tried before another panel of this tribunal.

III. Reflections

What a mercy it is that we do not decide how to allocate the resources of the dead by such a process as that set out in the last section. Worst of all would be the default provision whereby, if no successful claim were made to the Justice Tribunal, resources would be deemed to be ownerless and thereafter subject to a free-for-all. That would constitute one manifestation of what Garrett Hardin described as "the tragedy of the commons."[33] The principal concern of Hardin's essay was to argue that, in a world of finite resources, "[f]reedom to breed is intolerable."[34] However, as a step within his argument he claimed that disaster would have resulted if there had emerged no restraints on access to land,[35] and his essay has come to be treated as a classic statement of the supposed economic advantages of private property.

> We must admit that our legal system of private property plus inheritance is unjust, but we put up with it because we are not convinced at the moment that anyone has invented a better system. The alternative of the commons is too horrifying to contemplate. Injustice is preferable to total ruin.[36]

A full-blown tragedy of the commons arises, in Hardin's analysis, when a resource is the subject of unregulated access and a private property system is one means of preventing this. Precisely what the horror would be if private property were maintained, whilst inheritance was abolished, Hardin does not say. One of the things that emerges from the deliberations of the Justice Tribunal is that it would vary according to the types of resources. In relation to

---

33 See Garret Hardin, "The Tragedy of the Commons," *Science,* 162 (1968): 1243–48, reprinted in Bruce A. Ackerman, ed., *Economic Foundations of Property Law* (Boston: Little Brown and Co., 1975), pp. 2–11.

34 Ibid., p. 6.

35 Ibid., pp. 4–5.

36 Ibid., p. 9.

intellectual property, for example, there might be adverse effects on incentives but there would be no "tragedy" in Hardin's sense, since all may use ideational entities without treading on each other's toes. As far as property in cashable rights is concerned, there would also be no depletion of a common stock, but rather a windfall for debtors. For land, cash, and chattels, the "tragedy" would take the form of an unregulated scramble.

Some rules about will-making and intestacy we must have. Guidance about what those rules should be may be derived from our reactions to the proceedings of the Justice Tribunal. Limitations of space prevent any point-by-point discussion. In the present section, I shall concentrate on two major concerns, which I call "the historical-entitlement deficit" and "the egalitarian crunch."

(A) The Historical-Entitlement Deficit

Historical-entitlement theories of justice were invoked by Libertarian, C.J. Such theories raise many questions concerning the normative foundations of the entire process. Why should we accept that occupancy, with or without labor, of that which was previously unowned entails a unilateral power to subject other people to trespassory obligations banning them from all contact with the resource without leave of the appropriator? If first occupancy or labor is needed to trigger rest-of-the-world-exclusion, wherein arises the power to exclude that seemingly accrues to transferees from the original appropriator? Why should they step into his shoes? Is it that the unilateral power has timeless effects? By exercising it the first appropriator becomes entitled, not merely to exclude, but also to impose an eternal sequence of trespassory rules on all generations of mankind: No one may ever violate the possession of anyone to whom the resource is successively transferred. Can a single appropriative act have such consequences for a never-ending normative universe?[37]

The alchemy deployed by historical-entitlement theorists to deal with these problems is dogmatic insistence on a supposedly uncontestable and supra-temporal concept of ownership. Ownership just must comprise, not merely unlimited use-privileges and control-powers, but also unlimited powers of transmission. Original appropriation, at whatever past date it occurred, must have involved that concept of ownership. No normative argument need be supplied to establish these preconceived conceptual truths. It follows that the fostering of human autonomy becomes private property's supreme virtue.

Often cited is Blackstone's invocation of "that sole and despotic dominion which one man claims and exercises over the external things of the world, in total exclusion of the right of any other individual in the universe."[38] Blackstone, however, also argued that, in the state of nature, someone who first

37 See Alan Gibbard, "Natural Property Rights," *Noûs*, 10 (1977): 77–85.
38 Sir William Blackstone, *Commentaries on the Laws of England* (16th ed., London: J. Butterworth and Son, 1825), Book 2, p. 1.

occupied a determined spot, for rest, shade, or the like, "acquired therein a kind of transient property, that lasted so long as he was using it, and no longer."[39] Reference is also often made to a seminal essay of A. M. Honoré, which seeks to tabulate the "standard incidents" of "the liberal concept of full individual ownership."[40] But Honoré makes perfectly clear that the concept he analyzes is in no sense timeless. Less developed cultures – where original appropriations may have occurred – employed lesser ownership conceptions.[41]

I have argued that none of the received arguments succeed in establishing any free-standing natural right to "full-blooded ownership."[42] Suppose that, contrary to my view, ownership must, of conceptual necessity, be taken to include limitless powers of (at any rate) *inter vivos* transmission. What does a historical-entitlement theory have to offer, by way of moral prescription, when a person dies without having exercised such a power? If testamentary power is added, the same problem arises where a person dies intestate.

According to a historical-entitlement theory, original just titles can be acquired only by appropriative acts. A theorist can be comfortable with that for appropriations that are deemed to have occurred in the distant past; or if, in the modern world, they are limited to lost chattels or abandoned strips of land. We may even contemplate, as a practical measure, Murray Rothbard's proposal that the government of the United States should throw open to private homesteading all land now retained in the public domain.[43] But how, in principle, should such a theory deal with the countless instances which must inevitably arise of a person dying without exercising transmission powers as regards some, or all, of her property? No doubt the intestacy provisions of modern property institutions are frequently framed on the basis of what the average testator would have wished to happen to her property, or of obligations of support and maintenance that are assumed to have been incumbent on her, with the state taking *bona vacantia* in default of next of kin. However, as Libertarian, C.J.'s discussion of the problem reveals, a consistent historical-entitlement theory must respect only real choices and it cannot vest the state with power to sequestrate ownerless goods. The upshot must be this. If a full-blown "tragedy of the commons" is to be avoided, there must be a mechanism whereby individuals or groups can come to be owners of those continuing property items of which the deceased has not effectively disposed. Can we contemplate with equanimity that, whenever a person dies owning undisposed

39 Ibid., Book 2, p. 3.
40 A. M. Honoré, "Ownership," in A. G. Guest, ed., *Oxford Essays in Jurisprudence* (Oxford: Oxford University Press, 1961), pp. 107–47. A revised version of the essay appears in Tony Honoré, *Making Law Bind: Essays Legal and Philosophical* (Oxford: Clarendon Press, 1987), pp. 161–92. I have discussed Honoré's list of incidents in Harris, *Property and Justice,* pp. 125–30.
41 See Honoré, *Making Law Bind,* pp. 215–26.
42 See Harris, *Property and Justice,* Chapters 12 and 13.
43 See Rothbard, "Justice and Property Rights," at 118–19.

of assets, all such property is up for grabs? In other contexts we may call to mind the days of the wild west frontier, with intrepid pioneers winning the race to assert a claim in the gold fields. No doubt a first-come, first-take regime had its cost in social friction even then. But at least the pioneers may be supposed to have had equal starts. Not so those fortuitously connected with a dead person's property.

Libertarian, C.J. looked into the abyss. He could find no tolerable solution, on the assumption that Mrs. Jones's resources were now ownerless; and he was right. From the perspective of a pure historical-entitlement theory, there can be no moral basis for any rules of intestate succession. Let the vultures gather around the sick bed and grab as grab can when the last breath is exhaled.

A historical-entitlement theory would be pure if it rigorously restricted all just claims to own resources in the following way. The claimant must herself have appropriated unowned resources (in whatever manner the theory stipulates as just appropriation), or must have derived title by successive transfers from such an appropriator. Reallocation from someone who now holds a resource in favor of a claimant must be made when, but only when, the claimant can show an original or derived title while the present holder cannot. If property becomes unowned upon death then, as Libertarian, C.J.'s judgment demonstrates, no one (and especially not the state) can advance a just claim before the deceased's resources have actually been appropriated.

In the literature, however, historical-entitlement theories seldom come pure. Those consequentialist considerations, which Libertarian, C.J. noted but said were strictly unnecessary for determining just allocations, are often invoked to supplement the basic argument. Even Robert Nozick is constrained to do this. He deals with the classical Lockean requirement that an original appropriation, to be just, must leave "enough and as good" for others in the following way. So long as the appropriation did not (and continues not to) make other people worse off, all things considered, than they would have been had it not occurred (or were not still insisted on), then the appropriation is just; and in making this comparison one may take into account all the familiar incentive and market-instrumental advantages of private property institutions.[44]

All the more will consequences be prayed in aid by a theorist who seeks to marry his historical-entitlement morality with practical implementation. As Margaret Jane Radin has pointed out, such praying-in-aid informs the whole of Richard Epstein's celebrated critique of the United State's Supreme Court's interpretation of the "takings clause" in the U.S. Constitution.[45] Epstein founds moral claims to all private resource-holdings on first possession of unowned

---

44 See Nozick, *Anarchy, State, and Utopia*, pp. 175–82. For the argument that, consistently with the Lockean proviso, original just appropriation of land and non-renewable resources must be limited to usufructuary rights, see Clark Wolf, "Contemporary Property Rights, Lockean Provisos, and the Interest of Future Generations," *Ethics*, 105 (1995): 791–818, at 810–14.

45 See Margaret Jane Radin, *Reinterpreting Property* (Chicago: University of Chicago Press, 1993), pp. 98–104.

material objects, grace of the presupposed supra-temporal concept of full own-ership. Ownership of a thing "consists in a set of rights of infinite duration," comprising the incidents of "possession, use and disposition."[46] "The first possession rule" vests them all in the first occupant.[47] Why should we assume this? Because "linking rights of possession, use and disposition into a single body of rights offers powerful utilitarian advantages."[48] Past injustices, he maintains, should not be remedied by requiring present holders to disgorge, in favor of claimants who derive title from original appropriators, because such a program would impede productivity and public peace.[49] How does original appropriation of material objects yield intangible property such as cashable rights and intellectual property? There is sometimes a rather barren dispute about whether the label "property" should be applied to such items.[50] Epstein is clear that it should. All such items derive, he says, from exercises by the original appropriator of a material object, and his successors, of the right of disposition. They result in "patents, copyrights, trade secrets and other forms of intangible wealth which have value in use and disposition even if they cannot be reduced to physical possession."[51] However, even if unlimited transmission powers had a moral foundation in natural right, the common law and statutory complexities which channel their detailed implementation must surely have been framed with consequentialist considerations in mind. What about intes-tacy law? Epstein has recently suggested that "the roles of voluntary transfer" include, besides sale, gift and bequest, also "perhaps inheritance," by which he presumably intends intestate succession. He criticizes Blackstone for denying that "inheritance was not a natural right of property" but one which could be given or withheld by the state. Such a view is to be rejected, he says, because either submitting a deceased person's assets to an occupancy regime, or allow-ing them to be taxed by the state, would not be "conducive to overall creation of wealth."[52] He gives no indication why one set of intestacy rules would be more conducive to wealth creation (and hence a more "natural" right of prop-erty) than any other set would be.

An impure historical-entitlement theory might concede that ownerless re-sources of deceased persons, unlike other ownerless things, should not be open

46 Epstein, *Takings*, p. 58.
47 Ibid., p. 61.
48 Ibid.
49 Ibid., pp. 346–49.
50 In English, such resources are called "property," and in French *propriété*. German and Dutch law reserve the terms *Eigentum* and *eigendom* respectively for the ownership of material resources. Nevertheless, these intangible forms of wealth are, perforce, dealt with in those systems just as though they were "property." The difference is one in legal dogmatics, not in substance. See Wolfgang Mincke, "Property: Assets or Power? Objects or Relations as Sub-strata of Property Rights," in J. W. Harris, ed., *Property Problems: From Genes to Pension Funds* (London: Kluwer Law International, 1997), pp. 78–88.
51 Epstein, *Takings*, p. 62.
52 See Richard A. Epstein, "On the Optimal Mix of Private and Common Property," *Social Philosophy & Policy*, 11, no. 2 (Summer 1994): 17–41, at 32 and n. 34.

to individual appropriation – just to avoid the scrambles and unmerited wind-falls contemplated by Libertarian, C.J. As a prophylactic measure, let such *bona vacantia* be taken by the state. But then the theory, as a historical-entitlement theory, has nothing to offer by way of recommendation about how the state may justly apply or distribute the property it takes over. The whole point of such theories is to deny to the state a just redistributive role based on desert or need, of the sort envisaged by either Communitarian, J. or Egalitarian, J. It seems, then, that, from a historical-entitlement perspective, ownerless resources of deceased persons are altogether outside the agenda of just distribution – if the scramble solution is rejected. That is the historical-entitlement deficit.

Having looked into the abyss, Libertarian, C.J. proceeded to force a uni-lateral promise into the mold of a dispositive transfer. Since he felt able to do that only if there was no evidence that Mrs. Jones had changed her mind before she died, he was, in effect, inventing that which was unavailable within his jurisdiction – a testamentary bequest. The historical-entitlement deficit is re-duced if the concept of ownership deployed by a theory includes a power to bequeath, although it will still arise whenever a person dies wholly or partially intestate. That ownership does comprise this power is usually taken for granted, *en passant,* by historical-entitlement theorists,[53] as it is by other theorists who uphold property freedoms.[54] As pointed out at the beginning of this essay, however, unfettered testamentary power has not, historically, had this status. Its inclusion within a conception of ownership we wish to defend has to be supported by substantive normative arguments. Nozick has come to believe that bequests should be limited to those additions which a person makes to his inherited wealth.[55]

Hillel Steiner offers a historical-entitlement theory from which the power of bequest is altogether excluded. He contends that the set of jural relations that obtains between a property-owner and the rest of the world may be changed when an owner makes an *inter vivos* gift, for then the donee is substituted for the donor but otherwise the set remains unaltered. On the death of a testator, however, a new set of relations is supposed to arise, involving executors, heirs, and the state. This new set cannot include any jural relations to which the testator himself is a party, for he is now dead. Therefore, while ownership powers comprise *inter vivos* gift, they do not comprise bequest.[56] "'Dead' persons have no rights."[57]

53 See Nozick, *Anarchy, State, and Utopia,* p. 238; Rothbard, "Justice and Property Rights," at 114; Epstein, *Takings,* pp. 304, 347.
54 See, for example, F. A. Hayek, *The Constitution of Liberty* (London: Routledge and Kegan Paul, 1960), p. 91; Charles Fried, *Contract as Promise* (Cambridge, Mass.: Harvard University Press, 1981), p. 21.
55 See Robert Nozick, *The Examined Life* (New York: Simon and Schuster, 1989), pp. 30–31.
56 Steiner, *An Essay on Rights,* pp. 250–58.
57 Ibid., p. 250.

Steiner notes that the law overcomes the problem by the fiction of identifying the deceased with some living representative. He derides the idea that
moral rights could be based on fictions. "Can my just duty to pay a loan be
avoided by my creation of a fiction that I never undertook to do so when in fact
I did"?[58] "In short, there can be no moral counterpart to the legal power of
bequest, so the justification of bequest, if there is one, cannot lie in the de-
mands of justice and the property of the dead thereby joins raw natural resources in the category of initially unowned things."[59]

The exclusion of testamentary power is one of the important reasons advanced by Steiner for claiming that his particular version of an "historical
entitlement conception of justice" has "reasonably strong redistributive implications."[60] Whether that would be so in practice is questionable. If testation
were not available, familiar *inter vivos* settlements and trusts providing for
future generations might take its place, unless these too were held to flout the
requirements of justice by virtue of Steiner's claim that "future persons have no
rights."[61] Egalitarian, J. would applaud the suggestion that distributive choices
should not defer to the rights, or for that matter the duties, of persons now dead.
But every historical-entitlement theory assumes that the transactions of past
generations have enduring moral effects. Why should we suppose that they do
so if, but only if, they took the form of outright transfers of holdings? What, for
example, about executory contracts by dead people to pay money? Communitarian, J. thought that this must be an indisputable instance of a right
exigible against the assets of a deceased person. As we shall see, it seems to
follow from Steiner's analysis that even this should not be conceded.

According to Steiner, estates of deceased persons (and their bodies) join the
class of unowned things. In consequence, every adult person in the world at the
time of the death is at liberty to appropriate an equal share of them. He
recognizes, however, that, like other unowned things, they will not be readily
divisible into equalized portions. Hence, every person that succeeds in appropriating such assets must pay a contribution, representing the excess over his
equal share, into a global fund.[62] There is no question of the fund-holders
(whoever they may be) themselves appropriating the property for common use,
as both Communitarian, J. and Egalitarian, J. envisaged. Collective property
can, according to Steiner, only justly arise when individual owners pool that
which they have already appropriated.[63]

---

58 Ibid., p. 257.
59 Ibid., p. 258.
60 Ibid., p. 5.
61 Ibid., p. 250.
62 See ibid., pp. 257, 268, 273. The global fund also includes levies designed to redress those
    elements of value in people's holdings that are attributable to more than equal shares of natural
    resources, including levies on parents whose children have a better than average endowment of
    germ-line genetic information. Ibid., pp. 270–79.
63 See ibid., pp. 217–20

On this view, so far as Mrs. Jones's material property is concerned, the scramble must go on. But her intangible resources, it seems, will simply disappear. They depend on the persistence of rights, and "dead persons have no rights." In fact, there is a more fundamental problem with Steiner's account arising from what he says about the "compossibility" and the "material" substructure of rights. If these features of his conception of justice are taken at face value, it seems that property in intangible resources, and all cashable rights, are unaccountable mysteries.

Nozick condemned all talk of rights being founded on basic needs in the following terms:

> The major objection to speaking of everyone's having a right to various things such as equality of opportunity, life, and so on, and enforcing this right, is that these "rights" require a substructure of things and materials and actions; and other people may have rights and entitlements over these. The particular rights over things fill the space of rights, leaving no room for general rights to be in a certain material condition.[64]

Steiner builds on this spatial conception of compatible rights in the following way. The elementary particles of justice are, he says, a set of "compossible" moral rights.[65] This entails that the duties to which rights correlate must never conflict in the sense that any two of them could not be jointly performed; and the only way to ensure this requirement is to insist that every right must relate to the right-holder's separate physical domain.[66] A right must always be to the "physical components" of the duty-bearer's act.[67] All rights in a compossible set may be regarded as property rights, because they imply all other persons' duties of non-interference with the right-holder's "use of certain physical things."[68] On this view, we must not only banish from the justice agenda the entire law of bankruptcy and corporate insolvency (which presupposes obligations that cannot be jointly performed), but also, were Steiner consistent, claims to the payment of money are conceptually impossible rights.[69] I have use-rights over the coins in my pocket, because other persons' duties to refrain from taking them from me can be jointly performed. But my right that you pay me ten pounds, if it were taken to relate to coins in your pocket, might correlate with a duty which you could not perform jointly with a duty to pay someone else the same coins. In fact, the substructure of such rights never relates to particular physical tokens, so that the compossibility test could not be applied. The same is even more blatantly the case when people suppose they have rights

---

64 See Nozick, *Anarchy, State, and Utopia*, p. 238.
65 Steiner, *An Essay on Rights*, pp. 2–3.
66 Ibid., pp. 80–106.
67 Ibid., p. 91.
68 Ibid., p. 46.
69 Steiner is not consistent, for he assumes there can be redress rights to compensation – see ibid., pp. 204–6 – without demonstrating their physical domains or their compossibility; and he speaks throughout of sales and loans just as if there could be rights to be paid money.

to "money in the bank." The compossibility and materiality conditions are also incapable of being satisfied as regards those rights to receive dividends and participate in insolvency distributions which are entailed by ownership of shares.

Steiner notes that there are moral rules and values besides justice, and specifically that the practice of bequest might be supported on utilitarian grounds.[70] So it might be suggested that, even if it is incoherent to talk about justice or rights in the contexts of testamentary power, intestacy, bankruptcy, bank accounts, or company shares, we may employ some other epithet – such as "morally sound." But then Steiner insists that justice is the only proper business of judges and legislators[71] and that legal enforcement should be restricted to compossible moral rights.[72] If his compossibility requirement is a necessary feature of a pure historical-entitlement theory, such theories have nothing to say about what the law ought to be in respect of any resources other than material ones and Steiner ought not to have spoken, as he did in a passage cited earlier, of "my just duty to pay a loan." The historical-entitlement deficit yawns wide indeed.

(B) The Egalitarian Crunch

The testamentary power that modern legal systems confer upon owners is distinguishable from all other ownership powers in that it combines three attributes. It is unilateral; it is revocable; and it is ambulatory (that is, capable of extending to property that the disponor does not own at the time he exercises the power).[73] For all that, the fact that dead people have no rights in no way makes such a practice conceptually problematic. The law arms the owner with a power that he may exercise, and revoke, in a prescribed form. It correlates with a future liability of whomever the testator (or the law) designates as universal successor. It is no more a natural incident of ownership than is any other ownership power, although it is, historically, a late-comer. I have argued that there is no compelling moral argument for its total exclusion from histor- ically evolved conceptions of ownership interests. It is as much a *prima facie* valuable exercise of autonomy as any other ownership freedom.[74]

Dead people have no duties. Nevertheless, one of the moral limitations on testamentary power concerns obligations already incurred by a deceased per- son that ought justly to be discharged by appropriation of some of the assets she once owned. Some of those obligations arise from contract and some from other relationships. Their extent cannot be enunciated with precision. Com-

---

70 See ibid., p. 251.
71 See ibid., p. 3.
72 See ibid., pp. 202, 212–13.
73 See Gbolahan Elias, *Explaining Constructive Trusts* (Oxford: Clarendon Press, 1990), pp. 87–95.
74 See Harris, *Property and Justice,* pp. 249–56.

munitarian arguments address the problem, but their implications are inherently messy.

Of the obligations investigated by Communitarian, J., it may come as a surprise to those unfamiliar with English law that the only one for which legislative provision (overriding testamentary freedom) is made would be that owed to Septimus Tucker (the artist). The court may order reasonable financial provision for the maintenance of any person "who immediately before the death of the deceased was being maintained, either wholly or partly, by the deceased."[75] Jennifer Brown would not be eligible, because she needs no maintenance from her mother's estate. Able Handiman (the good neighbor) could only have succeeded, by invoking the doctrine of proprietary estoppel, if he established that he acted as he did on the faith of a representation that Mrs. Jones would provide for him in her will.[76] A mere promise, such as that made to William Jackson, would have no effect.[77]

I shall not investigate any of Communitarian, J.'s conclusions. Suffice it to say that, so far as it is true that deeply entrenched social attitudes about inheritance exist, they cannot be ignored by any would-be reformer. They can neither be challenged, nor supported, on the basis of natural right. Yet they are vulnerable to attack from another quarter. Inheritance is a major cause of wealth-disparity and, on that account, Egalitarian, J. condemned conventions which support it as "pernicious."

Among those who deploy some conception of equality of resources as a political value, few would align themselves with the Proudhonian stance of Egalitarian, J. And for good reason. His version of this ideal left too little for communal ties and independent initiatives. Most egalitarians suppose that a margin, great or small, should be left for ownership freedoms. For example, Ronald Dworkin has argued that inequalities resulting from industry, investment, or gambling – "option luck" – should be tolerated; in contrast measures should be adopted to counteract the effects of differences in talent – "brute luck."[78]

Here we are concerned with the redistribution-on-death theorists invoked by Egalitarian, J., Mill, Laski, Ackerman, and Haslett.[79] They uniformly accept that there is a prima facie right to bequeath, but recommend its overriding

---

75 Inheritance (Provision for Family and Dependants) Act 1975, 1(1)(e).

76 In *Re Basham decd,* [1987] 1 All E.R. 405, the deceased led his step-daughter to believe she would inherit his property, in reliance upon which the step-daughter and her husband performed unpaid services for the deceased. The court held that the step-daughter should receive the deceased's entire estate in preference to those entitled to it under intestacy law.

77 In *Taylor v. Dickens,* [1998] 1 FLR 806, the deceased promised to leave her house to a helpful neighbor, but later changed her will without telling him. The court held that the promise was not binding on those taking under the later will.

78 See R. M. Dworkin, "What Is Equality? Part 2 Equality of Resources," *Philosophy & Public Affairs,* 10 (1981): 283–355.

79 See the citation of these authors at note 30 above.

to the extent required to bring about a more desirable distribution of wealth. Theirs is a call to fellow citizens to recognize the injustice of some feature of wealth-distribution and accordingly to modify their present attitudes about inheritance. That is the egalitarian crunch.

A recent measured suggestion along these lines is that of W. D. Haslett. He considers two proposals, the first more stringent than the second. Both involve banning gifts, whether in the form of bequests or *inter vivos* transfers. He points out, rightly, that it would be question-begging to condemn such measures merely on the ground that they violate property rights, because what is at issue is whether such rights ought to include the power to make the banned gifts.[80]

Both proposals would exempt the following: (1) all small gifts (maximum not specified); (2) all gifts to spouses; (3) all gifts to charities; and (4) gifts setting up maintenance and education funds for dependants. The first proposal is that all other gifts should be prohibited by law, and that the part of any deceased person's estate that has not been bequeathed within one of the excepted categories should escheat to the state. The second proposal is that gifts made to any single donee throughout her lifetime should be limited to a total aggregate amount – say, $100,000 if calculated in 1990.[81] Gifts exceeding this quota should pass to the state. Haslett describes the first proposal as "abolishing" inheritance and the second as a "compromise."[82] In fact, neither proposal takes away the power of bequest altogether and both treat bequests and *inter vivos* gifts on the same terms.

The immediate objective of these proposals is the reduction in the huge disparities of wealth-holdings which now obtain. It has been suggested that this could be better achieved by graduated taxation.[83] Haslett argues against this on the ground that inheritance taxes notoriously allow for loopholes which negate their redistributive aims.[84] It is not clear why loopholeless legislation prohibiting gifts should be any easier to achieve than loopholeless taxation. Do not Haslett's proposals amount to a system of 100 percent tax, once the suggested limits have been exceeded?

The principal justification for the objective is that wealth-disparities militate against the "equal opportunity for all to pursue successfully the occupation of their choice."[85] Haslett accepts that such inequalities resulting from

---

80 See Haslett, *Capitalism with Morality,* pp. 242, 247–8.
81 The second proposal is similar to the one made by Mill, noted at the beginning of this essay, except that Mill would allow each individual donee to receive "the means of comfortable independence."
82 See Haslett, *Capitalism with Morality,* pp. 245–7, 257–62.
83 See Stephen R. Munzer, *A Theory of Property* (Cambridge: Cambridge University Press, 1990), Chapter 13.
84 Haslett, *Capitalism with Morality,* pp. 237, 259.
85 Ibid., p. 239.

differential endowment or parental nurture cannot be avoided, but claims that his proposals would substantially diminish those that are caused by parental gifts.[86]

It can be objected that what is at stake here is not "equality" as such. I have suggested that the trespassory rules of a property institution are morally binding on those to whom they are addressed, generally speaking, only if the community shoulders "justice costs," which includes meeting all persons' basic needs.[87] Haslett himself contends (and I would agree) that public provision should be made for educational and professional training so that anyone with the relevant aptitudes may qualify for the career of her choice.[88] Now, as Joseph Raz has pointed out, if we say that a certain good should be made available to all, the adverb "equally" adds nothing but a (possibly useful) rhetorical flourish.[89] If suitable education and training were so extended that no one was prevented from pursuing the career of her choice by lack of means – the extension being financed, *inter alia,* by taxing inheritance – such wealth-disparities as remained could not be condemned on the ground that they resulted in unequal opportunities to pursue the career of one's choice.[90]

Nevertheless, whether one argues that large holdings of inherited wealth should be partly expropriated to finance justice costs, or that this should be done because equalizing holdings is itself a necessary step to particular just outcomes, in either case the advocated measures would probably be called "egalitarian." Haslett correctly identifies the problem. Having surveyed objections that might be taken to his first proposal, he concludes that the "abolition" of inheritance would, on balance, be justified.[91] He opts, however, for the second "compromise" proposal. He does so because, among other things, current social attitudes are so wedded to the idea that people are entitled to pass on their wealth as they choose that public opinion would not stomach the first proposal. We must, he says, persist in pointing out the unacceptability of this attitude, given its unjust distributive consequences. We must win people round to seeing the errors of their present assumptions.[92]

Haslett says nothing about the other half of the inheritance problem, namely, rules of intestate succession – though no doubt they could be adapted

86 See ibid., pp. 239–41, 243–4, 248–9.
87 See Harris, *Property and Justice,* pp. 279–89.
88 See Haslett, *Capitalism with Morality,* pp. 98–9, 261–2.
89 See Joseph Raz, *The Morality of Freedom* (Oxford: Clarendon Press, 1986), Chapter 9.
90 At one point, Haslett suggests that unequally open careers include that of being a passive "big-time investor." *Capitalism with Morality,* p. 241. That amounts to the question-begging claim that being excessively rich is unacceptable because it gives a person an unequal opportunity to be excessively rich. I have argued that other objections to major wealth-disparities are either contingent on a social context or else presuppose "equality of resources" as a dominating value. Harris, *Property and Justice,* pp. 258–64, 308–17.
91 See Haslett, *Capitalism with Morality,* pp. 247–57.
92 See ibid., pp. 249–51.

in accordance with either of his proposals. Would the same difficulty of confronting entrenched social attitudes be encountered? I am not aware of surveys
of public opinion that specifically put the question: "If you omitted to make a
will, would you want your property to go to the government?" For what it is
worth, I have put that question to colleagues, acquaintances, and pupils over
the years, and the pretty uniform answer has been "no". That is partly, I
suspect, because the proper expenditure of justice costs is not factored into
people's surface reactions. Could that be changed?

So far as direct descendants and spouses (and probably siblings) are concerned, my suspicion is that a popular response would be as follows: "Let the
Treasury exact just taxation from my estate; but, after that, keep its hands off. I
would prefer that [or, perhaps, I am morally obliged to ensure that] what is left
goes to the family." However, intestacy rules extend in England to descendants
of common grandparents – cousins of all degrees. We might convince people
that such windfalls are totally unmerited, that the Treasury really has worthy
ways of spending resources and that therefore, in this respect, intestacy rules
should be changed.[93] That is the place where, I suggest, we should first bring
the egalitarian crunch to bear. Be that as it may, the argument is, in my view,
not one about equality at all, but one about the interplay between deeply
entrenched assumptions about passing on of wealth and the state's need to raise
revenue to discharge justice costs.

IV. Conclusion

It is the business of property theory (1) to identify its subject, (2) to investigate
moral considerations pertinent to that subject, and (3) to address contemporary
political culture in the light of (1) and (2). That is what I attempted in my
Property and Justice.[94] In the present essay I have employed a thought-
experiment to isolate the problem of inheritance from our familiar legal ma-
chinery and the cultural assumptions that go with it. When an owner dies, must
his property persist? If it does, should we defer to his wishes, to blood ties, to
any of his obligations, to others' needs, to the claims of the community, or to all
of these? How should any of these considerations be ranked? If the reader is
sure that the members of the Justice Tribunal erred about any of these matters,
the grounds for the reader's certainty are part of his or her understanding of the
political culture we should foster.

In the introduction to the essay, I espoused an approach to property theory
that rejects single-track stances. I hope to have shown that the stereotypical
visions of the three members of the Justice Tribunal bear this out. Whether or

---

93 There is nothing novel in such a suggestion. See Sidgwick, *The Elements of Politics,* pp.
   106–7.
94 See note 11 above.

not they erred in their detailed discriminations, at least each of them sought to stick consistently to a singular view of the proper purpose of property institutions. In so doing they were, in my contention, bound to reach unsatisfactory outcomes. The mix of sound property-specific justice reasons which ought to govern all questions of property-institutional design encompasses some aspects of all their opinions, and much else besides.

5

Lockean Arguments for Private Intellectual Property

SEANA VALENTINE SHIFFRIN

It has been pretended . . . that inventors have a natural and exclusive right to their inventions. . . . If nature has made any one thing less susceptible than others of exclusive property, it is the action of the thinking power called an idea. . . . Its peculiar character . . . is that no one possesses the less, because every other possesses the whole of it. He who receives an idea from me, receives instruction himself without lessening mine; as he who lights his taper at mine, receives light without darkening me. That ideas should be freely spread from one to another over the globe, for the moral and mutual instruction of man, and improvement of his condition, seems to have been . . . designed by nature. . . . *Inventions then cannot, in nature, be a subject of property.* Society may give an exclusive right to the profits arising from them, as an encouragement . . . to pursue ideas which may produce utility, but this may or may not be done, according to the will and convenience of the society, without claim or complaint from anybody.[1]

I. Introduction

Thomas Jefferson was the first administrator of the U.S. patent system and a Lockean sympathizer. Nevertheless, he was fiercely critical of natural rights approaches to intellectual property. Many contemporary legal and philosophical commentators, however, seem to suppose the contrary: that Lockean justificatory foundations straightforwardly support a wide range of strong intellectual property rights.[2]

I am grateful for constructive, stimulating comments from Tyler Burge, David Dolinko, William Fisher, Wendy Gordon, Barbara Herman, Timothy Hinton, Michael Jacovides, David Kaplan, Jerry Kang, Matthew Kramer, Mark Lemley, Gillian Lester, Eric Mack, Miles Morgan, Steve Munzer, Calvin Normore, Michael Otsuka, James Penner, Monroe Price, Steven Shiffrin, Lloyd Weinreb, Jonathan Wilwerding, Eugene Volokh, Clark Wolf, the Law and Philosophy Discussion Group of Los Angeles, and anonymous reviewers for Cambridge University Press.
1 Thomas Jefferson, "The Invention of Elevators" (Letter, 1813), in Saul K. Padover, ed., *The Complete Jefferson* (New York: Dell, Sloan & Pearce, 1943), p. 1015 (emphasis added).
2 See, for example, Lawrence C. Becker, "Deserving to Own Intellectual Property," *University of Chicago-Kent Law Review,* 68 (1993): 609–29, at 610–12 & 616; James Child, "The Moral Foundations of Intangible Property," *The Monist,* 73 (1990): 578–600, William W. Fisher III, "Reconstructing the Fair Use Doctrine," *Harvard Law Review,* 101 (1988): 1661–795, at 1688– 90; Justin Hughes, "The Philosophy of Intellectual Property," *Georgetown Law Journal* 77

The desire to use Lockean theory to ground intellectual property rights is understandable in light of its theoretical and practical advantages. Locke's approach to property appears to offer a strong, principled justification for private property rights. It does not presuppose the justifiability of private property. Instead, it aims to arrive at justifications for both the institution, and the appropriation conditions, of private property from premises that assume a starting point of common ownership of resources. Moreover, it appears to offer a principled alternative to consequentialist approaches, one that might reduce the need for empirical investigation. Consequentialist foundations for property rights rely upon contingent, empirical facts that may fluctuate with variations in the economic context – for example, how effectively various incentives stimulate production, or whether restrictions on derivative use propel or deter innovation over time. These facts may be difficult and costly to investigate. By contrast, Lockean arguments seem to offer the prospect of justifying private ownership with little appeal to these potentially varying facts.

To many commentators, these advantages appear to be in easy reach. Intellectual property seems, at first, particularly well suited to the application of Locke's theory. In fact, it seems easier to satisfy Lockean conditions on appropriation for intellectual property than for real property. It is generally thought that Lockean principles permit private appropriation of property from the common stock of property, so long as the "Lockean proviso" is met. This proviso is understood to allow one to appropriate so long as one leaves "enough, and as good" for others and one does not appropriate so much that goods waste or spoil.[3] For three main reasons, many believe that these

(1988): 287–366, at 291, 300, 325, 365; Adam Moore, "Toward a Lockean Theory of Intellectual Property," in Adam Moore, ed., *Intellectual Property* (Lanham: Rowman and Littlefield, 1997), pp. 81–103, Robert Nozick, *Anarchy, State, and Utopia* (New York: Basic Books, 1974), pp. 181–2; Alan Ryan, *Property* (Milton Keynes: Open University Press, 1987), pp. 68–9; *Ruckelshaus v. Monsanto,* 467 U.S. 986, 1002–03 (1984). For accounts of the historical influence of Lockean theory on the development of intellectual property rights, see Mark Rose, *Authors and Owners* (Cambridge, Mass: Harvard University Press, 1993), pp. 4–5, 8, and Diane L. Zimmerman, "Information as Speech, Information as Goods: Some Thoughts on Marketplaces and the Bill of Rights," *William & Mary Law Review,* 33 (1992): 665–740, at 676–7, 690–703, 705–6, 712. See also William Fisher's discussion in "Theories of Intellectual Property" in this volume.

Even some powerful critics of strong intellectual property rights acknowledge the prima facie permissibility of Lockean appropriation of intellectual property, although they dispute that the conditions of justified individual appropriation are met as often as is usually presumed. See, for example, Wendy Gordon, "An Inquiry into the Merits of Copyright: The Challenges of Consistency, Consent and Encouragement Theory," *Stanford Law Review,* 41 (1989): 1343–469, at 1388–9 (1989); Wendy Gordon, "A Property Right in Self-Expression: Equality and Individualism in the Natural Law of Intellectual Property," *Yale Law Journal,* 102 (1993): 1533–609 at 1533, 1535, 1538, 1540; Edwin C. Hettinger, "Justifying Intellectual Property," *Philosophy & Public Affairs,* 18 (1989): 31–52, at 34–7, 41–2, 51; Jeremy Waldron, "From Authors to Copiers," *University of Chicago-Kent Law Review,* 68 (1993): 841–87, at 879.

3 John Locke, *Two Treatises of Government* [1698] ed. Peter Laslett 2nd ed. (Cambridge: Cambridge University Press, 1994) at II.33, II.31. Further citations to this text will simply be in the form of Locke's name, followed by the treatise number (I or II), and then the section number (e.g. 33).

conditions are easier to fulfill for intellectual property than for real property. First, meaningful satisfaction of the proviso's "enough and as good" component may preclude substantive amounts of appropriation when real property is scarce. This problem appears less formidable for intellectual property because the terrain of intellectual stock for acquisition (or creation) does not seem at risk of depletion. On some views, it can even be regenerated or expanded through our efforts.[4] As an early British supporter of strong copyright protection urged, "The Field of Knowledge is large enough for all the World to find Ground in it to plant and improve."[5] Second, some regard intellectual products as less subject to waste through spoilage because, generally, their usefulness does not expire or decay in the way that, say, apples do.[6] Third, some regard it as easier, with intellectual products than with products involving work on real property, to isolate the value due to human labor from the value of the initial materials that are worked upon.[7] In many cases, the creation of intellectual products does not involve laboring on independent, physical materials.[8]

4 See, for example, Becker, "Deserving to Own Intellectual Property," at 616; Gordon, "A Property Right in Self-Expression," at 1566; Child, "The Moral Foundations of Intangible Property," at 589; and Hughes, "The Philosophy of Intellectual Property," at 315, 325, 329, 365. I discuss the characterization of the intellectual common in Section III.

5 Anonymous, "A letter from an author to a Member of Parliament. Occasioned by a late letter concerning the Bill now depending in the House of Commons, for the encouragement of learning, &c.," (London: April 17, 1735). (Goldsmiths-Kress Library of Economic Literature 7279; Hanson 4793; ESTCN 20589). Indeed, if the stock of intellectual property were *that* expansive, it could buttress the viability of Lockean theory for real property. Complaints that real property appropriation would not leave enough and as good for others could be answered, since plenty of valuable, tradeable, intellectual property is available for use and even appropriation.

6 Hughes, "The Philosophy of Intellectual Property," at 328. But, although intellectual products may not spoil in the same way as agricultural products, they are not immune from spoilage or waste. The value of information may be time-dependent – consider stock tips or information about irrevocable decisions; if such information is hoarded, it may "spoil" or become useless. Some software programs may be useful only in combination with current hardware technology. Other intellectual products may be more useful at particular times – when, for instance, they draw upon or react to current events or contemporary culture. As I discuss in Section III, conditions of exclusive use may waste or significantly underuse some intellectual products.

7 See, for example, Becker, "Deserving to Own Intellectual Property," at 611; Hughes, "The Philosophy of Intellectual Property," at 300; Waldron, "From Authors to Copiers," at 879; Ryan, *Property*, p. 68, and Jeremy Waldron, *The Right to Private Property* (Oxford: Oxford University Press, 1988), p. 279, n. 45. In brief, the problem for real property rights is that ownership of one's labor may not entail that one completely owns the products of one's labor. If one combined one's labor with raw resources to generate a product, one may only be entitled to the portion attributable to one's labor. If so, the part of a product's value attributable to labor must be disentangled from what is contributed by the material resources.

8 This argument has difficulties. Paintings and sculptures generally involve substantial use of material objects. Also, similar difficulties arise because intellectual products typically involve substantial borrowing and interweaving with prior elements in the culture. See Hettinger, "Justifying Intellectual Property," Waldron, "From Authors to Copiers," and Jessica Litman, "The Public Domain," *Emory Law Journal*, 39 (1990): 965–1023. I propose here, though, to bracket concerns about dependence on prior works and to consider cases involving either the first generation of creators or contemporary, but purely original, intellectual products. In Section III, I address related issues concerning whether intellectual production involves mixing labor with elements of an intellectual, nonmaterial common.

Despite the attractions of a Lockean approach and its apparent amenability to intellectual property, I side with Jefferson. I will challenge the claim that Lockean foundations straightforwardly support most strong natural rights over intellectual works – such things as articles, plays, books, songs, paintings, methods, processes, and other inventions. I will also challenge the related claim that Lockean foundations for strong property rights come easier for these forms of intellectual property than for real property. As Jefferson observed and as I hope to explain, the nature of intellectual works makes them less, rather than more, susceptible to Lockean justifications for private appropriation.

Making this argument requires an extended excursion into the underlying motivations and structure of Locke's general theory of property. I do this first before addressing intellectual property specifically. In Section II, I lay out an interpretation of the Lockean defense for private property that places a strong emphasis on the significance of common property as a starting point. This interpretation generates special difficulties for asserting strong Lockean rights to intellectual property. In Section III, I return to the subject of intellectual property and discuss these difficulties in detail.

Before embarking on this task, I should clarify my subject matter and method. I mean to criticize the claim that Lockean theory, as I suggest it is most plausibly interpreted, generally supports the assertion of strong, natural rights over most intellectual products. For ease of expression, I speak broadly of "intellectual products" and "intellectual property," but I focus upon the rights associated with copyright and patent. Parts of my argument pertain to trademark protections, but little of it bears on trade secret law or its justifications.

In investigating *Lockean* theory, I mean to explore John Locke's theory of property and its animating themes, as I think they can be best interpreted and developed to provide a justification for private appropriation. My aim is to reconstruct Locke's strongest line of argument. I do not try to ascertain what John Locke, the person, would say if we put various questions to him about property rights and their justification.[9] Rather, I am primarily interested in interpreting the *Two Treatises*. This text has had a lasting appeal and pull on our sensibilities. I aim to interpret the text in a way that presents it in its best light (or at least, in a way that is illuminating and explains some of its appeal). In doing so, I de-emphasize what I take to be some of Locke's less felicitous as well as his less central views and remarks, in order to follow and expand upon what I take to be the foundational motivations of his account.[10] I put to the side some contrary lines of argument and interpretation for two reasons. First, it is

9 In Section III, I discuss some letters of John Locke's that concern copyright. While these are also relevant to the project of identifying Locke's actual, historical intentions, I refer to them for a different reason. They help to elaborate my interpretation and the line of argument that I locate in the *Treatises*. They also shed light on how a thinker could embrace the line of arguments in the *Treatises* and still be critical of strong intellectual property rights.

10 My description of Lockean theory follows A. John Simmons, *A Lockean Theory of Rights* (Princeton: Princeton University Press, 1992), p. 4.

not clear to me that all of Locke's remarks can be reconciled. Second, my principal aim is to develop a less-emphasized line of thought in Locke's text — one that, I believe is true to Locke's starting point and provides his strongest, most appealing argument for property rights.

By *strong intellectual property rights,* I mean those core intellectual property rights that empower their bearers to exert exclusive control over access to and use of intellectual works. Those rights include the rights: to interfere with and to control the dissemination and use of intellectual products, whether through injunctions or by setting potentially prohibitive prices for access; to interfere with and even prevent others' production and distribution of similar or derivative works; and to sell, transfer, or devise these rights to others. For example, I have in mind the exclusive rights in the copyright law to reproduce and distribute copies of copyrighted works, to prepare derivative works, and to perform or display works. I also have in mind the power to enforce these rights through injunctions, impounding infringing articles, suits for damages, and the criminal law,[11] and the rights in the patent law to prevent others from using or making a patented invention or process, even if it is independently, subsequently discovered.[12]

So, to deny that creators have, as a natural right, strong property rights is not to deny that creators should be compensated and acknowledged for their work.[13] Of course, they should be compensated. But they may be compensated without affording them full, unrestricted abilities to control the use of such works, to charge any price for access, and to sell these rights to others. For example, compensation is divorced from strong rights under the U.S. compulsory licensing scheme that governs recordings of non-dramatic musical works.[14] They may be recorded and sold without the creator's or copyright owner's consent — thereby making the works widely available for public, common use. But, as compensation, the copyright owner receives a mandatory royalty for each use. Furthermore, the denial that there are strong, natural rights to intellectual property does not entail that there are no other grounds for positing strong intellectual property rights. Perhaps, a legal system that grants strong intellectual property rights generates unique incentives to production, or has other advantages. If so, as Jefferson argued, the public might then have good reasons to consent to and to create strong intellectual property rights *beyond* the sphere of natural rights.

---

11 See 17 U.S.C. Secs. 106, 502–506 (West 2000).
12 See 35 U.S.C. Secs. 271, 283–84 (West 2000).
13 Many others have made the point that labor may deserve compensation but that this need not entail strong property rights, including rights of exclusive use and control. See, for example, Hettinger, "Justifying Intellectual Property," at 38, and Judith Jarvis Thomson, *The Realm of Rights* (Cambridge, Harvard University Press: 1991), pp. 325–6. A sufficiently high wage for labor and acknowledgment of authorship are other reasonable ways to compensate labor and investment.
14 See 17 U.S.C. Sec. 115 (West: 2000).

II. Lockean Arguments for Private Property

My view of Locke's theory of property, in general, and of its application to intellectual property, in particular, relies upon a distinction between two justificatory conditions on appropriation. To justify a person's appropriation of a thing, two conditions must be met: First, things *of that sort* must be susceptible to justified private ownership. Second, the person must satisfy the conditions necessary to appropriate that specific thing. Proponents of Lockean rights to intellectual property often seem to muddle these conditions. In particular, they neglect serious consideration of the first condition. The proviso, which represents the Lockean criteria for satisfying the second condition, may be simpler to satisfy for intellectual property than for real property. But there are prior issues of justification, regarding the institution of intellectual private property. These pose a more formidable challenge to asserting a broad range of strong intellectual property rights.

This section will sketch an interpretation of Locke's theory of the first condition about what justifies an institution of private property for certain sorts of things. As I interpret Locke's view, it supports a more limited scope of appropriation than is commonly attributed to him and than he, at times, may have aimed to defend.[15] Because it is unclear that there is a single, consistent position running through the *Treatises,* I will not attempt to reconcile all of Locke's remarks with my account. I will attempt, instead, to identify a deep, attractive, and foundational strand of his thought. I will stress neglected, but foundational, themes about the initial state of common ownership and outline what strikes me as the most defensible reconstruction of the *Treatises'* argument for private appropriation. On my reading, Locke's view does not endorse Lockean appropriation of most intellectual products.

My version of Locke's theory of private appropriation differs from standard accounts by assigning greater prominence to the common ownership thesis, namely, the view that the world is initially owned in common. The defense of this view, against critics like Robert Filmer, was a major impetus behind Locke's work and shapes his defense of private property. The account I will offer, unlike accounts that give pride of place to the themes of labor and self-ownership, preserves the importance of the common ownership thesis. I will claim that the conditions of effective use of common property, coupled with appeal to the right of self-preservation, initially justify some private appropriation out of the commonly held stock. Labor plays a subsidiary role. Labor is used, primarily, to justify the appropriation by one individual rather than

15 Locke may have thought (if so, I think mistakenly) that his arguments yielded a more comprehensive justification for strong property rights in most or all things. Locke did, however, work against the renewal of strong copyright-like provisions of the Licensing Act of 1662 as I discuss in Section III.

another, assuming that some private appropriation of the given sort of property has been antecedently justified.

Locke is explicit that the *Treatises'* aim is to show that the world is initially held in common by all people.[16] His attack on Filmer's patriarchal theory of authority and property ownership is central to the *Treatises.*[17] Locke takes pains to emphasize the egalitarian nature of his contrary position.[18] He faults Filmer's patriarchal theory for exalting Adam above other human beings who share the same intellectual qualities as Adam. Locke maintains that God[19] grants human beings superiority over animals, "the inferior creatures." The community of human beings *together* enjoy dominion over the world. Locke also emphasizes that people have rights of subsistence or rights of self-preservation. These rights of subsistence, coupled with the right and duty to make use of God's grant, are what seem to motivate his endorsement of a right of private property in such things as fruits, animals, and land.

Locke acknowledges that the thesis of common ownership creates a puzzle about the justification of private property.[20] In the *Second Treatise,* he declares that he will attempt to show how people "might come to have a property in several parts of that which God gave to Mankind in common. . . ."[21] This

---

16 For examples, see John Locke, I.24 ("I shall shew . . . that by this Grant God gave [Adam] . . . a right [over the inferior creatures] in common with all Mankind."), I.29 ("Whatever God gave by the words of [his] Grant, it was not to Adam in particular . . . but a Dominion in common with the rest of Mankind."), 1.30 ("God in this donation, gave the World to Mankind in common . . . ," in which Locke emphasizes that all people are intellectual creatures, equally in God's image), I.40 ("God gives us all things richly to enjoy . . . this [Biblical] text is so far from proving Adam Sole Proprietor, that on the contrary, it is a Confirmation of the Original Community of all things amongst the Sons of Men . . ."), II.4, II.25 (". . . 'tis very clear, that God . . . has given the Earth to the Children of Men, given it to Mankind in Common."), II.26 ("God, who has given the World to Men in common, hath also given them reason to make use of it to the best advantage of Life and convenience . . . [its fruits and animals] belong to Mankind in common . . . and no body has originally a private Dominion, exclusive of the rest of Mankind . . .), II.27 ("[T]he Earth, and all inferior Creatures be common to all Men . . .").

17 This attack dominates the First Treatise. The Second Treatise contains few direct references to Filmer, but begins by reiterating the rejection of Filmer's theses. Locke at II.1–3.

18 See, for example, Locke, II.4. (The state of nature is a "state of perfect freedom" and a state of equality. "[T]here being nothing more evident, than that Creatures of the same species and rank promiscuously born to all the same advantages of Nature, and the use of the same faculties, should also be equal one amongst another without Subordination or Subjection . . . "). See also II.5, II.6 ("being furnished with like faculties, sharing all in one Community of Nature . . .").

19 I retain references to *God's* grant as the simplest method of exegesis. I do not think religious premises are necessary for the argument. *Lockean* arguments could do without them. One could defend the common ownership thesis as the most plausible initial starting position, one that best reflects commitments to interpersonal and intergenerational equality. One could also appeal to secular premises about the value of using common property and secular rights of self-preservation. I do not attempt to supply those arguments here. Jeremy Waldron, however, has expressed skepticism about secular reformulations of Locke's position, *The Right to Private Property,* p. 142.

20 Locke at II.25.

21 Ibid.

effort is crucial to the enterprise of defending the common ownership thesis. Filmer, as well as other critics, criticized the common ownership thesis on the ground that if it were true, then use of property could not be made without the consent of humankind.[22] Such a requirement of consent would be absurd, especially if subsistence materials could not be used without everyone's consent.[23] A consent requirement would also create tension with the egalitarian motivations of the theory: common ownership, so construed, could lend itself to subordinating exercises of power. A group or individual could use the veto power to deny the fulfillment of individuals' needs or to make others beholden to them.

To some versions of Filmer's objection, one may reply that they presuppose an inaccurate view of common ownership, one under which all use of the commons is impermissible without the consent of the members of humankind. Common ownership does not necessarily require common consent for all individual use, such as walking across a commonly owned plot of land. Some individual uses that do not destroy or diminish the common are consistent with common ownership, although individual appropriation of parts of it without consent of the common is not. Yet this reply, which I accept, does not answer all forms, including the most potent forms, of the objection. For there are important forms of use, such as the consumption of food, that do require appropriation and exclusive use and that are crucial to human survival and flourishing.

Locke's reply and his development of an account of justified private appropriation draw on individuals' natural rights of self-preservation and on the idea that the grant of common ownership should be meaningful. The argument runs roughly as follows: God gave the world in common to humankind for its *benefit.*[24] God's grant would be frustrated were the world not used to benefit people.[25] But, importantly, some articles cannot be used to benefit people if they must be used in common or be available for common use. Their use must be exclusive. Furthermore, each person enjoys a natural right for his or her subsistence needs to be met. Part of what propels God's grant is that it serves to

---

22 See Robert Filmer, "The Originall of Government," in Robert Filmer, *Patriarcha and Other Writings,* ed. Johann P. Sommerville (New York: Cambridge University Press, 1991), p. 234; see also Alan Ryan, *Property and Political Theory* (New York: B. Blackwell, 1984), pp. 16–17; James Tully, *A Discourse on Property* (New York: Cambridge University Press, 1980), p. 97 (discussing similar objections by Pufendorf and Tyrell). On such views, it is unclear whether such consent would need to flow from just living people (all or a majority?) or also, hypothetically, from future generations. (Problems relating to future generations may lessen if property reverts to the common after a lifetime.)

23 Locke at II.28. Locke correctly observes that this problem attaches as strongly to Filmer's theory as it does to Locke's. Filmer's theory hinges the fulfillment of subsistence needs upon the discretion of a single patriarch and his heirs. It, too, cannot guarantee the fulfillment of natural rights of self-preservation. Locke, I.41, II.25.

24 Ibid. at II.26. See also I.86.

25 Ibid.

fulfill the right of self-preservation.[26] But food cannot nourish unless it is fully appropriated by a single person and incorporated into his or her body. Significantly, Locke points to this type of example *to introduce* his argument for appropriation:

The earth and all that is therein is given to men for the support and comfort of their being. And though all the fruits it naturally produces and beasts it feeds belong to mankind in common, as they are produced by the spontaneious hand of nature; and not anybody has originally a private dominion exclusive of the rest of mankind in any of them, as they are thus in their natural state; yet, being given for the use of men, there must of necessity be a means to appropriate them some way or other, *before they can be of any use or at all beneficial.* The fruit, or venison, which nourishes the wild Indian . . . must be his and so his, i.e. a part of him, that another can no longer have any right to it, before it can do him any good for the support of his life.[27]

Two paragraphs later, Locke remarks similarly that "it is the taking any part of what is common, and removing it out of the state nature leaves it in which begins the property; without which the common is of *no use.*"[28] Where beneficial use requires exclusive possession, it is consistent with the grant's purposes to remove the item from the stock of commonly owned things and dedicate it to a particular individual's exclusive use. So, for those items that have a use that requires exclusive possession, the institution of private property would be

---

26 Ibid., especially, I.86, I.88, I.92 and also I.41, I.42, II.25 and II.26. Gopal Sreenivasan also emphasizes common ownership as a starting point. He places more weight on the right to self-preservation. *The Limits of Lockean Rights in Private Property* (New York: Oxford University Press, 1995). He argues that Locke's solution to the "consent problem" lies in claiming that appropriation that leaves sufficient materials for others' subsistence is legitimate and does not require consent. If one leaves enough for others' subsistence, one does not violate the right of common ownership for "[t]his natural right to property in common, which everyone enjoys, is *equivalent* to the natural right to the means of preservation." p. 140. Although his reading is subtle, I find it unsatisfying. First, this justification for appropriation is only negative: It explains why appropriation does not violate rights but it does not supply a positive rationale for appropriation. It renders the common ownership claim relatively thin, as though it were a mere side-constraint. Second, the text he cites to support this reading of equivalence, II.26, is ambiguous. It could also be read to suggest that the earth was granted in common in order, partly, to fulfill the natural right to the means of support. Third, the equivalence claim suggests, oddly, that if all the world became privately owned in such a way that each denizen privately owned enough for her subsistence, then we would all still be in a state of common ownership. This interpretation vitiates the distinction between common and private ownership. It also makes it strange that Locke regards private property – even in the means of subsistence – as needing justification against the backdrop of common ownership. If they are identical, where is the puzzle?

27 Jeremy Waldron and David Snyder also call attention to this preliminary justification for exclusive appropriation. See Waldron, *The Right to Private Property*, pp. 168–71; David Snyder, "Locke on Natural Law and Property Rights," *Canadian Journal of Philosophy*, 16 (1986): 723–50. David Snyder seems to assert without explanation that most other goods "must be owned to be useful," at 737, whereas Waldron worries that this argument's power is limited to the case of food, p. 168. I attempt to supply some of the missing further explanation of how this account could extend to other sorts of property besides food, and thereby to facilitate a more integrated interpretation of Locke's justification for property.

28 II.28 (emphasis added).

justified and consistent with the purposes of God's grant. An institution of private appropriation in *some parts* of the common stock is justified on two grounds: because it comports with the underlying motivation of the common grant and because it is necessary to fulfill the natural right of self-preservation. The grant of common ownership should not be construed in such a way that it would make that grant nonsensical and counterproductive to its purposes.[29]

It remains to be explained what criteria govern individual appropriation, that is, how a specific individual may justifiably come to have a property right to a specific thing. Individual appropriation must proceed according to a criterion that respects the equal claims of all people to the means to subsistence and to the common. Furthermore, no more should be taken from the commonly owned stock than is justified. Here, the criteria of labor and spoilage become pertinent. Locke stresses that people are self-owners and that labor has moral value. But these facts alone do not themselves necessitate private appropriation. Rather, in the context in which private property is justified, labor is then an appropriate means to stake a claim. Between two individuals, the one who has exerted labor and improved the thing's value has a stronger claim over the thing than a rival who has not labored. Locke notes that "labour put a *distinction* between [acorns collected by a person] and the common."[30] The justification for collecting items and exerting one's labor toward those things in the first place stems from the right as a beneficiary to consume them so as to make God's grant worthwhile. Still, this method of staking a claim is not arbitrary. It connects to Locke's fundamental justification for privatization; for, as I will discuss below, Locke celebrates labor for bringing out the value of a thing and making it useful.

So, too, the "enough and as good" and waste conditions of the Lockean proviso serve to limit appropriation in ways related to Locke's justifications for private appropriation. These criteria ensure that appropriation does not disadvantage the equal rights of others to appropriate some goods and to use others, and to ensure that the common stock is not depleted past the point of fruitful use. Wasteful appropriation would frustrate the charge to make the common grant work to humankind's benefit.[31]

---

29 See II.28 and II.29. This argument could be fleshed out in four ways and the text is not decisive among them. The claim might be that since the grant would be meaningless unless it could be used, we could infer hypothetical consent to that exclusive use necessary to make use possible. Locke does endeavor to show why an "express" compact is unnecessary. See II.27. Or, perhaps the grant is circumscribed by the conditions for its meaningful use. Or, the claim might be that refusal to give consent would be wrong (for it would violate the duty in natural law to make use of God's grant) and therefore unnecessary. Or, the grant of common ownership might be trumped by a prior, superior right to the means of self-preservation; this is an unlikely interpretation, though, for the language of II.25 suggests that the grant is partly in the service of, and not at odds with, the right to self-preservation.

30 II.28.

31 This interpretation has the advantage of not rendering the waste criterion redundant. Views like Gopal Sreenivasan's, which locate the constraint on appropriation solely in the right of self-

This interpretation differs from more standard accounts. On those accounts, the Lockean argument for private ownership goes roughly as follows. Each person enjoys the natural right of self-ownership. One's labor is a part of one's self and so one owns one's labor. Because one owns one's labor, one owns the products of one's labor. Others' use of one's labor or its products without one's permission is an encroachment upon one's self-ownership. It is as though they use *the person* without permission and thereby fail to respect the principle of self-ownership. The commonly perceived difficulty here is thought to lie in the step from ownership of one's labor to ownership of the fruits of one's labor. For, usually, to produce from one's labor, one needs to combine that labor with some part of the material common. But, it may be objected, what right does one have to approach the common and expend one's labor upon it? Why does one thereby gain the property by presumptuous expenditure instead of losing one's labor? Here, the proviso is thought to provide the answer. So long as there is enough and as good for others and so long as one's expenditure of labor will not lead to a wasteful appropriation, no harm is done to others through exertion of labor upon a nonprivately owned thing as a justified precursor to and constituent of appropriation.

If one has a standard account in mind, it is easy to see why some think Lockean natural rights to intellectual property are easily derived, given the abundance of sources for making intellectual products and the intimate connection between individual labor and intellectual products. Standard interpretations like these, however, neglect or effectively play down the *Treatises'* motivation to defend the thesis of initial common ownership. Although Locke's frequent remarks about labor and its connection to property strongly encourage aspects of the standard interpretation, that story, taken in full, is not consistent with Locke's stated fundamental concerns. On the standard interpretation, the claim of initial common ownership has almost no significance. At best, it underwrites the need for the Lockean proviso. But the proviso, it seems, could as easily have been posited from a no-ownership starting point – motivated by concerns of fairness about who should come to own the unowned. Likewise, if there is no presumption for common ownership and no presumption against private appropriation, it is difficult to understand why Locke stressed the right of self-preservation and the purpose of the grant in the context of his discussion of justified appropriation.

---

preservation, have a difficult time motivating Locke's insertion of the waste criterion alongside the "enough and as good" criterion. If others have enough to ensure their subsistence (and such holdings suffice to respect the right to common ownership, as Sreenivasan claims), then what explains the prohibition on taking more than one can use? In my view, taking more than one can use removes material from the common and prevents its use by others. Such behavior thereby frustrates the command and permission to make full use of the common grant. Edward McCaffery's "Must We Have a Right to Waste?," in this volume, investigates the significance of prohibitions on waste in a contemporary context.

Assigning such a role to the claim of common ownership, however, seems unduly subordinate given the prominence the claim plays in Locke's stated motivations. Locke was fully aware of the challenge common ownership posed to the permissibility of private appropriation, and he explicitly aimed to answer the challenge. It would be perverse to treat common ownership as relevant merely to the shape of the conditions of individual appropriation, absent an explanation of why a departure from the celebrated initial scheme of common ownership is justified.

Thus, I think that the standard account is called into question because it is unable to acknowledge the primacy of the thesis of common ownership and to explain how Locke understands the compatibility of private appropriation with this notion. An account more sensitive to Locke's own starting point can be culled from the text. However, such an account does not justify privatization of all sorts of property – at least as a matter of distinctively Lockean natural right. It only justifies privatization where, because of the nature of the property, it is necessary to make effective use of the grant of resources and to fulfill the right of self-preservation. Locke himself gives some indication that his justificatory account for property signals some such limits to the range of permissible appropriation. In discussing the land that remains common in England and may not be further inclosed or appropriated, he first notes that it remains common by "compact, i.e. by the law of the land. . . ." Importantly, though, he goes on to point out that "[b]esides, the remainder, after such inclosure, would not be as good to the rest of the Commoners as the whole was, when they could all make use of the whole: whereas in the beginning and first peopling of the great Common of the World, it was quite otherwise. The Law Man was under, was rather for appropriating."[32] I understand Locke to be saying that initially, there is a great need to appropriate from and labor upon the initial common in order to fulfill God's command that his grant be well-used. But, at some point – as with the common remaining in England – what property remains may only be properly used if it is left in common.[33]

---

32 Locke, II.35.
33 I take this passage, in conjunction with the general argumentative structure of the *Second Treatise,* as evidence that Locke endorsed neither the standard ideal of positive community nor that of negative community. These ideals were identified by Locke's contemporary, Samuel Pufendorf. Positive community is an ideal of strict joint ownership. In its strictest form, positive community involves complete control by the group over use and appropriation. Under a negative community, the common is open to use *and* appropriation by all, but none of it is yet connected to or designated for any particular person. See Stephen Buckle, *Natural Law and the Theory of Property* (Oxford: Clarendon Press, 1991), pp. 91–108. Locke is conspicuously silent with respect to these terms. His implicit conception of what owning in common involves seems to fall somewhere in between these ideals. On the one hand, his reply to Filmer and his description of the remaining common of England suggest that he rejects the ideal of pure positive community. Although he points out that the remaining common's status as a common traces to an agreement, he analogizes its conditions to those of the original common. He declares that it is open to use by all its members, seemingly at their individual instigation, although not their individual appropriation. On the other hand, it is difficult to make full sense

Against my more restrictive interpretation of Locke's view, it may be asked why Locke permits appropriation beyond that necessary to fulfill one's subsistence needs and to satisfy the right of self-preservation. It is clear that Locke envisions that further appropriation may be justified when it can be accomplished without waste. Indeed, Locke celebrates the introduction of money for facilitating additional appropriation and use without waste.[34] This suggests that Locke's vision of the permissible scope of appropriation was not especially constricted.

Of course, it may be that Locke's good arguments run out here. Or, this may be the spot at which a tension surfaces between the common ownership foundations and the other strands of argument that connect labor and self-ownership to justified appropriation. Both of these seem like possibilities, but I believe there is a reading of the text that reconciles Locke's endorsement of further appropriation with the interpretation I defend.

First, to elaborate on the problem: a puzzle for my reading seems to be as follows. On the one hand, one might read the two facts supporting appropriation (the need for exclusive use of some things to make certain sorts of use of them and the need for certain sorts of use to fulfill the rights of self-preservation) as both setting necessary conditions for appropriation. Yet, if they both must be in place, then it is unclear how Locke could justifiably approve of appropriation beyond subsistence needs. On the other hand, if the two facts are read as posing disjunctive requirements, then it is unclear why the right to self-preservation merits special mention. Isn't its inclusion otiose, since its preconditions would already be met by the disjunctive permission to appropriate things for those uses that require exclusive use? Furthermore, on either reading, why does Locke seem to endorse appropriation in cases where exclusive use does not seem strictly necessary for use?

---

of Locke's concerns if one assumes, in the alternative, that he had Pufendorf's idea of negative community in mind, as some have claimed. See, for example, Buckle, pp. 165, 175, 183–7. If Locke did have this in mind, it is odd that he did not say so. Further, it is odd that his discussion of the norms of the remaining common includes a bar on individual appropriation, without any remark that this is out of the ordinary. Moreover, such an assumption is hard to square with what seem to be efforts to explain and justify appropriation. If the world is just available for appropriation and the only question is how to establish clear methods of title, then it seems odd that he introduces his account of how appropriation is justified with examples so specific as those in which exclusive use is necessary for use. Rather, the text seems to suggest a distinctive conception of common ownership in which the common is available to nonaltering use by each and all. To complement this negative right, there is a positive right, jointly owned, over the rights of exclusive use. This positive right complements the negative right by ensuring that no one may unilaterally infringe on the common right of use by appropriating things that could be used in common. Rights over exclusive use are jointly owned, subject to the proviso that their exercise is limited by the purpose of the common grant: to ensure the world's use for its benefit. In other words, the negative right of access trumps the positive right when the positive right does not complement the negative right, that is, only when we must either permit exclusive rights or frustrate the purpose of God's grant.

34 Locke at II.45–6.

Locke does not, to put it mildly, confront this problem squarely. An interpretative solution to this puzzle, involving two speculative steps, runs as follows. God has given us the world in common to make use of it for our benefit. Some uses may require exclusive use and so might justify appropriation, assuming that these uses are appropriate ones. One clearly valid use for things is to fulfill the right of self-preservation. So far, on this reading, the two facts do not pose joint, necessary conditions. Rather, the first identifies a condition of appropriation (that exclusive use is required for a valid use) and the second identifies one especially clear and pertinent, valid use, supported by a natural right. This argument represents the first speculative step. It explains why Locke would not have regarded the reference to self-preservation as otiose. It also opens up the possibility that there might be appropriation for other purposes. For, on this reading, it would still be possible for other uses to justify appropriation if exclusive use were necessary for them and if they were valid purposes. This reading renders the reference to self-preservation sensible and non-redundant. It does, however, reveal a gap in Locke's account, namely the absence of a fuller, explicit account of what other uses are valid and appropriate.

The second speculative step of this reading attributes to him an expansive understanding of the way in which exclusive use is necessary to fulfill the purpose of God's grant. Although this interpretation is speculative, it, unlike most other interpretations, renders Locke's stance thematically consistent with the initial passages about appropriation for subsistence. One way to explain Locke's acceptance of "extra" private appropriation – that is, private appropriation beyond that needed for subsistence and beyond that needed to make the materials minimally useful – is to emphasize his apparent belief about how God's grant is to be fully, effectively exploited. Locke asserts that the main value of land is reaped through the addition and application of labor to it. This endorsement of further appropriation need not be understood as an unadorned endorsement of the view that labor deserves the reward of property. Rather, these passages suggest that Locke's emphasis was that such appropriation and the labor it engenders here are *very substantially* more efficient in realizing the productive potential of the land. That is, appropriation prevents the waste of land and enables the full realization of God's purpose to ensure that the common grant be used to benefit humankind.[35]

Locke's writings are quite difficult to interpret here. But his implicit argument for private ownership of more land than is necessary for a particular

35 I have in mind especially II.35–37 and II.40–45, especially when read together with I.41, I.42, II.32 and II.34. II.34 contrasts, interestingly, those who productively labor with the "fancy or covetousness of the quarrelsom and contentious," and advises that others "ought not to *meddle* with what was already improved by another's labor." It is interesting that Locke advises against meddling and not just appropriating or using. This emphasis supports the hypothesis that Locke was concerned with some individuals interfering with others' plans for and management of land and not only concerned with individuals making use of others' labor.

individual's subsistence does not appear to draw on the idea that profit incentives are necessary to induce people to labor and produce on land. The text does not mention the incentive argument. This omission is not surprising, because a profit incentive argument would mark a sharp departure from the arguments offered earlier in Locke's exposition. It would locate the impetus for exclusive use not in the nature of the thing to be used and the natural requirements of its use but in contingent decisions and psychological features of the laborer.

Furthermore, to attribute to Locke the implicit stance that an incentive argument attributes to the laborer – a reasonable unwillingness to work unless more is received than is needed to ensure self-preservation and to sustain fully productive labor – would be in some tension with the Locke's view of the laborer's natural *duty* to make full use of God's grant.[36] A better interpretation would maintain more symmetry with the arguments about the nature of subsistence materials and the inherent, rather than imposed, conditions on the use of property.

Why, then, must the use of "extra" land be exclusive to facilitate full exploitation of God's gift? Locke does not squarely address this question, but he makes some suggestive remarks. He associates land remaining in common as "uncultivated" and then, significantly, asserts that "subduing or cultivating the Earth, and having Dominion, we see are joyned together."[37] In discussing the use he has in mind, he mentions the need to plow, plant, till, and perform other sorts of directed, long-term activities on the land. I suspect that he thought that fully effective use required exclusive control by someone with a determinate plan for the land. The land would not be as effectively used if a user's plans could be disrupted by the imposition of another's inconsistent plans or spontaneous use.[38] It would then make some sense that he endorsed private, nonconsensual appropriation of some things beyond what is necessary to subsist. Their appropriation would be justified where exclusive use of such things is necessary for their *fully* effective use.[39]

---

36 In another context, G. A. Cohen argues that although incentives are often treated as a response to a given, fixed aspect of the economic context, the putative need for incentives in fact represents a choice on the part of a worker to withhold work that could be provided. Cohen contends that if the talented require incentives in the Rawlsian scheme, they do not behave as members of a well-ordered society. They act inconsistently with their acceptance of the difference principle and its underlying rationale. See G. A. Cohen, "Where the Action Is: On the Site of Distributive Justice," *Philosophy & Public Affairs,* 26 (1997): 3–30; "The Pareto Argument for Inequality," *Social Philosophy & Policy,* 12 (no. 1)(1995): 160–85; "Incentives, Inequality, and Community," in Grethe B. Peterson, ed., *The Tanner Lectures on Human Values,* vol. 13 (Salt Lake City: University of Utah Press, 1992): 261–329.

37 See Locke at II.34 and II.35.

38 See Locke at II.32 and II.34.

39 Of course, fully effective use may not require exclusive control by an individual – groups of individuals could cooperate. Even so, groups would need the ability to exclude noncooperators who sought to use that land for their own ends. A more comprehensive, state-run system of coordination could also achieve the same end. But, such a system would also involve taking the property out of the common (although not through *private* appropriation). In any

On my reading, the passages stressing labor's vast enhancement of land's value are meant to combine with both the mandate to make full, effective use of resources and an implicit view that the land requires exclusive control for such use. This combination yields a positive argument for privatizing more out of common stock than is necessary for subsistence. "Extra" appropriation is justified because it is necessary to fulfill our shared aim and duty of exploiting our common resources. Interestingly, the value of the land he draws attention to is its ability to produce agricultural goods. It is, thus, connected to a use he has already explicitly endorsed – the collection and production of goods that contribute to the fulfillment of people's needs.

Other suggested readings of these passages, by G. A. Cohen and Andrew Williams,[40] attribute a different strategy to Locke. On their readings, the enhancement of labor does all or most of the work to propel a more negative argument for appropriation. They maintain, roughly, that, for Locke, appropriation is justified when other individuals have no valid complaint against another's appropriation. Appropriation of land is justified because it takes little of value and thus deprives others of little; for, either the land itself is nearly worthless (Cohen) or it is not of unconditional value, that is, it has no value without labor (Williams).

Although these readings have strong textual support, my reading has certain advantages over them. Because my reading does not depend upon claiming that the land alone is worthless, it rescues Locke from what would be, as Cohen notes, a terrible argument for this claim.[41] It also makes Locke less vulnerable to another, severe criticism Cohen lodges, that Locke is insensitive to the opportunity costs involved in appropriating undeveloped land.[42] Furthermore, as Cohen notes, if Locke is making the argument that land alone is worthless, such a position would be in tension with the "as good" component of the proviso.[43] For, what exactly would it mean to leave enough and "as good" of that which is virtually worthless?

Most important, my reading provides an interpretation of the passages that Cohen and Williams draw upon. But, my reading is both consistent and continuous with Locke's initial argument for appropriation – the argument in which he justifies privatization of foods that are, without labor, already valuable. Locke provides a positive justification for appropriation, adducing the ground that appropriation is necessary for such goods to be properly used. He does not make the mere negative claim that such appropriation would not take

case, that suggestion is rather far removed from Locke's context here, namely the state of nature.

40 G. A. Cohen, *Self-Ownership, Freedom and Equality* (Cambridge: Cambridge University Press, 1995), Ch. 7; Andrew Williams, "Cohen on Locke, Land, and Labour," *Political Studies,* 49 (1992): 51–66.

41 Cohen, *Self-Ownership, Freedom and Equality,* pp. 182–5.

42 Ibid., pp. 186–7.

43 Ibid.

anything valuable and therefore will not disadvantage others. If he had such a negative claim in mind, it would be odd not to voice it and it would be odd to instead offer a separate line of argument that gave a positive reason for appropriation. As Williams admits,[44] his interpretation does not fit well with the passages from II.26–31 about the appropriation of apples and venison. His reading locates the justification of appropriation in that it takes that which is only of conditional value – that is, that which depends on labor to be made valuable. This lack of fit presents a striking problem for these interpretations, I think, since Locke's first, main effort to justify appropriation tackles the problem of things of unconditional value, like food. He uses this case as the primary case to answer Filmer's challenge and to build his own account.

My interpretation maintains continuity with the common-property impetus of Locke's project. It places more emphasis on the nature of the property to be appropriated and the natural conditions of its effective use than do the more standard labor-desert interpretations. The nature of the property and the conditions of its full, effective use justify its removal from common ownership and render it susceptible to private appropriation.

My analysis of the Lockean account of what makes a given kind of property appropriable makes a difference when contemplating intellectual products and their susceptibility to private appropriation. Section III takes up the ramifications of this interpretation for intellectual property.

III. A Lockean Approach to Intellectual Property

Locke did not direct sustained theoretical attention to intellectual property. But in 1694 he wrote a letter opposing the renewal of the Licensing Act of 1662.[45] In addition to criticizing the Act's censorship provisions, Locke objected to its "patent" (copyright-like) clauses on the grounds that they granted a monopoly to publishers and prevented scholars from obtaining "true or good copies of the best ancient Latin authors, unless they pay . . . 6s. 8d a book."[46] Locke declared that

nobody should have any peculiar right in any book which has been in print fifty years, but any one as well as another might have the liberty to print it; for by such titles as these, which lie dormant, and hinder others, many good books come quite to be lost. [N]or can there be any reason in nature why I might not print [classic texts] as well as the

44 Williams, "Cohen on Locke and Labor," at 56, n. 18.
45 An Act for preventing the frequent abuses in printing seditious treasonable and unlicensed Bookes and Pamphlets and for regulating of Printing and Printing Presses, 1662, 14 Car. II, Ch. 33 (Eng.).
46 John Locke, "His Observations on the Censorship," in Peter King, *The Life and Letters of John Locke,* [1884] 2nd ed. (New York: B. Franklin, 1972), p. 205. Also in John Locke, *Political Essays,* ed. Mark Goldie (Cambridge: Cambridge University Press, 1997), pp. 329–39.

Company of Stationers, if I thought fit. This liberty, to any one, of printing them, is certainly the way to have them the cheaper and the better.[47]

Locke's remarks have three very interesting features. First, Locke's proposal that anyone may publish a book after fifty years does not comfortably fit with the view that Locke's theory endorses most strong natural rights to intellectual property.[48] Second, Locke contends that there is no "reason in *nature*" to preclude a freer system of use, albeit to classical works.[49] Third, he complains that strong patent provisions obstruct access to and full use of these works.

I do not want to make too much of these brief, political remarks on their own.[50] Nevertheless, on my reading of Locke's approach to property, these remarks are not out of character. It is unsurprising that similar themes reverberate in a later anonymous pamphlet that resists copyright expansion on grounds appealing to natural rights (as well as in Jefferson's even later remarks).[51] Locke's concern about strong rights inducing the loss or substantial underuse

---

47 Ibid.

48 Locke's proposal – a term of years followed by lapse into the public domain – does not differ in kind from current legal protections, although it is significantly shorter. I question whether the stock story of Lockean appropriation can easily explain the endorsement of a reversion, especially since his proposal specifies a term of years, not a life term. Locke's concerns about lack of access to individual works also do not fit the stock story, given that other works may be available or created.

49 It is possible, though, that he was denying that *publishers* had any natural right to benefit from a longer term. Much of the debate in the late seventeenth and early eighteenth centuries over copyright was phrased in terms of authors' rights but was waged between smaller and larger publishers. Those opposed to longer terms feared it would solidify the monopolies of large booksellers who would inflate prices and obstruct access to books. See generally Mark Rose, *Authors and Owners* (Cambridge, Mass.: Harvard University Press, 1993). Still, the substance of Locke's point has wider application beyond publishers. And, even if the point were limited to publishers' rights, it suggests that even if authors had full-fledged natural rights, they were not fully transferable.

50 They were not, however, isolated remarks or private notes. Locke sent them to the parliamentarian Edward Clarke, who delivered them to a joint conference of the Parliamentary houses. "The lords at once gave way." H. R. F. Bourne, *The Life of John Locke,* vol. 2, pp. 315–16 [1876] (Aalen: Scientia-Verl, 1969). See also Thomas Fowler, *Locke,* (1888) (New York: AMS Press, 1968), pp. 82–3. Locke wrote rival, but unpassed, legislation to grant a limited period of copyright to authors, restricted to the right to reprint or authorize reprinting. See Locke, *Political Essays,* ed. Mark Goldie, pp. 329–30, 338–9. An earlier letter complains that the Licensing Act "put in the hands of ignorant and lazy stationers" a monopoly over ancient Latin works which are "excessively dear to scholars." He urges Clarke to "have some care of book-buyers" and worries that the copyright-holders will not generate "fairer or more correct editions." He objects that scholars (like himself) cannot publish new editions of the work, enacting a "great oppression on scholars." Locke, "Locke to Clarke," 2nd Jan. 1692[-3] in Benjamin Rand, ed., *The Correspondence of John Locke and Edward Clarke* (Cambridge, Mass.: Harvard University Press, 1927), pp. 366–7.

51 The pamphlet author complained that copyright expansion would solidify booksellers' monopolies, raise prices, and discourage reprinting, thereby threatening to "notoriously invade the natural Rights of Mankind." Anonymous, "A letter to a Member of Parliament concerning the bill now depending . . . an Act for the encouragement of learning . . ." (London: 1735) (Goldsmiths-Kress Library of Economic Literature 7300; Hanson 4792; ESTCT 53548).

of works is in keeping with his concern that property be used, so as to fulfill the purpose behind God's grant.

Under an interpretation stressing the common property presumption, Lockean justifications for private property are more strained for intellectual property than for real property. For real property, private appropriation proceeds because it is necessary for proper and full use to be made of the common. Failure to permit some private appropriation would be absurd, since it would frustrate the purpose for which common ownership of the resource was granted. "Extra" appropriation beyond that needed directly for subsistence, if it is permitted, appeals to analogous grounds – private appropriation facilitates the development and the full use of a resource.

For most forms of intellectual property, the analogous argument falls flat, even if one adopts the broad reading that permits "extra" appropriation beyond subsistence needs.[52] The fully effective use of an idea, proposition, concept, expression, method, invention, melody, picture, or sculpture generally does not require, by its nature, prolonged exclusive use or control. Generally, one's use or consumption of an idea, proposition, concept, expression, method, and so forth, is fully compatible with others' use, even their simultaneous use. Moreover, intellectual products often require at least some fairly concurrent, shared (though not necessarily coordinated) use for their full value to be achieved and appreciated. Ideas and their expressions are usually most effective when contemplated by many – when their truths are commonly appreciated and implemented, and their flaws discovered and shared. Indeed, there is a social presumption that ideas and expressions are the object of open dialogue, exchange, and discussion. Attempts to control, suppress, manipulate, or monopolize ideas and information run counter to the intellectual spirit of open public discussions that promote learning and appreciation for the truth.[53]

---

52 Pursuing the analogy may require identifying the intellectual analog to the real property common. I discuss the intellectual common below. To simplify, I focus on appropriations of the first intellectual products and the *initial* intellectual common. Questions about contemporary, created works raise further complications about how much an intellectual product owes to prior works, and at what point, if at all, intellectual products revert into the common or the public domain. The resolution of these complications hinges upon how rights over initial products and the initial common are conceived.

53 The First Amendment of the U.S. Constitution also embodies an attitude of openness. Its philosophical spirit counsels resistance to departures from the common ownership presumption. A growing literature comments on the tensions between the First Amendment and strong copyright protections. See Yochai Benkler, "Free as the Air to Common Use: First Amendment Constraints on Enclosure of the Public Domain," *New York University Law Review* 74 (1999): 354–446; Robert Denicola, "Copyright and Free Speech: Constitutional Limitations on the Protection of Expression," *California Law Review,* 67 (1979): 283–316; Gordon, "Property Right in Self-Expression," at 1533–9; Mark Lemley and Eugene Volokh, "Freedom of Speech and Injunctions in Intellectual Property Cases," *Duke Law Journal,* 48 (1999): 147–242; Melville Nimmer, "Does Copyright Abridge the First Amendment Guaranties of Free Speech and the Press?," *UCLA Law Review,* 17 (1970): 1180–204; Zimmerman, "Information as Speech," at 665–6.

For the bulk of intellectual products, then, the basic Lockean justification for parceling them out to specific individuals for exclusive control is missing. The abilities to prevent the use of given intellectual works by others and to prevent the creation of derivative works run counter to the presumption of common ownership and the concomitant concern to make full use of resources. Even if the proviso-based conditions for individual appropriation could easily be met, that would not suffice to justify individually initiated departures from the default presumption of common ownership and common use.[54]

To be sure, there are important exceptions to the generalization that intellectual works do not require exclusive possession or control for effective use. Works in progress may require exclusive control by the author or creator to be brought to full fruition. Premature forced publication, input from too many directions, and interference by others may impede proper development of a work by disrupting an author's full expression or a creator's process of discovery. In addition, some works may, by their nature, require prolonged exclusive or highly restricted use for their production to be possible, for their communicative purpose to be achieved, or for their meaning to be fully realized. Diaries, the transmission of secrets, and intimate letters come to mind. Were such materials public and not under the exclusive control of specific individuals, the public's use, scrutiny, and contributions could disrupt the pure, full expression of the author's personality. Valuable relations of intimacy partly constituted by the fact that they feature some privileged, exclusive communications would thereby be precluded. The use of such materials, then, would be only partial. Surprisingly, on grounds different from those that others have identified, some rights of privacy and control could derive from Lockean foundations for property, even as I strictly construed them. On related grounds, there might also be a Lockean argument for trademark protection that prevents consumer confusion.[55]

Of course, there may be hard cases in which it is unclear what promotes the full and effective use of a work. The proliferate use of some works may even lessen their impact, by making them cliched or overfamiliar. Perhaps the recent overexposure of the image of Edvard Munch's *The Scream* on stickers, t-shirts, mousepads, and even blow-up dolls represents such a example. Generally, though, the Lockean approach, as I have construed it, carries a presumption of common ownership. The nature of most intellectual products and the conditions

---

54 By contrast, compulsory licensing schemes, like the one that currently governs recordings of nondramatic musical works, are more amenable to the Lockean approach. They take advantage of the fact that intellectual products may be fully used simultaneously by many users and creators. A copyright owner receives a royalty for each use, but musical works may be recorded and distributed without the owner's consent, thereby making the works widely available for public, common use. 17 U.S.C. Sec. 115 (West 2000).

55 This argument may not support, however, the greater protection antidilution statutes offer. They grant companies exclusive use of a name, phrase, or symbol, even when there is little risk of consumer confusion.

conducive to their full use fail to supply direct, positive grounds for surmounting this presumption.

An Objection

The argument I have sketched assumes that the presumption of initial common ownership applies to intellectual property. I now turn to examining this presumption and some variants on it. It may be objected this argument presupposes, in error, that intellectual products, or at least the foundational stuff from which they are made, are like real property and other raw physical materials, namely that they exist independently of human efforts. It may seem as though I (wrongly) assume there is some initial realm of commonly owned intellectual property in the same way that there is an initial expanse of commonly owned land. After all, it is the common grant of things that creates the common ownership presumption. If there is no common abstract expanse – if the initial, intellectual common is empty – then perhaps Locke's initial presumption against private appropriation does not apply.

Suppose ideas, expressions, methods, processes, and so on, were the pure *sui generis* creations of individual thinkers-cum-laborers. As one early British copyright advocate argued, ". . . in some Cases [the author] may be said rather to create, than to discover or plant his Land; and it cannot be said, that an Author's Work was ever common, as the Earth originally was to all the World."[56] If this were true, then it might seem that the intellectual products of fully self-owned labor could be owned without violating the common ownership thesis.

My counterargument to this objection will take some time to explain. The leading idea of my reply is that metaphysical facts do not settle the issue about property rights. We might agree that intellectual products or their bases are not independent of us; still, this would not imply that we have Lockean property rights over them. On the reading of Locke that I have developed, there is a Lockean reason to think that, *morally,* such creations should be regarded as commonly owned, irrespective of their origins.[57] To develop this argument, I begin by characterizing the initial intellectual common. There is more than one way to do this. On each characterization, there is a Lockean argument against expansive intellectual property rights.

The rival characterizations of the initial intellectual common could be crudely characterized as follows. The first characterization would place all

---

56 Anon., "A letter from an author to a Member of Parliament. Occasioned by a late letter concerning the Bill now depending in the House of Commons, for the encouragement of learning, &c.," (London: April 17, 1735).

57 For this reason, I bypass the challenge of exploring Locke's metaphysics, epistemology, and theology for indications about how he would have characterized the intellectual common. It would, however, be an important task for a full, historical treatment of Locke's approach to the subject.

intellectual products in the intellectual commons. Authors discover and bring such products out of the commons, but do not create, develop, or refine them. A second characterization would locate only the subject matter and materials of intellectual products in the commons, for example, facts, concepts, ideas, propositions, literary themes, musical themes, and values. Authors discover these things and their interconnections. They make them publicly accessible by expressing them, often, in unique ways. The third characterization presents the initial common as empty. Intellectual products are completely the inventions of their authors. The creation of intellectual products does not involve any use of common resources.

Of course, there is a final, plausible, hybrid view that holds that the appropriate characterization depends on the sort of intellectual product. Each of the first three characterizations, it might be thought, roughly describes some products, or, at least, some aspects of their creation. Some intellectual products mainly draw upon facts about the physical world that are discovered and not created by a single mind. The subjects of (some) patents may be like this. These products seem fruitfully analyzed under the first characterization.[58] Other intellectual products draw on common resources but also importantly depend upon authorial development, refinement, and expression – for example, the nonfictional reporting of facts, fictional treatments of love and betrayal, and portraits of landscapes. These seem like instances of the second characterization. Still other products, perhaps abstract paintings or performance art, may seem to be entirely authorial inventions.

Rendering these distinctions less crude and sorting out what products fall under what characterization would be a large, daunting task, far beyond the scope of this paper. As I hope to bring out through the discussion of these characterizations, though, I doubt the matter ultimately turns upon getting the classifications right. I will discuss these disparate characterizations in turn.

The First Characterization of the Initial Common (all products are in the initial common)

Suppose that all products are in the initial common. If this were true, the Lockean argument (as I have construed it) against private appropriation would be fairly straightforward. Authors exert labor through discovering and delivering intellectual products to the public. For their labor they may deserve compensation, attribution, and admiration. Yet, because such products generally do not require exclusive use for fully effective use, the argument for a natural, strong right to appropriate would be a nonstarter.

One may object to this analysis that some appropriation of the intellectual common may make other parts of it newly accessible, facilitating its fuller use.

---

58 Of course, to gain a patent, one must not just have an idea or discover a method or process. One's idea must be fixed in tangible form through expression. Nonetheless, patent protection is not limited to the description of the method or process, but extends to the method itself.

A profound insight or a probing discussion can spark ideas and open up new areas of thought. Thus, appropriation here might not reduce the total, accessible, usable common. Appropriation would, in fact, contribute to the Lockean aim of facilitating fuller use of the common.

But it is not the author's appropriation, *per se,* that expands the usable common. It is her distinctive *use* of the idea or expression, for example, and its communication to others that opens the way to the new appreciation and discovery of other facts and ideas. Again, this use need not be exclusive or subject to an individual's exclusive control to achieve this effect. To the contrary, the effect is generally compounded the less exclusive and more public the use is. Hence, it seems that on the first characterization Lockean arguments for strong intellectual property rights do not gain any firm footing.

Of course, the first characterization strikes most as unacceptably Platonist. Many find it implausible that musical works, diary entries, novels, scientific articles, and logos all have independent existence prior to the efforts of authors, creators, or "discoverers." Yet, it may seem difficult to resist the view that there are propositions about the world (broadly construed) that can be discovered and then expressed. The view that most such propositions can be owned by individuals is unattractive and rather hard to entertain.[59] This may make the second characterization (ideas, but not expressions, are common) more attractive, since it distinguishes between the underlying ideas, facts, and propositions that lie in the common and the expressions of them that are the product of creative labor.

But before proceeding to the second characterization, it is important to take stock. This analysis of the first characterization of the common, in which all is discovered and not made, yields rather significant results. Even if the first characterization implausibly describes intellectual products themselves, wholly or in part, its analysis still matters. The analysis suggests some minimal limitations on the permissible range of intellectual property rights. In law, intellectual property rights often extend protection to the author or creator beyond mere protection against use and copying of the actual product itself. Often, they extend protection against the creation of related, derivative works. Although this is a fuzzy area, this protection afforded to the creator may encompass enough that, in effect, it appropriates the sorts of things that seem to fall within the first characterization (even if the primary product itself does not squarely fall within the first characterization). Copyright law gives the owner an exclusive right to the production of derivative works.[60] In some cases, the specific plot or character sketches are protected. In patent law, protection will extend not just to the specific patented invention but it allows the patent owner

---

59 Certain sorts of personal, private facts might be thought to "belong" to individuals, however. Examples may include information about one's grooming habits, one's purely personal relationships, or one's medical decisions and prescriptions.
60 See 17 U.S.C. Sec. 106(2) (West 2000).

to prevent the use, manufacture, or sale of sufficiently similar devices, processes, or inventions. If the analysis of the first characterization is right, Lockean arguments may reject this wider range of protection that extends the rights of exclusive use beyond that of control over the specific product.

The Second Characterization of the Initial Common (the underlying ideas but not the works themselves are in the initial common)

The second characterization of the common may seem especially amenable to a Lockean justification for intellectual property rights. It fits nicely with commonplace copyright distinctions between ideas and expressions, where the latter, but not the former, are deemed ownable.[61] On this characterization, expressions seem to resemble agricultural products. There is commonly owned material – the terrain of ideas, facts, propositions – that an intellectual laborer works on. The result is new material that, like harvested crops, is the product of interaction between individual labor and the common. In this case, though, these products – the expressions – even enhance the value of the common by rendering it more accessible.

Nevertheless, there is a significant difference between intellectual property, on the lights of the second characterization, and the paradigm real property case. The contents of the intellectual common (here, the ideas) need not be exclusively owned or controlled to be made useful. With real property, though, the products of agricultural efforts arise from materials, such as land, that Locke suggests must themselves be exclusively owned to be properly developed and fully used.

One might object that this disanalogy between real and intellectual property has little significance. Why should it matter that the initial property to be worked on need not be exclusively owned to be made useful? Might it even cut the other way, given that, with intellectual materials (unlike real property), many can labor over the same stretch of the intellectual common, simultaneously and without mutual interference? My contemplation of an idea does not preclude your contemplation of that same idea. Furthermore, my expression of that idea (and even my ownership of that expression) does not preclude your independent expression of that idea. Since ownership of an expression does not preclude others from access to the same underlying terrain of ideas, doesn't that strengthen the argument for private ownership of expressions?

I believe that it does not. Although this feature is important, it does not supply a positive, initial impetus for privatization. As I stressed in Section II, Locke's argument begins with a common property presumption, grounded in positive moral (albeit theologically grounded) motivations. Deviations from this default position are justified when full and effective use of the property

---

61 See, for example, 17 U.S.C. Sec. 102 (West 2000). In practice, though, copyright protection over derivative works may be in tension with this distinction.

requires private appropriation. If the Lockean position were the contrary, namely that one could come to own material unless such private ownership interfered with the use of the common, then the ability to work simultaneously and without mutual interference on the same stretch of the intellectual common would be more significant.

But as I understand Locke's approach (and what makes it attractive), it has a different cast. Reasons of equality ground a common property presumption that is overcome because the nature of the property suggests it. The fact that the contents of the initial intellectual common need not be exclusively owned or controlled to be made useful matters because it precludes appropriation of ideas from the common, as was previously discussed. It also provides reason to resist ownership of expressions that make use of this nonappropriable common; the ownership of the expression is not necessary to make full, effective use of the idea or its expression. By contrast, for real property, Locke's belief that the underlying land must be exclusively owned does some work to justify exclusive ownership of the products of labor on it – ownership of the products is connected to the project of efficiently managing the productive land.

The fact that intellectual products can normally be used simultaneously lends even stronger support to the Lockean argument against a natural right to intellectual property. Apart from the previously noted exceptions of works-in-progress, the products of intellectual labor need not be exclusively owned for proper use of either these products themselves or of the underlying common. Often the opposite is true: intellectual products are put to their best use through common use and contemplation. So, again, there is no reason emanating from the nature of the property itself and the conditions of its full, effective use for departing from the common property presumption.

But is the contrast between real and intellectual property fair in this respect? Are the products of labor on real property always or generally the sorts of things that need to be exclusively owned to be properly used? We might consider a range of cases. Locke's prominent case was agriculture – in which labor either improved land that needed to be, he assumed, exclusively owned, or produced crops like food that required exclusive ownership for proper use. Of course, the producer need not have been the exclusive owner of her products; others could perform this service. But, as earlier suggested, Locke seems to have supposed that exclusive ownership of the products was part of the process of managing the underlying property that, itself, required exclusive control. For Locke's prototypical case, then, there is a difference between agricultural, real products and intellectual products: The nature of the former property directly or indirectly generates a need for exclusive control, whereas the nature of intellectual products does not directly or indirectly require exclusive control for effective use.

What about nonagricultural uses? Suppose a landowner builds a mansion, a park, or a wide path up a mountain on his or her property. Does the owner have less of an exclusive claim to these products because they, like intellectual products, are more amenable to common use? Without much stretching, one can construct a neo-Lockean argument to justify the intuition that the legitimate landowner can exert exclusive control over the mansion – albeit by appealing to different values served by some sorts of property than just the value of self-preservation that Locke himself invoked. The mansion can be occupied by many people at once. But one cannot reliably achieve the sense of privacy, belonging, and the sense of an identity that it is part of the function of a home to provide, unless one may exert strong control over the number and identity of its occupants. But the park and the path pose harder cases. Although it is not the typical view of Lockean rights, on the account I have sketched it might matter for Lockean purposes that such places would be significantly underused were their creator to exert control over them by excluding the public from their enjoyment and use. Lockean concerns about waste and about the full, proper use of the property would be activated.

Returning to the copyright case, suppose we thought of expressions metaphorically – as ways to get to ideas. An expression is like a new, convenient path forged into a mountain in order to reach its valuable, commonly owned apex. Other paths, perhaps less direct or elegant, could be forged, maybe with great difficulty. Although it seems permissible to make this path and to charge compensation for the work, we might balk at the pathbreaker's being able to block access indefinitely, at his discretion, or to charge high fees for access that would deter fruitful use. One would need to give a positive reason for the full private appropriation of the path. Mere appeal to labor and the existence of alternatives would not suffice. On Lockean grounds, the pathbreaker's ability to appropriate might be blocked or restricted to require public access so long as these public-oriented uses were on it.[62]

As must be evident, my argument leans heavily on the common property presumption. One might worry that this presumption, for Locke, arises in response to a pre-existing set of things that is not, initially, clearly associated with or specially connected to particular individuals. We all stand in the same relation, initially, to land, most facts, the laws of nature, and so on. So we all have an equal claim to them. It might be objected that, under the second conception (and the third conception) of the initial common, this equal relation does not hold with respect to intellectual products. Under it, there is a special connection between a creator and her product. Other people do not stand in the same relation as the creator to intellectual products.

---

62 These cases are more complex than the analogous intellectual property cases. The landowner might need to exert control over access to the park or the path in order to ensure the proper management of the underlying land – unregulated use might damage the land. In the case of intellectual property, it seems less likely that permissive public access to expression will damage the underlying ideas or impede their apprehension. There are parallel hazards, though; overuse of some intellectual products may make them hackneyed.

Yet, there is another plausible understanding of the impetus behind the common property presumption, one that views the presumption as a reflection and an expression of the equal moral status of individuals. On this alternative explanation, it should matter less whether intellectual products were in a preexisting initial common or whether they were partly or wholly human creations. Creations could become part of the common – available equally to all – when their nature did not require exclusive use, to symbolize the equal moral status of individuals.

Locke's writings do not directly develop the foundations of the common property presumption. But there is reason to favor the second understanding. It, unlike the first, reflects the themes that initially animate Locke: the emphasis on equality, the connection between equality and common ownership, and reasoning about property in light of its nature – that is, in light of what is necessary to make full and robust use of it. The qualities of intellectual property strongly engage these Lockean themes – especially the facts that exclusive use is generally unnecessary for its proper use and that, to the contrary, its full exploitation commonly depends on nonexclusive use. These features generate moral reasons to regard intellectual products as part of the intellectual common, even if they are pure authorial creations.

Since expressions do not require exclusive use for full, effective use, the Lockean impetus to make full, robust use of property may suggest that although an individual's unique expressions of the ideas are not preexisting components of the intellectual common, these works should be viewed as incorporated into the common upon their creation. They are properly viewed as becoming part of the common for two reasons. First, their nature is like the nature of other things properly left in common, that is, compatible with joint use. Second, their becoming part of the common jibes with the motivation of Locke's account of property – that things should be shared, equally, unless there is a strong reason to do otherwise.

The Third Characterization (the initial common is empty)

On the third characterization, the initial intellectual common is empty. Nothing is used or taken from it when intellectual products are formed; intellectual products are pure authorial creations. This characterization does seem extreme – at least for many intellectual products and their subject matter, especially historical works and other nonfictional prose. Suppose it were, though, a plausible description of at least some intellectual products, perhaps abstract paintings. Such products would seem like paradigm cases for the more traditional version of the Lockean story: that property, and hence property rights, arise through and as a reaction to the justifiable exertion of self-owned labor. But this alone, as I have contended, does not indicate that intellectual products are strongly owned by their producers, since they do not have to be exclusively owned for their proper use. The argument I have just given would instead suggest that they should be viewed as incorporated into the common upon creation, even if they do not exist in some initial intellectual common, prior to human efforts.

This may be an apt place to consider a final reply, one that appeals to another important Lockean theme to which I have not paid much attention. Perhaps the Lockean right of self-ownership provides a normative reason to characterize the common as including only preexisting things. If intellectual products flow entirely from the creator's mind and labor, then they might be viewed as an extension of the self.[63] They are owned not through appropriation but because the author is a self-owner and these are aspects of his or herself. If intellectual products do flow entirely from a creator, I think such an argument may indeed provide an additional, independent Lockean ground for property rights over works-in-progress, private works, and perhaps unpublished works (of the living) altogether. These works are not yet completely distinct from the person. But completion and publication of a work seems to effect a separation from the private self.[64] It is not clear that the values animating the right of self-ownership can sensibly be extended to protect individuals' ability to disperse aspects of themselves into the public domain while simultaneously retaining complete control over them.

By analogy, suppose a person grows an extra length of hair, cuts it off from his or her head, and deliberately throws it onto the beach for public view. Is it clear that he or she should be able to prevent passersby from touching it or using it? Suppose this person discards many such lengths of hair onto the common, creating aisles of long, silky hair. Does the right of self-ownership really yield a natural right to restrict access to or control what is done to these clumps? How many such hair-aisles may she introduce into public space yet continue to subject to her control? Of course, when the hair is still attached to the body, there are reasons associated with the values underlying self-ownership to permit the owner to restrict access to it, to protect his or her autonomy and physical security. Such reasons hold even if the attached hair has been fashioned into an artwork or sculpture that others might appreciate. But once a person has deliberately separated from his or her products, it is harder to believe that the right to self-ownership grants rights to continue to control these things. To permit that control would be, in part, to grant a person exclusive

---

63 Locke's remarks at II.44 might be read this way (". . . though the things of Nature are given in common, yet Man had still in himself *the great Foundation of Property*; . . . that which made up the great part of what he applyed to the Support and Comfort of his being, when Invention and Arts had improved the conveniencies of Life, was perfectly his own, and did not belong in common with others.")

64 There are difficult questions about what constitutes publication, especially in digital media where web sites may be under constant construction and revision. These questions would require further discussion. One possible criterion might be whether the material has been deposited within the public domain or distributed to a wide group of people, as opposed to a discrete group of friends or associates.

control over an aspect of the public domain or the common. A person with such rights could introduce things into them, occupy their space, and control what was done to them. Such rights of control seem inconsistent with the norms of common ownership – those of free public access and use that govern what remains of the public commons.

Granted, an important asymmetry remains. Separating off one's body parts and putting them on display is not a typical part of individual development or self-expression. By contrast, creative expression in the public forum often does contribute importantly to the development and full expression of the self. It might be plausibly submitted that publication – unlike the public scattering of body parts – may be intimately connected to values that the right of self-ownership protects. Still, I do not think this asymmetry makes a salient difference here. To make such a difference, not only would publication have to be essential to self-development, but publication *coupled with strong rights of control* would have to be essential to self-development. The connection between self-development and public expression may undergird fundamental protection to publish and distribute creative materials into the public common, or the public culture. To develop oneself and one's talents fully, one may need the freedom to display and expose oneself and one's intellectual products to others. One may also need the opportunity to provoke and gauge the reaction of other people – just as if there were a connection between self-development and body-part scattering, this might yield a right to use the common in a way that could not be abridged by public regulation. The further right to control others' use, however, would follow only if full "use" of the self required control of others' use of the published material. This, it seems to me, is an implausible claim. For these reasons, I resist even the suggestion that the third characterization is fully amenable to Lockean arguments for the normal panoply of strong intellectual property rights.

IV. Conclusion

Although my arguments do not land intellectual products conclusively in the common property camp over the private property camp, there are two main Lockean arguments for resolving the balance of reasons in favor of common ownership. First, in contrast to the assumptions about real property and its effective use, the full, effective use of intellectual works generally depends upon *shared* use, not exclusive, private use. If effective exploitation of the grant of the world is a value that propels Locke's arguments for ownership, then, since free, shared use of intellectual products contributes to their effective exploitation, this sort of property seems unamenable to private appropriation that manifests in strong rights.

Second, the interpretation that I have urged suggests that the place of common ownership in Locke's scheme cuts against the argument for private ownership of intellectual property. Common ownership, for Locke, is not, I think, best seen as a mere starting place or an easily overturned default rule. It is also a concrete expression of the equal standing of, and the community relationship between, all people. Important resources may not be monopolized without good reason. They should, if possible, be available to all for use freely. The symbolic significance of common ownership may be affirmed in a more manifest way within the intellectual property domain than with much real property. That is, where real property is appropriable, it may matter even more that intellectual property is not appropriable, so that the common ownership foundation behind property rights is not obscured or forgotten. Retaining some explicit common ownership underscores the common grant of the world and serves as a reminder of our equal status.

These Lockean arguments leave open the possibility of other arguments for strong privatization or for the public's consenting to create private intellectual property. But the force of my arguments is not restricted to undermining Lockean defenses of most strong intellectual property rights. Their further implication is that those who do subscribe to initial principles of common ownership may not just point to these other possible foundations for private intellectual property rights. They may also have to show that these alternative grounds offer sufficiently strong and well-supported reasons to override the value of the tangible symbol of equality manifested by the common ownership presumption.

6

Theories of Intellectual Property

WILLIAM FISHER

The term "intellectual property" refers to a loose cluster of legal doctrines that regulate the uses of different sorts of ideas and insignia. The law of copyright protects various "original forms of expression," including novels, movies, musical compositions, and computer software programs. Patent law protects inventions and some kinds of discoveries. Trademark law protects words and symbols that identify for consumers the goods and services manufactured or supplied by particular persons or firms. Trade-secret law protects commercially valuable information (soft-drink formulas, confidential marketing strategies, etc.) that companies attempt to conceal from their competitors. The "right of publicity" protects celebrities' interests in their images and identities.

The economic and cultural importance of this collection of rules is increasing rapidly. The fortunes of many businesses now depend heavily on intellectual-property rights. A growing percentage of the legal profession specializes in intellectual-property disputes. And lawmakers throughout the world are busily revising their intellectual-property laws.[1]

Partly as a result of these trends, scholarly interest in the field has risen dramatically in recent years. In law reviews and in journals of economics and philosophy, articles deploying "theories" of intellectual property have proliferated. This essay canvasses those theories, evaluates them, and considers the roles they do and ought to play in lawmaking.

This essay has benefited substantially from the comments of Charles Fried, Paul Goldstein, Jim Harris, Ned Hettinger, Edmund Kitch, Ed McCaffery, Stephen Munzer, Samuel Oddi, J. E. Penner, John T. Sanders, F. M. Scherer, Seanna Shiffrin, Stewart Sterk, and a generous group of anonymous outside readers.

1 The history of these doctrines in the United States – and possible reasons for their growing importance – are considered in William Fisher, "Geistiges Eigentum – ein ausufernder Rechtsbereich: Die Geschichte des Ideenschutzes in den Vereinigten Staaten," in *Eigentum im internationalen Vergleich* (Göttingen: Vandenhoeck and Ruprecht, 1999) (available in English at http://www.law.harvard.edu/Academic_Affairs/coursepages/tfisher/iphistory.html).

I. A Preliminary Survey

Most of the recent theoretical writing consists of struggles among and within four approaches. The first and most popular of the four employs the familiar utilitarian guideline that lawmakers' beacon when shaping property rights should be the maximization of net social welfare. Pursuit of that end in the context of intellectual property, it is generally thought, requires lawmakers to strike an optimal balance between, on one hand, the power of exclusive rights to stimulate the creation of inventions and works of art and, on the other, the partially offsetting tendency of such rights to curtail widespread public enjoyment of those creations.

A good example of scholarship in this vein is William Landes's and Richard Posner's essay on copyright law. The distinctive characteristics of most intellectual products, Landes and Posner argue, are that they are easily replicated and that enjoyment of them by one person does not prevent enjoyment of them by other persons. Those characteristics in combination create a danger that the creators of such products will be unable to recoup their "costs of expression" (the time and effort devoted to writing or composing and the costs of negotiating with publishers or record companies), because they will be undercut by copyists who bear only the low "costs of production" (the costs of manufacturing and distributing books or CDs) and thus can offer consumers identical products at very low prices. Awareness of that danger will deter creators from making socially valuable intellectual products in the first instance. We can avoid this economically inefficient outcome by allocating to the creators (for limited times) the exclusive right to make copies of their creations. The creators of works that consumers find valuable – that is, for which there are not, in the opinions of consumers, equally attractive substitutes – will be empowered thereby to charge prices for access to those works substantially greater than they could in a competitive market. All of the various alternative ways in which creators might be empowered to recover their costs, Landes and Posner contend, are, for one reason or another, more wasteful of social resources. This utilitarian rationale, they argue, should be – and, for the most part, has been – used to shape specific doctrines within the field.[2]

A related argument dominates the same authors' study of trademark law. The primary economic benefits of trademarks, they contend, are (1) the reduction of consumers' "search costs" (because it's easier to pick a box of "Cheerios" off the grocery shelf than to read the list of ingredients on each container, and because consumers can rely upon their prior experiences with

---

2 William Landes and Richard Posner, "An Economic Analysis of Copyright Law," *Journal of Legal Studies*, 18 (1989): 325. This argument is derived in substantial part from Jeremy Bentham, *A Manual of Political Economy* (New York: Putnam, 1839); John Stuart Mill, *Principles of Political Economy*, 5th ed. (New York: Appleton, 1862); and A. C. Pigou, *The Economics of Welfare*, 2d ed. (London: Macmillan and Co., 1924).

various brands of cereal when deciding which box to buy in the future) and (2) the creation of an incentive for businesses to produce consistently high-quality goods and services (because they know that their competitors cannot, by imitating their distinctive marks, take a free ride on the consumer good will that results from consistent quality). Trademarks, Landes and Posner claim, also have an unusual ancillary social benefit: they improve the quality of our language. By increasing our stock of nouns and by "creating words or phrases that people value for their intrinsic pleasingness as well as their information value," they simultaneously economize on communication costs and make conversation more pleasurable. To be sure, trademarks can sometimes be socially harmful – for example, by enabling the first entrant into a market to discourage competition by appropriating for itself an especially attractive or informative brand name. Awareness of these benefits and harms should (and usually does), Landes and Posner claim, guide legislators and judges when tuning trademark law; marks should be (and usually are) protected when they are socially beneficial and not when they are, on balance, deleterious.[3]

The second of the four approaches that currently dominate the theoretical literature springs from the propositions that a person who labors upon resources that are either unowned or "held in common" has a natural property right to the fruits of his or her efforts – and that the state has a duty to respect and enforce that natural right. These ideas, originating in the writings of John Locke, are widely thought to be especially applicable to the field of intellectual property, where the pertinent raw materials (facts and concepts) do seem in some sense to be "held in common" and where labor seems to contribute so importantly to the value of finished products.[4]

A good illustration of this perspective is Robert Nozick's brief but influential discussion of patent law in *Anarchy, State, and Utopia*.[5] After associating himself with Locke's argument, Nozick turns his attention to Locke's famously ambiguous "proviso" – the proposition that a person may legitimately acquire property rights by mixing his labor with resources held "in common" only if, after the acquisition, "there is enough and as good left in common for others."[6] Nozick contends that the correct interpretation of this limitation ("correct" in the senses (a) that it probably corresponds to Locke's original intent and (b)

---

3 William Landes and Richard Posner, "Trademark Law: An Economic Perspective," *Journal of Law & Economics,* 30 (1987): 265. Other works that address trademark law in similar terms include Nicholas Economides, "The Economics of Trademarks," *Trademark Reporter,* 78 (1988): 523–39 and Daniel McClure, "Trademarks and Competition: The Recent History," *Law and Contemporary Problems,* 59 (1996): 13–43.
4 See, for example, Justin Hughes, "The Philosophy of Intellectual Property," *Georgetown Law Journal,* 77 (1988): 287, at 299–330. These initial impressions are examined in more detail in Section III below.
5 Robert Nozick, *Anarchy, State, and Utopia* (New York: Basic Books, 1974), pp. 178–82.
6 John Locke, *Two Treatises of Government* (P. Laslett, ed., Cambridge: Cambridge University Press, 1970), *Second Treatise,* Sec. 27.

that, in any event, it is entailed by "an adequate theory of justice") is that the acquisition of property through labor is legitimate if and only if other persons do not suffer thereby any net harm. "Net harm" for these purposes includes such injuries as being left poorer than they would have been under a regime that did not permit the acquisition of property through labor or a constriction of the set of resources available for their *use* – but does not include a diminution in their opportunities to acquire property rights in unowned resources by being the first to labor upon them. Construed in this fashion, the Lockean proviso is not violated, Nozick argues, by the assignment of a patent right to an inventor because, although other persons' access to the invention is undoubtedly limited by the issuance of the patent, the invention would not have existed at all without the efforts of the inventor. In other words, consumers are helped, not hurt, by the grant of the patent. Nozick contends, however, that fidelity to Locke's theory would mandate two limitations on the inventor's entitlements. First, persons who subsequently invented the same device independently must be permitted to make and sell it. Otherwise the assignment of the patent to the first inventor would leave them worse off. Second, for the same reason, patents should not last longer than, on average, it would have taken someone else to invent the same device had knowledge of the invention not disabled them from inventing it independently. Although Nozick may not have been aware of it, implementation of the first of these limitations would require a substantial reform of current patent law – which, unlike copyright law, does not contain a safe harbor for persons who dream up the same idea on their own.

The premise of the third approach – derived loosely from the writings of Kant and Hegel – is that private property rights are crucial to the satisfaction of some fundamental human needs; policymakers should thus strive to create and allocate entitlements to resources in the fashion that best enables people to fulfill those needs. From this standpoint, intellectual property rights may be justified either on the ground that they shield from appropriation or modification artifacts through which authors and artists have expressed their "wills" (an activity thought central to "personhood") or on the ground that they create social and economic conditions conducive to creative intellectual activity, which in turn is important to human flourishing.[7]

In perhaps the most fully developed argument of this sort, Justin Hughes derives from Hegel's *Philosophy of Right* the following guidelines concerning the proper shape of an intellectual-property system: (a) We should be more willing to accord legal protection to the fruits of highly expressive intellectual activities, such as the writing of novels, than to the fruits of less expressive activities, such as genetic research. (b) Because a person's "persona" – his "public image, including his physical features, mannerisms, and history" – is

---

7 See Margaret Jane Radin, *Reinterpreting Property* (Chicago: University of Chicago Press, 1993); Jeremy Waldron, *The Right to Private Property* (Oxford: Clarendon, 1988).

an important "receptacle for personality," it deserves generous legal protection, despite the fact that ordinarily it does not result from labor. (c) Authors and inventors should be permitted to earn respect, honor, admiration, and money from the public by selling or giving away copies of their works, but should not be permitted to surrender their right to prevent others from mutilating or misattributing their works.[8]

The last of the four approaches is rooted in the proposition that property rights in general – and intellectual-property rights in particular – can and should be shaped so as to help foster the achievement of a just and attractive culture. Theorists who work this vein typically draw inspiration from an eclectic cluster of political and legal theorists, including Jefferson, the early Marx, the Legal Realists, and the various proponents (ancient and modern) of classical republicanism.[9] This approach is similar to utilitarianism in its teleological orientation, but dissimilar in its willingness to deploy visions of a desirable society richer than the conceptions of "social welfare" deployed by utilitarians.

A provocative example may be found in Neil Netanel's recent essay, "Copyright and a Democratic Civil Society." Netanel begins by sketching a picture of "a robust, participatory, and pluralist civil society," teeming with "unions, churches, political and social movements, civic and neighborhood associations, schools of thought, and educational institutions." In this world, all persons would enjoy both some degree of financial independence and considerable responsibility in shaping their local social and economic environments. A civil society of this sort is vital, Netanel claims, to the perpetuation of democratic political institutions. It will not, however, emerge spontaneously; it must be nourished by government. In two ways, copyright law can help foster it.

The first is a production function. Copyright provides an incentive for creative expression on a wide array of political, social, and aesthetic issues, thus bolstering the discursive foundations for democratic culture and civic association. The second function is structural. Copyright supports a sector of creative and communicative activity that is relatively free from reliance on state subsidy, elite patronage, and cultural hierarchy.

Promotion of these two objectives does not require that we retain all aspects of the current copyright system. On the contrary, Netanel suggests, they would be advanced more effectively by a copyright regime trimmed along the following lines: The copyright term should be shortened, thereby increasing the size

---

8 See Hughes, "Philosophy of Intellectual Property," at 330–50.

9 See, for example, James Harrington, *Oceana* (Westport, Conn.: Hyperion Press, 1979); Thomas Jefferson, *Notes on the State of Virginia* (New York: Norton, 1972); Karl Marx, *Economic and Philosophic Manuscripts of 1844* (New York: International Publishers, 1964); Morris Cohen, "Property & Sovereignty," *Cornell Law Quarterly,* 13 (1927): 8; Frank Michelman, "Law's Republic," *Yale Law Journal,* 97 (1988): 1493; William Fisher, Morton Horwitz, and Thomas Reed, eds., *American Legal Realism* (New York: Oxford University Press, 1993).

of the "public domain" available for creative manipulation. Copyright owners' authority to control the preparation of "derivative works" should be reduced for the same reason. Finally, compulsory licensing systems should be employed more frequently to balance the interests of artists and "consumers" of their works.[10]

Other writers who have approached intellectual-property law from similar perspectives include Keith Aoki, Rosemary Coombe, Niva Elkin-Koren, Michael Madow, and myself.[11] As yet, however, this fourth approach is less well established and recognized than the other three. It does not even have a commonly accepted label. To describe a closely analogous perspective developed in the context of land law, Greg Alexander suggests the term "Proprietarian" theory.[12] I find more helpful the phrase, "Social Planning Theory."

II. Explaining the Pattern

Those, then, are (in order of prominence and influence) the four perspectives that currently dominate theoretical writing about intellectual property: Utilitarianism; Labor Theory; Personality Theory; and Social Planning Theory. What accounts for the influence of these particular approaches? In large part, their prominence derives from the fact that they grow out of and draw support from lines of argument that have long figured in the raw materials of intellectual property law – constitutional provisions, case reports, preambles to legislation, and so forth.

The dependence of theorists on ideas formulated and popularized by judges, legislators, and lawyers is especially obvious in the case of utilitarianism. References to the role of intellectual-property rights in stimulating the production of socially valuable works riddle American law. Thus, for example, the constitutional provision upon which the copyright and patent statutes rest indicates that the purpose of those laws is to provide incentives for creative intellectual efforts that will benefit the society at large.[13] The United States

10 "Copyright and a Democratic Civil Society," *Yale Law Journal,* 106 (1996): 283. See also idem., "Asserting Copyright's Democratic Principles in the Global Arena," *Vanderbilt Law Review,* 51 (1998): 217–329.

11 See, for example, Rosemary J. Coombe, "Objects of Property and Subjects of Politics: Intellectual Property Laws and Democratic Dialogue," *Texas Law Review,* 69 (1991): 1853; Niva Elkin-Koren, "Copyright Law and Social Dialogue on the Information Superhighway: The Case Against Copyright Liability of Bulletin Board Operators," *Cardozo Arts & Entertainment Law Journal,* 13 (1995): 345; Michael Madow, "Private Ownership of Public Image: Popular Culture and Publicity Rights," *California Law Review,* 81 (1993): 125; William Fisher, "Reconstructing the Fair Use Doctrine," *Harvard Law Review,* 101 (1988): 1659–795, at 1744–94.

12 Gregory S. Alexander, *Commodity and Propriety* (Chicago: University of Chicago Press, 1997), p. 1.

13 Article I, Section 8, Clause 8 of the United States Constitution empowers Congress "to Promote the Progress of Science and useful Arts, by securing for limited Times to Authors and Inventors the exclusive Right to their respective Writings and Discoveries."

Supreme Court, when construing the copyright and patent statutes, has repeatedly insisted that their primary objective is inducing the production and dissemination of works of the intellect.[14] A host of lower courts have agreed.[15]

References to the importance of rewarding authors and inventors for their labor are almost as common. Proponents of legislative extensions of copyright or patent protection routinely make arguments like: "Our American society is founded on the principle that the one who creates something of value is entitled to enjoy the fruits of his labor."[16] The United States Supreme Court often uses a similar vocabulary. For example, Justice Reed ended his opinion in *Mazer v. Stein* with the solemn statement: "Sacrificial days devoted to . . . creative activities deserve rewards commensurate with the services rendered."[17] Lower court opinions and appellate arguments frequently take the same tack.[18]

Until recently, the personality theory had much less currency in American law. By contrast, it has long figured very prominently in Europe. The French and German copyright regimes, for example, have been strongly shaped by the writings of Kant and Hegel. This influence is especially evident in the generous protection those countries provide for "moral rights" — authors' and artists' rights to control the public disclosure of their works, to withdraw their works from public circulation, to receive appropriate credit for their creations, and above all to protect their works against mutilation or destruction. This cluster of entitlements has traditionally been justified on the ground that a work of art embodies and helps to realize its creator's personality or will. In the past two decades, "moral-rights" doctrine — and the philosophic perspective on which it rests — have found increasing favor with American lawmakers, as evidenced most clearly by the proliferation of state art-preservation statutes and the recent adoption of the federal Visual Artists Rights Act.[19]

---

14 See, for example, *Fox Film Corp. v. Doyal,* 286 U.S. 123, 127–28 (1932); *Kendall v. Winsor,* 62 U.S. (21 How.) 322, 327–28 (1858).

15 See, for example, *Hustler Magazine v. Moral Majority,* 796 F.2d 1148, 1151 (9th Cir. 1986); *Consumers Union of United States v. General Signal Corp.,* 724 F.2d 1044, 1048 (2d Cir. 1983).

16 Testimony of Elizabeth Janeway, Copyright Law Revision: Hearings on H.R. 4347, 5680, 6831, 6835 Before Subcomm. No. 3 of the House Comm. on the Judiciary, 89th Cong., 1st Sess. (1965), reprinted in George S. Grossman, *Omnibus Copyright Revision Legislative History,* vol. 5 (1976), p. 100.

17 347 U.S. 201, 219 (1954). For a similar argument in the patent context, see *Motion Picture Patents Co. v. Universal Film Manufacturing Co.,* 243 U.S. 502 (1917).

18 Many examples are set forth in Stewart E. Sterk, "Rhetoric and Reality in Copyright Law," *Michigan Law Review,* 94 (1996): 1197; Alfred C. Yen, "Restoring the Natural Law: Copyright as Labor and Possession," *Ohio State Law Journal,* 51 (1990): 517; and Lloyd L. Weinreb, "Copyright for Functional Expression," *Harvard Law Review,* 111 (1998): 1149–1254, at 1211–14.

19 See Thomas Cotter, "Pragmatism, Economics, and the *Droit Moral,*" *North Carolina Law Review,* 76 (1997): 1, at 6–27; Jeri D. Yonover, "The 'Dissing' of Da Vinci: The Imaginary Case of Leonardo v. Duchamp: Moral Rights, Parody, and Fair Use," *Valparaiso University Law Review,* 29 (1995): 935–1004.

Finally, deliberate efforts to craft or construe rules in order to advance a vision of a just and attractive culture – the orientation that underlies Social Planning Theory – can be found in almost all of the provinces of intellectual property law. Such impulses underlie, for example, both the harsh response of most courts when applying copyright or trademark law to scatological humor and the generally favorable treatment they have accorded criticism, commentary, and education. Social-planning arguments also figure prominently in current debates concerning the appropriate scope of intellectual-property rights on the Internet.[20]

To summarize, one source of the prominence of utilitarian, labor, personality, and social-planning theories in recent theoretical literature is the strength of similar themes in judicial opinions, statutes, and appellate briefs. But two circumstances suggest that such parallelism and resonance cannot fully explain the configuration of contemporary theories. First, there exist in the materials of intellectual-property law several important themes that have not been echoed and amplified by a significant number of theorists. Many American courts, for example, strive when construing copyright or trademark law to reflect and reinforce custom – either customary business practices or customary standards of "good faith" and "fair dealing."[21] That orientation has deep roots both in the common law in general and in the early-twentieth-century writings of the American Legal Realists.[22] Yet, few contemporary intellectual-property theorists pay significant attention to custom.[23] Much the same can be said of concern for privacy interests. Long a major concern of legislators and courts,[24] protection of privacy has been given short shrift by contemporary American theorists.

The second circumstance is that, in legislative and judicial materials, arguments of the various sorts we have been considering typically are blended. Here, for example, is the preamble to Connecticut's first copyright statute:

Whereas it is perfectly agreeable to the principles of natural equity and justice, that every author should be secured in receiving the profits that may arise from the sale of his works, and such security may encourage men of learning and genius to publish their writings; which may do honor to their country, and service to mankind. . . .[25]

20 See Niva Elkin-Koren, "Cyberlaw and Social Change: A Democratic Approach to Copyright Law in Cyberspace," *Cardozo Arts & Entertainment Law Journal,* 14 (1996): 215.
21 *Harper & Row v. Nation Enterprises,* 471 U.S. 539, 563 (1985). See also *Time v. Bernard Geis Associates,* 293 F.Supp. 130, 146 (S.D.N.Y. 1968); *Rosemont Enterprises v. Random House,* 366 F.2d 303, 307 (2d Cir. 1966); *Holdridge v. Knight Publishing Corp.,* 214 F.Supp. 921, 924 (S.D.Cal. 1963).
22 See Fisher et al., *American Legal Realism,* p. 170.
23 But cf. Lloyd L. Weinreb, "Fair's Fair: A Comment on the Fair Use Doctrine," *Harvard Law Review,* 103 (1990): 1137–61.
24 See *Harper & Row v. Nation Enterprises,* 471 U.S. 539, 564 (1985); *Salinger v. Random House,* 811 F.2d 90, 97 (2d Cir. 1987).
25 1783 Conn. Pub. Acts Jan. Sess., reprinted in U.S. Copyright Office, *Copyright Enactments of the United States,* 1783–1906, at 11 (2nd ed., Washington: Government Printing Office, 1906).

Two hundred years later, in the *Harper & Row* case, the Supreme Court took a similar line:

> We agree with the Court of Appeals that copyright is intended to increase and not to impede the harvest of knowledge. But we believe the Second Circuit gave insufficient deference to the scheme established by the Copyright Act for fostering the original works that provide the seed and substance of this harvest. The rights conferred by copyright are designed to assure contributors to the store of knowledge a fair return for their labors.[26]

Fairness, incentives, culture-shaping – in these and countless other passages, they swirl together. In contemporary theoretical writing, by contrast, such themes are typically disentangled and juxtaposed.

How can we account for these two respects in which intellectual-property theory deviates from extant legal materials? The answer seems to be that the theorists are seeing the law through glasses supplied by political philosophy. In contemporary philosophic debates, natural law, utilitarianism, and theories of the good are generally seen as incompatible perspectives.[27] It is not surprising that legal theorists, familiar with those debates, should separate ideas about intellectual property into similar piles.

One additional circumstance also likely plays a part: Many contemporary *intellectual*-property theorists also participate in similar arguments about the appropriate shape of property law in general. In that arena, there is now a well-established canon of rival perspectives, again drawn in large part from Anglo-American political philosophy. Labor theory, utilitarianism, and personality theory are the primary contenders.[28] We should not be surprised to see them replicated in the context of intellectual property.

III. Gaps, Conflicts, and Ambiguities

Lawmakers are confronted these days with many difficult questions involving rights to control information. Should the creators of electronic databases be able to demand compensation from users or copyists? What degree of similarity between two plots or two fictional characters should be necessary to trigger a finding that one infringes the other? Should computer software be

---

26 *Harper & Row v. Nation Enterprises,* 471 U.S. 539, 545–46 (1985).
27 The pertinent literature is enormous. A few entries, suggesting the importance of the divisions drawn in the text, are H. L. A. Hart, "Between Utility and Rights," *Columbia Law Review,* 79 (1979): 828; Michael Sandel, *Liberalism and the Limits of Justice* (Cambridge: Cambridge University Press, 1982).
28 For discussions and illustrations of the canon, see J. Roland Pennock and John W. Chapman, eds., *Property* (Nomos XXII) (New York: New York University Press, 1980); Alan Ryan, *Property and Political Theory* (Oxford: Blackwell, 1984); Waldron, *Right to Private Property.* To be sure, not all property theorists are inclined to maintain the traditional boundaries between natural law, utilitarianism, and theories of the good. For one prominent pluralist theory, see Stephen R. Munzer, *A Theory of Property* (Cambridge: Cambridge University Press, 1990).

governed by copyright law, patent law, or a *sui generis* legal regime? Should we expand or contract intellectual-property protection for the configurations of consumer products? Should time-sensitive information (e.g., sports scores, news, financial data) gathered by one party be shielded from copying by others? Many other, similar problems demand attention.

The proponents of all four of the leading theories of intellectual property purport to provide lawmakers with answers to questions of these sorts. In other words, they understand their arguments to be, not merely systematic accounts of the impulses that have shaped extant legal doctrines, but guides that legislators and judges can use in modifying or extending those doctrines in response to new technologies and circumstances. Unfortunately, all four theories prove in practice to be less helpful in this regard than their proponents claim. Ambiguities, internal inconsistencies, and the lack of crucial empirical information severely limit their prescriptive power. Subsections III.A. – III.D., below, explore those limitations. Section IV contends that the theories nevertheless have considerable value.

A.

The first task in developing a utilitarian theory of intellectual property is translating the Benthamite ideal of the "greatest good of the greatest number" into a more precise and administrable standard. Most contemporary writers select for this purpose either the "wealth-maximization" criterion, which counsels lawmakers to select the system of rules that maximizes aggregate welfare measured by consumers' ability and willingness to pay for goods, services, and conditions,[29] or the "Kaldor–Hicks" criterion, under which one state of affairs is preferred to a second state of affairs if, by moving from the second to the first, the "gainer" from the move *can,* by a lump-sum transfer, compensate the "loser" for his loss of utility and still be better off.[30]

This preliminary analytical maneuver is vulnerable to various objections. First, the wealth-maximization and Kaldor–Hicks criteria, though similar, are not identical, and much may turn on the choice between them. Next, skeptics commonly object to both criteria on the grounds that they ignore the incommensurability of utility functions and bias analysis in favor of the desires of the rich, who, on average, value each dollar less than the poor. Finally, some economists and political theorists who draw inspiration from the rich tradition of utilitarianism contend that both criteria (but especially the first) define social welfare too narrowly and would prefer a more encompassing analytical net. But because these objections are by no means limited to the field of intellectual

29 For more thorough discussion of this standard, see Richard Posner, *Economic Analysis of Law* (3rd ed., Boston: Little, Brown, 1986), pp. 11–15.
30 See Nicholas Kaldor, "Welfare Propositions in Economics and Interpersonal Comparisons of Utility," *Economic Journal,* 69 (1939): 549–52.

property and because they have been well aired elsewhere, I will not pause to explore them here.[31]

Assume that we are comfortable with at least one of these criteria as our beacon. How might it be applied to intellectual-property law? What system of rules, in other words, will most improve social welfare? It turns out that there are at least three general ways in which we might try to answer that question:[32]

1. Incentive Theory. The first and most common of the three approaches is well illustrated by William Nordhaus' classic treatment of patent law.[33] Norhaus was primarily concerned with determining the optimal duration of a patent, but his analysis can be applied more generally. Each increase in the duration or strength of patents, he observed, stimulates an increase in inventive activity. The resultant gains to social welfare include the discounted present value of the consumer surplus and producer surplus associated with the distribution of the intellectual products whose creation is thereby induced. At the same time, however, social welfare is reduced by such things as larger administrative costs and larger deadweight losses associated with the higher prices of intellectual products that would have been created even in the absence of the enhanced incentive. Ideally, patent duration or strength should be increased up to the point where the marginal benefits equal the marginal costs.[34]

2. Optimizing Patterns of Productivity. Many years ago, Harold Demsetz argued that the copyright and patent systems play the important roles of letting

31 For explorations of these difficulties, see, for example, C. Edwin Baker, "Starting Points in Economic Analysis of Law," *Hofstra Law Review,* 8 (1980): 939, at 966–72; Duncan Kennedy, "Cost-Benefit Analysis of Entitlement Problems: A Critique," *Stanford Law Review,* 33 (1981): 387; Ronald Dworkin, "Is Wealth a Value?," *Journal of Legal Studies,* 9 (1980): 191; Louis Kaplow and Steven Shavell, "Principles of Fairness versus Human Welfare: On the Evaluation of Legal Policy," John M. Olin Foundation, Discussion Paper No. 277 (2000).

32 A thorough review of the many varieties of economic analysis may be found in Peter Menell, "Intellectual Property: General Theories," *Encyclopedia of Law & Economics* (forthcoming 2000).

33 William D. Nordhaus, *Invention, Growth, and Welfare: A Theoretical Treatment of Technological Change* (Cambridge: M.I.T. Press, 1969).

34 Among the lessons that Nordhaus derived from his analysis are that "commodities that have lower elasticity of demand have higher optimal [patent] lives" and that "patents for industries having more progressive (or easier) invention should have shorter lives." Ibid., p. 79.

   A wide array of essays in both the patent and copyright fields attempt to refine or apply the general approach developed by Nordhaus. See, for example, Pankaj Tandon, "Optimal Patents with Compulsory Licensing," *Journal of Political Economy,* 90 (1982): 470–86; Richard Gilbert and Carl Shapiro, "Optimal Patent Protection and Breadth," *RAND Journal of Economics,* 21 (1990): 106–12; Paul Klemperer, "How Broad Should the Scope of Patent Protection Be?," *RAND Journal of Economics,* 21 (1990): 113–30; Landes and Posner, "Economic Analysis of Copyright Law"; William Fisher, "Reconstructing the Fair Use Doctrine," at 1698–1744; S. J. Liebowitz, "Copying and Indirect Appropriability: Photocopying of Journals," *Journal of Political Economy,* 93 (1985), 945; A. Samuel Oddi, "Beyond Obviousness: Invention Protection in the Twenty-First Century," *American University Law Review,* 38 (1989): 1097, at 1101–2, 1114–16; and Frederic M. Scherer, *Industrial Market Structure and Economic Performance* (2nd ed., Chicago: Rand McNally, 1980), pp. 439–58. The history of this perspective is traced in Gillian K. Hadfield, "The Economics of Copyright: An Historical Perspective," *Copyright Law Symposium (ASCAP),* 38 (1992): 1–46.

potential producers of intellectual products know what consumers want and thus channelling productive efforts in directions most likely to enhance consumer welfare.[35] In the past decade, a growing group of theorists has argued that recognition of this function justifies expanding the copyright and patent systems. In Paul Goldstein's words:

The logic of property rights dictates their extension into every corner in which people derive enjoyment and value from literary and artistic works. To stop short of these ends would deprive producers of the signals of consumer preference that trigger and direct their investments.[36]

Won't adoption of this strategy impede public dissemination of intellectual products? Not at all, say the proponents of this approach. Sales and licenses will ensure that goods get into the hands of people who want them and are able to pay for them. Only in the rare situations in which transaction costs would prevent such voluntary exchanges should intellectual-property owners be denied absolute control over the uses of their works – either through an outright privilege (such as the fair-use doctrine) or through a compulsory licensing system.[37]

3. Rivalrous Invention. The final approach is related to but distinguishable from the second. Its objective is to eliminate or reduce the tendency of intellectual-property rights to foster duplicative or uncoordinated inventive activity. The foundation for this approach was laid by a group of economists, led by Yoram Barzel, who over the last three decades have explored the ways in which competition among firms complicates the impact of the patent system upon inventive activity.[38] This body of literature has sensitized legal theorists

35 See Harold Demsetz, "Information and Efficiency: Another Viewpoint," *Journal of Law and Economics,* 12 (1969): 1.

36 See Paul Goldstein, *Copyright's Highway* (New York: Hill & Wang, 1994), pp. 178–9.

37 See Wendy J. Gordon, "An Inquiry into the Merits of Copyright: The Challenges of Consistency, Consent, and Encouragement Theory," *Stanford Law Review,* 41 (1989): 1343, at 1439–49; Robert P. Merges, "Are You Making Fun of Me?: Notes on Market Failure and the Parody Defense in Copyright," *American Intellectual Property Law Association Quarterly Journal,* 21 (1993): 305, at 306–7; Netanel, "Copyright and Democratic Civil Society," at 308–10. In this vein, Robert Merges has argued that lawmakers should not be quick to institute compulsory licensing systems. Private institutions such as collective-rights management organizations are likely to be superior to any governmentally mandated regime – and will often spring up spontaneously if lawmakers refuse to intervene.

38 The work of this group of economists is well summarized in Menell, "General Theories," at 7–8. Among the leading works are: Yoram Barzel, "Optimal Timing of Innovations," *Review of Economics and Statistics,* 50 (1968): 348–55; Partha Dasgupta, "Patents, Priority and Imitation or, The Economics of Races and Waiting Games," *Economics Journal* 98 (1988): 66, at 74–8; Partha Dasgupta and Joseph Stiglitz, "Uncertainty, Industrial Structure and the Speed of R & D," *Bell Journal of Economics,* 11 (1980); 1, at 12–13; Drew Fundenberg, Richard Gilbert, Joseph Stiglitz, and Jean Tirole, "Preemption, Leapfrogging, and Competition in Patent Races," *European Economic Review,* 77 (1983): 176–83; Michael L. Katz and Carl Shapiro, "R & D Rivalry with Licensing or Imitation," *American Economic Review,* 77 (1987): 402; Steven A. Lippman and Kevin F. McCardle, "Dropout Behavior in R & D Races with

to three stages in the inventive process at which economic waste can occur. First, the pot of gold represented by a patent on a pioneering, commercially valuable invention may lure an inefficiently large number of persons and organizations into the race to be the first to reach the invention in question. Second, the race to develop a lucrative improvement on an existing technology may generate a similar scramble for similar reasons at the "secondary" level. Finally, firms may try to "invent around" technologies patented by their rivals – that is, to develop functionally equivalent but non-infringing technologies – efforts that, although rational from the standpoint of the individual firm, represent a waste of social resources. Heightened awareness of these risks has prompted legal scholars to search for possible reforms of intellectual property law – or of related doctrines, such as antitrust law – that would mitigate the dissipation of resources at these various sites.[39]

Serious difficulties attend efforts to extract from any one of these approaches answers to concrete doctrinal problems. With respect to incentive theory, the primary problem is lack of the information necessary to apply the analytic. To what extent is the production of specific sorts of intellectual products dependent upon maintenance of copyright or patent protection? With respect to some fields, some commentators have answered: very little. Other monetary or nonmonetary rewards – such as profits attributable to lead time, inventors' opportunities to speculate in markets that will be affected by the revelation of their inventions, the prestige enjoyed by artistic and scientific innovators, academic tenure, and the love of art – would be sufficient to sustain current levels of production even in the absence of intellectual-property protection.[40] Other commentators sharply disagree.[41] The truth is that we don't have enough information to know who is right. Empirical work has suggested that

Learning," *RAND Journal of Economics,* 18 (1987): 287; Glenn C. Loury, "Market Structure and Innovation," *Quarterly Journal of Economics,* 93 (1979): 395; Frederic M. Scherer, "Research and Development Resource Allocation Under Rivalry," *Quarterly Journal of Economics,* 81 (1967): 359, at 364–6; Pankaj Tandon, "Rivalry and the Excessive Allocation of Resources to Research," *Bell Journal of Economics,* 14 (1983): 152; Brian D. Wright, "The Resource Allocation Problem in R & D," in *The Economics of R & D Policy,* 41, 50 (George S. Tolley, James H. Hodge & James F. Oehmke eds., 1985).

39 See Louis Kaplow, "The Patent–Antitrust Intersection: A Reappraisal," *Harvard Law Review,* 97 (1984): 1813–92; Edmund Kitch, "The Nature and Function of the Patent System," *Journal of Law and Economics,* 20 (1977): 265; idem, "Patents, Prospects, and Economic Surplus: A Reply," *Journal of Law and Economics,* 23 (1980): 205; Mark F. Grady & J. I. Alexander, "Patent Law and Rent Dissipation," *Virginia Law Review,* 78 (1992): 305; Robert Merges and Richard Nelson, "On the Complex Economics of Patent Scope," *Columbia Law Review,* 90 (1990): 839–916; Mark Lemley, "The Economics of Improvement in Intellectual Property Law," *Texas Law Review,* 75 (1997): 993–1084.

40 See, for example, Joan Robinson, *The Economics of Imperfect Competition* (London: Macmillan, 1933); Arnold Plant, "The Economic Aspects of Copyright in Books," in *Economica (n.s.)* (1934): 30–51; Jack Hirshleifer, "The Private and Social Value of Information and the Reward to Inventive Activity," *American Economic Review,* 63 (1973): 31–51; Stephen Breyer, "The Uneasy Case for Copyright," *Harvard Law Review,* 87 (1970): 281–351.

41 See, for example, Barry Tyerman, "The Economic Rationale for Copyright Protection for Published Books: A Reply to Professor Breyer," *UCLA Law Review,* 18 (1971): 1100.

patent law has been more important in stimulating innovation in certain industries (e.g., pharmaceuticals and chemicals) than in others, but has failed to answer the ultimate question of whether the stimulus to innovation is worth its costs.[42] With respect to forms of intellectual-property protection other than patents, we know even less.

Even if we were able to surmount this enormous hurdle – and concluded that society would be better off, on balance, by supplying authors and inventors some sort of special reward – major sources of uncertainty would remain. Is an intellectual-property system the best way of providing that reward or might it be better, as Steven Shavell and Tanguy van Ypersele have recently suggested, for a government agency to estimate the social value of each innovation and pay the innovators that sum out of tax revenues?[43] If the former, how far should creators' entitlements extend? Should they include the right to prepare "derivative works"? To block "experimental uses" of their technologies? To suppress their inventions? Some scholars continue to seek the data necessary to begin to answer questions of this sort. Most have given up the game, despairing of acquiring the kinds of information one would need.[44] Almost everyone agrees that such information is not yet at our disposal. Until it is, lawmakers will gain little guidance from the first variant of the utilitarian approach.

Theorists who seek to optimize patterns of productivity confront less severe informational problems. To be sure, they are obliged to make difficult judgments – often with thin data – on such questions as whether the failure of creators to license certain uses of their works results from the fact that such

42 The relevant literature includes John Kay, "The Economics of Intellectual Property Rights," *International Review of Law & Economics,* 13 (1993): 337, at 344–6; R. C. Levin, A. K. Klevorick, R. R. Nelson, and S. G. Winter, "Appropriating the Returns from Industrial Research and Development," *Brookings Papers Economic Activity* (1987): 783–831; Edwin Mansfield, "Patents and Innovation: An Empirical Study," *Management Science,* 32 (1986): 173–81; George L. Priest, "What Economists Can Tell Lawyers About Intellectual Property," *Research in Law and Economics,* Vol. 8 (John Palmer, ed., 1986), pp. 19, 21; Antoon A. Quaedvlieg, "The Economic Analysis of Intellectual Property Law," in Willem F. Korthals Altes et al., eds., *Information Law Towards the 21st Century* (Boston: Kluwer Law and Taxation Publishers, 1992), pp. 379, 393; D. Schwartzmann, *Innovation in the Pharmaceutical Industry* (Baltimore: Johns Hopkins University Press, 1976); C. Taylor and Z. Silberston, *The Economic Impact of the Patent System* (London: Cambridge University Press, 1973).

43 More specifically, Shavell and Ypersele contend that a regime in which, after an invention had been commercialized, the government used sales data and surveys to assess its social value and then periodically paid the inventor accordingly might be better, despite the familiar difficulties associated with governmental estimates of this sort, than a patent regime – and that a system in which each inventor had the option of either obtaining a traditional patent or collecting the government's reward would certainly be better than a simple patent system. See "Rewards versus Intellectual Property Rights," *National Bureau of Economic Research,* Working Paper 6956 (February 1999).

44 See, for example, Robert M. Hurt and Robert M. Schuchman, "The Economic Rationale of Copyright," *American Economic Review,* 56 (1966): 425–6; Jessica Litman, "The Public Domain," *Emory Law Journal,* 34 (1990): 997; Lloyd L. Weinreb, "Copyright for Functional Expression," at 1232–6; John Shepard Wiley, Jr., "Bonito Boats: Uninformed but Mandatory Innovation Policy," *Supreme Court Review* (1989), 283.

uses are worth less to consumers than preventing them is worth to creators (in which case, the absence of licenses is socially desirable) or from excessively high transaction costs (in which case, the creators should be compelled to grant licenses – for free or for a governmentally determined fee). But inquiries of this sort are not as frighteningly complex as those that confront incentive theorists. However, scholars and lawmakers who take this road confront an additional problem: What is the set of productive activities the incentives for which we are trying to adjust? For the reasons sketched above, if we confine our attention to intellectual products, the optimal legal doctrine may be one that confers upon creators a very generous set of entitlements. Only thereby will potential producers be provided refined signals concerning how consumers wish to make use of which sorts of intellectual products. However, as Glynn Lunney has argued, if we expand our frame of reference, that solution proves highly problematic.[45] In virtually no field of economic activity are innovators empowered to collect the full social value of their innovations. The elementary schoolteacher who develops a new technique for teaching mathematics, the civil-rights activist who discovers a way to reduce racial tension, the physicist who finds a way to integrate our understandings of gravity and quantum mechanics – all of these confer on society benefits that vastly exceed the innovators' incomes. Enlarging the entitlements of intellectual-property owners thus might refine the signals sent to the creators of different sorts of fiction, movies, and software concerning consumers' preferences, but would lead to even more serious *over*investment in intellectual products as opposed to such things as education, community activism, and primary research. Unfortunately, Lunney's proposed response to this problem – reducing copyright protection until the creators of entertainment receive rewards no greater than the returns available to innovators in other fields – would sacrifice most of the economic benefits highlighted by Demsetz and Goldstein. The optimal solution is thus far from clear.

Theorists bent on avoiding redundant inventive activity have problems of their own. The most serious difficulty arises from the fact that reducing social waste at one stage of the inventive process commonly increases it at another. Thus, for example, in the leading article in this subfield, Edmund Kitch highlighted the advantages of granting to the developer of a pioneering invention an expansive set of entitlements, thereby enabling him or her to coordinate research and development dedicated to improving the invention, thus reducing the dissipation of rents at the secondary level.[46] However, as Robert Merges argues, granting generous patents on pioneering inventions will exacerbate rent

---

45 See Glynn Lunney, Jr., "Reexamining Copyright's Incentives-Access Paradigm," *Vanderbilt Law Review,* 49 (1996): 483.
46 See Kitch, "The Nature and Function of the Patent System." See also Suzanne Scotchmer, "Protecting Early Innovators: Should Second-Generation Products Be Patentable?," *RAND Journal of Economics,* 27 (1996): 322–31.

dissipation at the primary level. An even greater – and more socially wasteful – number of persons or firms will now race to be the first to develop pioneering patents. Mark Grady and Jay Alexander have developed an ingenious theory for determining which of these dangers is more salient in particular cases.[47] Primary inventions that have only modest social value but that "signal" a large potential for improvement are likely to draw potential improvers like flies. To cut down on the swarms, the developer of the primary invention should be granted a broad patent of the sort commended by Kitch. Primary inventions with large social value but minimal "signalling" power should, instead, be given only narrow patents – to reduce the risk of duplicative activity at the primary level. Finally, and most surprisingly, socially valuable inventions so well conceived they cannot be improved upon should be given no patents whatsoever, thereby discouraging rent dissipation at both levels. This typology, though intriguing, has many defects, both practical and theoretical. To begin with, it is difficult to determine in advance which inventions "signal" possibilities for improvement. Next, what are we to do with cases in which the invention at issue is of a type that both is highly socially valuable (thus creating a danger of waste at the primary level) and signals a large number of improvements (thus creating a danger of waste at the secondary level)? Finally, Robert Merges and Richard Nelson point out that efforts, through broad patent grants, to mitigate rent dissipation at the secondary level may have serious economic side effects. Instead of enabling the original inventor to coordinate efficiently the exploitation of the technology, it may lead to "satisficing" behavior[48] and an inefficiently narrow focus on improvements related to the primary inventor's principal line of business.[49] In short, a combination of limited information and theoretical tensions render this third approach just as indeterminate in practice as the other two.[50]

Even if the difficulties specific to each of the three economic approaches could be resolved, an even more formidable problem would remain: there exists no general theory that integrates the three lines of inquiry. How should the law be adjusted in order simultaneously (i) to balance optimally incentives for creativity and concomitant efficiency losses, (ii) to send potential producers

---

47 Grady and Alexander, "Patent Law and Rent Dissipation."
48 First developed by Herbert A. Simon, the concept of "satisficing" has come to be associated with behavior under which a decision maker ceases activity after meeting a minimum requirement – such as the laziness displayed by lions when prey is abundant. See David Ward et al., "The Role of Satisficing in Foraging Theory," *Oikos,* 63:2 (1992): 312–17.
49 Merges and Nelson, "Complex Economics of Patent Scope."
50 For debate on these issues, see Donald G. McFetridge and Douglas A. Smith, "Patents, Prospects, and Economic Surplus: A Comment," *Journal of Law & Economics,* 23 (1980): 197; A. Samuel Oddi, "Un-Unified Economic Theories of Patents – The Not-Quite-Holy Grail," *Notre Dame Law Review,* 71 (1996): 267, at 283 (disagreeing with Merges and Nelson); Donald L. Martin, "Reducing Anticipated Rewards from Innovation Through Patents: Or Less is More," *Virginia Law Review,* 78 (1992): 351, at 356; Robert P. Merges, "Rent Control in the Patent District: Observations on the Grady–Alexander Thesis," *Virginia Law Review,* 78 (1992): 359, at 376–7.

of all kinds of goods accurate signals concerning what consumers want, and (iii) to minimize rent dissipation? To date, no theorist has even attempted to answer this overarching question. Until that challenge is successfully met, the power of the utilitarian approach to provide guidance to lawmakers will be sharply limited.[51]

B.

Similar difficulties afflict efforts to apply labor theory to intellectual property. The problems begin at the threshold. As was true of utilitarianism, it is not altogether clear that the labor theory supports *any* sort of intellectual-property law. The source of the difficulty is ambiguity in Locke's original rationale for property rights – from which this entire theory springs. Why exactly should labor upon a resource held "in common" entitle the laborer to a property right in the resource itself? Scattered in Chapter 5 of the *Second Treatise* can be found six related but distinguishable answers to that question.

(1) "Natural reason" tells us that men have "a right to their Preservation," and the only practicable way in which they can sustain themselves is by individually "appropriating" materials necessary to provide them food and shelter.[52]

(2) Religious obligation reinforces the foregoing proposition. God did not merely give the Earth to man in common, but "commanded" him to "subdue" it – that is, "improve it for the benefit of Life" – which man can do only by both labouring upon it and appropriating the fruits of that labor.[53]

(3) Intuitions regarding self-ownership point in the same direction. Each person plainly has "a Property in his own Person," including the "Labour of his Body, and the Work of his Hands." It seems only natural that whatever he mixes that Labour with should belong to him as well.[54]

(4) The moral value of work reinforces the foregoing insight. God gave the World to "the Industrious and Rational, . . . not to the Fancy or Covetousness of the Quarrelsom and Contentious." It is thus fitting that the former acquire, through their labour, title to that which they labor upon.[55]

(5) A sense of proportionality and fairness also figures in the inquiry. Most of the value of things useful to men derives not from the value of the raw materials from which they are made, but from the labour expended on them. It is thus not "so Strange" that, when determining whether ownership should be assigned to the worker or the community, the individual "Property of labour should be able to over-balance the Community of Land."[56]

(6) Finally, Locke relies throughout the chapter on an imagery of productive transformation. By labouring upon unclaimed land or other resources, the worker changes

51 See Oddi, "Un-Unified Economic Theories of Patents."
52 *Two Treatises of Government,* Sections 25–6.
53 Ibid., Sections 32, 35.
54 Ibid., Sections 27, 44.
55 Ibid., Section 34.
56 Ibid., Sections 38, 40–43.

them from wild to domestic, from raw to cultivated, from chaotic to ordered, from pointless to purposeful. The self-evident desirability of that transformation supports a reward for the worker.[57]

Whether Locke's theory provides support for *intellectual* property depends upon which of these various rationales one regards as primary. If, for example, one sees arguments 4 and 5 as the crux of the matter, then the *Second Treatise* would seem to provide strong support for most sorts of intellectual property. After all, most authors and inventors work hard, and their intellectual labor typically is a far more important contributor to the total value of their creations than the raw materials they have employed. On the other hand, if arguments 1 and 2 are stressed, the case for intellectual-property rights is far weaker. As Seana Shiffrin shows, crucial to these two arguments is the proposition that certain articles essential to life, such as food, cannot be enjoyed in common; "their use must, of necessity, be exclusive."[58] Yet, intellectual products plainly are not like that. Not only is access to them typically not necessary for survival, but they can be used by an infinite number of persons, simultaneously or in sequence, without being used up.

Whether Locke's theory provides support for *any* intellectual-property rights is thus uncertain. It depends on which aspects of Locke's original theory are dominant. Locke did not say, and no interpreter of his work has yet provided us a convincing way of ascertaining his original intent.[59] Assume, however, that we somehow surmount the barricade identified by Shiffrin and conclude that intellectual labor does give rise to a natural entitlement to its fruits – an entitlement that the state must recognize and enforce. Other difficulties await us.

Perhaps the most formidable is the question: What, for these purposes, counts as "intellectual labor"? There are at least four plausible candidates: (1) time and effort (hours spent in front of the computer or in the lab); (2) activity in which one would rather not engage (hours spent in the studio when one would rather be sailing); (3) activity that results in social benefits (work on socially valuable inventions); and (4) creative activity (the production of new ideas). The first of the four may be closest to Locke's original intent, but he was not focusing on *intellectual* labor. Justin Hughes has shown that serious arguments can be made in support of the both the second and the third. And Lawrence Becker reminds us how important the fourth is to our images of deserving authors and inventors.[60] No grounds on which we might select one or another are readily apparent.

---

57 See Ryan, *Property and Political Theory*, at 22 ff.
58 See Seana Shiffrin, "Lockean Arguments for Private Intellectual Property," in this volume.
59 See Tom Palmer, "Are Patents and Copyrights Morally Justified?," *Harvard Journal of Law and Public Policy*, 13 (1990): 817–65, at 832.
60 Lawrence Becker, "Deserving to Own Intellectual Property," *Chicago-Kent Law Review*, 68 (1993): 609.

Unfortunately, our choice among these four options will often make a big difference. The third, for instance, suggests that we should insist, before issuing a patent or other intellectual-property right, that the discovery in question satisfy a meaningful "utility" requirement; the other three would not. The second would counsel against conferring legal rights on artists who love their work; the other three point in the opposite direction. The fourth would suggest that we add to copyright law a requirement analogous to the patent doctrine of "nonobviousness"; the others would not. In short, a lawmaker's inability to choose among the four will often be disabling.

Similar troubles arise when one tries to apply Locke's conception of "the commons" to the field of intellectual property. What exactly are the raw materials, owned by the community as a whole, with which individual workers mix their labor in order to produce intellectual products? At least seven possibilities come to mind:

a. the universe of "facts";[61]
b. languages — the vocabularies and grammars we use to communicate and from which we fashion novel intellectual products;
c. our cultural heritage — the set of artifacts (novels, paintings, musical compositions, movies, etc.) that we "share" and that gives our culture meaning and coherence;
d. the set of ideas currently apprehended by at least one person but not owned by anyone;
e. the set of ideas currently apprehended by at least one person;
f. the set of all "reachable" ideas — that is, all ideas that lie within the grasp of people today;
g. the set of all "possible ideas" — that is, all ideas that someone might think of.[62]

When applying the Lockean argument to intellectual property, it will often make a difference which of these options one selects. For example, option (c) is difficult to reconcile with contemporary copyright and trademark law, under which much of our cultural heritage — Mickey Mouse, "Gone with the Wind," the shape of a Coke bottle — is owned, not by the community, but by individual persons or organizations; options (a) and (b) present no such difficulty. Patent law is consistent with option (d) but not (e) — insofar as it permits ownership of many extant "ideas." Copyright law, which (at least formally) does not allow

---

61 The first of these options — though common in the discourse of copyright law — is vulnerable to criticism as naively Platonist. See, for example, Jessica Litman, "The Public Domain," *Emory Law Journal,* 39 (1990): 965, at 996; Jane Ginsburg, "Sabotaging and Reconstructing History," *Bulletin of the Copyright Society,* 29 (1982): 647, at 658.
62 Plainly these options are not mutually exclusive. For example, one intuitively plausible interpretation of the "the commons" would be a + b + c. Some of the options nest. For example, d is a subset of e, which is a subset of f, which is a subset of g.

the ownership of any "ideas" (only distinctive ways of "expressing" them) meshes comfortably with either (d) or (e). As Justin Hughes has shown, the Lockean "sufficiency" proviso can be satisfied fairly easily if one chooses option (f) – on the theory that the deployment of most ideas enables other people to "reach" an even larger set of ideas and, thus, enlarges rather than subtracts from the commons. By contrast, if one adopts option (g) – as both Wendy Gordon and Robert Nozick appear to do – the sufficiency proviso becomes a good deal more constraining (a topic to which we will return in a minute). Which is the correct approach? Who knows?[63]

Suppose we arbitrarily select one interpretation – say, option (d). Trying to fit it into the Lockean analytic quickly gives rise to three additional, related problems. First, the act of mixing labor with a piece of the commons does not, under any of the various extant intellectual-property regimes, work the way Locke supposed real-property law works. When one mixes one's physical labor with a plot of virgin land, one should acquire, Locke suggested, a natural right not merely to the crops one produces but to the land itself. By contrast, when one mixes one's intellectual labor with an existing idea, one acquires a property right only to the "original" or "novel" material one has generated, not to the idea with which one began. Second, the set of entitlements one acquires does not have the kind of exclusivity Locke apparently attributed to real-property rights.[64] For example, the issuance of a patent on a better mousetrap prevents others from making that mousetrap, but not from reading the patent and using the information contained therein to make an even better mousetrap. The issuance of a copyright on a novel prevents others from copying it but not from reading it, discussing it, parodying it, and so on. Finally, Locke suggested that the property rights one acquires through labor upon resources held in common do and should last forever – that is, are alienable, devisable, and inheritable indefinitely.[65] Most intellectual-property rights, by contrast, sooner or later expire.

One might respond that none of these observations indicates that the application of labor-desert theory to intellectual property is indeterminate. They indicate merely that intellectual-property law would have to be radically revised to conform to the Lockean scheme. Perhaps. But the scale of the necessary revision is daunting. Is it plausible – on Lockean or any other premises – that by working to express in distinctive form the idea that infidelity usually

---

63 For discussions of alternative understandings of "the commons," see Yen, "Restoring the Natural Law"; Wendy Gordon, " A Property Right in Self-Expression: Equality and Individualism in the Natural Law of Intellectual Property," *Yale Law Journal,* 102 (1993): 1533–1609; Hughes, "Philosophy of Intellectual Property"; Shiffrin, "Lockean Arguments."

64 Closely examined, real-property rights also lack the exclusivity Locke attributed to them, but the difficulty is more apparent in the case of property in ideas. See William Fisher, "Property and Contract on the Internet," *Chicago-Kent Law Review,* 73 (1998) 1203, at 1207.

65 Seana Shiffrin points out, however, that some evidence that Locke understood property rights to be more temporally limited may be found in *Two Treatises of Government, First Treatise,* Secs. 88–9.

corrodes a marriage, one would acquire ownership of the idea itself? Is it plausible that, by registering the trademark "Nike," one could prevent others from using it in any way – including reproducing it in an essay on intellectual property? If not, then what set of more limited entitlements would satisfy the obligation of the state to "determine" and "settle" natural property rights? Locke's argument contains few clues.

We have not exhausted, unfortunately, the troubles associated with the "sufficiency" proviso. Some of the commentators who have sought to harness Locke's argument to intellectual property have seen little difficulty in the requirement that a laborer leave "as much and as good" for others. Justin Hughes, for example, emphasizes the myriad ways in which the expansion of the set of available ideas stimulated by intellectual property improves the lot of everyone. Robert Nozick, as suggested above, sees the sufficiency proviso as somewhat more constraining, but has identified to his satisfaction a way of structuring patent law that avoids violating it. Wendy Gordon, by contrast, construes the proviso as a much more serious limitation on the scope of intellectual-property rights. Conferring monopoly privileges on the creators of intellectual products, she claims, can hurt more than help the public. Take the word "Olympics." If the term did not exist, we would have contrived other ways to communicate the notion of periodic amateur international sports competitions untainted by ideology or warfare. But because the word does exist, we have become dependent on it. No other word or collection of words quite captures the idea. Consequently, if we now prohibit "unauthorized" uses of the word – for example, in connection with the "Gay Olympics" or on a t-shirt highlighting the hypocritical way in which the ideal has been applied in recent years – we have left the public worse off than if the word never existed. Fidelity to the Lockean proviso (and to a more general "no-harm" principle that runs through Locke's work), Gordon insists, requires that we withhold property rights in situations such as these. Once again, a wide range of interpretations of an important component of Locke's theory is available, and no one member of the set seems plainly superior to the others.[66]

We come, finally, to the well-known problem of proportionality. Nozick asks: If I pour my can of tomato juice into the ocean, do I own the ocean? Analogous questions abound in the field of intellectual property. If I invent a drug that prevents impotence, do I deserve to collect for twenty years the extraordinary amount of money that men throughout the world would pay for access to the drug? If I write a novel about a war between two space empires, may I legitimately demand compensation from people who wish to prepare motion-picture adaptations, write sequels, manufacture dolls based on my

---

66 For exploration of these issues, see Gordon, "Property Right in Self-Expression"; Edwin C. Hettinger, "Justifying Intellectual Property," *Philosophy and Public Affairs*, 18 (1989), 31–52; Sterk, "Rhetoric and Reality"; Weinreb, "Copyright in Functional Expression," at 1218.

characters, or produce t-shirts emblazoned with bits of my dialogue? How far, in short, do my rights go? Locke gives us little guidance.[67]

C.

Private property rights, argue contemporary personality theorists, should be recognized when and only when they would promote human flourishing by protecting or fostering fundamental human needs or interests. The first step in the application of this perspective to intellectual property is identification of the specific needs or interests one wishes to promote. As Jeremy Waldron has argued, a wide variety of interests might be deemed fundamental, each of which arguably could be advanced by a system of property rights. Here are some:

1. *Peace of Mind.* An exclusive right to determine how certain resources shall be used might be thought essential to avoid moral exhaustion – the sense of guilt that arises from awareness that one's actions, one's use of the commons, disadvantages countless other people.[68]
2. *Privacy.* Property rights may be necessary to provide persons "refuge[s] from the general society of mankind" – places where they can either be alone or enjoy intimacy with others.[69]
3. *Self-Reliance.* An exclusive right to control certain resources may be thought necessary to enable persons to become independent, self-directing.[70]
4. *Self-Realization as a Social Being.* The freedom to own and thus trade things may be necessary to enable persons to help shape their social environments and establish their places in communities.[71]
5. *Self-Realization as an Individual.* Ownership of property may be necessary to enable a person to assert his or her will and to be recognized as a free agent by others.[72]
6. *Security and Leisure.* Control over a certain amount of resources may be necessary to free persons from obsession with obtaining the means of

---

67 See Hughes, "Philosophy of Intellectual Property"; Becker, "Deserving Intellectual Property." Cf. James W. Child, "The Moral Foundations of Intangible Property," *The Monist* (1990); Wendy Gordon, "Property Right in Self-Expression."
68 See Waldron, *The Right to Private Property,* at 295; cf. Charles Fried, *Right and Wrong* (Cambridge, Mass.: Harvard University Press, 1978), p. 1.
69 See Waldron, *The Right to Private Property,* at 296.
70 See ibid., at 300–01; cf. Abraham Lincoln, "Address to the Wisconsin State Fair, 1859," in Richard N. Current, ed., *The Political Thought of Abraham Lincoln* (Indianapolis: Bobbs-Merrill, 1967), p. 134.
71 See Waldron, *The Right to Private Property.* pp. 296–7; Carol Rose, *Property and Persuasion* (Boulder, Colo.: Westview Press, 1994), pp. 146–7.
72 See Waldron, *The Right to Private Property,* pp. 302–3; Margaret Jane Radin, *Reinterpreting Property.*

survival, the "impulsion of desire," and thus to enable them to attend to higher pursuits.[73]

7. *Responsibility.* Virtues like prudence, self-direction, and foresight may be cultivated by the opportunity and obligation to manage one's own resources.[74]

8. *Identity.* Selfhood may be thought to depend upon the ability to project a continuing life plan into the future, which in turn is fostered by connection to and responsibility for property.[75]

9. *Citizenship.* Ownership of a certain amount of resources might be thought necessary to put a person in an economic and psychological position to participate effectively in the polity.[76]

10. *Benevolence.* Property rights may be thought essential to enable a person to express ideas of what is beautiful or to enact benevolent wishes.[77]

Six of these ten arguments – 1, 3, 4, 6, 7, 9 – provide support for some system of intellectual-property rights but give us little guidance in deciding *which* entitlements to recognize. To the extent that intellectual-property rights have economic value and may be bought and sold, gained and lost, they may contribute to their owners' abilities to avoid guilt, become autonomous, engage in independent political action, etc. But those values could be promoted equally well by providing persons rights to land or shares in private corporations. Consequently, a lawmaker persuaded by one of these claims would be inspired to construct some system of private ownership of resources, but would have little help in determining which resources to privatize and which to leave to the public.

Personhood-based guidelines for crafting intellectual-property rights thus must be found, if anywhere, in some combination of themes 2, 5, 8, and 10: the interests of privacy, individual self-realization, identity, and benevolence. But the writers who have sought to extract from those sources answers to specific questions have come to widely divergent conclusions. Here are some examples:

When an author has revealed her work to the world, does it nevertheless continue to fall within the zone of her "personhood" – so that she may legitimately claim a right to restrict its further communication? Neil Netanel, relying on an exploration of the ideal of "autonomy," thinks yes. Lloyd Weinreb, reasoning that, "once the individual has

73 See Waldron, *Right to Private Property,* pp. 304–6; cf. George Fitzhugh, *Cannibals All!* (1857), C. Vann Woodward, ed. (Cambridge, Mass.: Harvard University Press, 1960) (defending the ownership of slaves on similar grounds).
74 See Waldron, *Right to Private Property,* pp. 308–10; Thomas Hill Green, *Lectures on the Principles of Political Obligation* (Ann Arbor: Univ. of Michigan Press, 1967), Lecture N.
75 See Radin, *Reinterpreting Property.*
76 See Hannah Arendt, *On Revolution* (New York: Viking Press, 1965); Alexander, *Commodity and Propriety,* pp. 43–71.
77 See Green, *Lectures on Political Obligation,* at Sec. 220.

communicated her expression publicly, it takes on a 'life of its own' and . . . its further communication does not involve her autonomous self," thinks no.[78]

Assume the answer to the previous question is yes. May the author *alienate* his right to control the copying of his work? Kant, reasoning that "an author's interest in deciding how and when to speak [is] an inalienable part of his personality," thought no. Hegel, reasoning that expressions of mental aptitudes (as opposed to the aptitudes themselves) were "external to the author and therefore freely alienable," thought yes.[79]

Should an artist's investment of his self in a work of visual art – say, a painting or sculpture – prevent others from imitating his creation? Hegel thought not – on the ground that the copy would be "essentially a product of the copyist's own mental and technical ability." Justin Hughes seems to take the opposite position.[80]

Is the protection of trade secrets necessary to protect privacy interests? Edwin Hettinger thinks no – on the ground that most trade secrets are owned by corporations, which do not have the "personal features privacy is intended to protect." Lynn Sharp Paine disagrees. She argues that the right to privacy includes the freedom to reveal information to a limited circle of friends or associates without fear that it will be exposed to the world – a freedom that trade-secret law shields.[81]

Is a celebrity's persona a sufficiently important repository of selfhood that other persons ought not be permitted to exploit that persona commercially without permission? Justin Hughes suggests yes, reasoning that "[a]s long as an individual identifies with his personal image, he will have a personality stake in that image." Michael Madow, insisting that the "creative (and autonomous) role of the media and the audience in the meaning-making process" are at least as important as the "personality" of the celebrity, sharply disagrees.[82]

Two related problems underlie these and many other disagreements. First, the conceptions of the self – the images of "personhood" that, through adjustments of intellectual-property doctrine, we are trying to nurture or protect – that underlie most avatars of personality theory are too abstract and thin to provide answers to many specific questions. Either a more fully articulated

---

78 Neil Netanel, "Copyright Alienability Restrictions and the Enhancement of Author Autonomy: A Normative Evaluation," *Rutgers Law Review,* 24 (1993): 347; Weinreb, "Copyright for Functional Expression," at 1221. Good illustrations of both positions may be found in the current debate over the legitimacy of Gary Larson's effort to persuade his fans not to post copies of his cartoons on their websites. For a sample of the debate, see http://stud.unisg.ch/rportmann/gary.html.
79 See Cotter, "Pragmatism and the *Droit Moral,*" at 8–9. For other treatments of the divergence of Kant and Hegel, see Palmer, "Are Patents Morally Justified?," at 837–41; Sterk, "Rhetoric and Reality in Copyright Law," at 1243.
80 Hughes, "Philosophy of Intellectual Property," at 338, 340.
81 Hettinger, "Justifying Intellectual Property"; Paine, "Trade Secrets and the Justification of Intellectual Property," *Philosophy & Public Affairs,* 20 (1991): 247, at 251–3.
82 Hughes, "Philosophy of Intellectual Property," at 340–41; Madow, "Private Ownership of Public Image," at 182–97 & n. 338.

vision of human nature (that would forthrightly address such grand questions as the importance of creativity to the soul) or a conception of personhood tied more tightly to a particular culture and time seems necessary if we are to provide lawmakers guidance on the kinds of issue that beset them.

Second, no personality theorist has yet dealt adequately with what Margaret Radin once called the problem of fetishism.[83] Which of the many tastes exhibited by current members of American culture should be indulged, and which should not? The quest for individuality? Nationalism? Nostalgia for a real or imagined ethnic or racial identity? The hope that audiences will treat one's creations with respect? The hunger for fifteen minutes (or more) of fame? Yearnings or orientations of all of these sorts are implicated by intellectual-property disputes. Deciding which merit our deference is essential to determining how those disputes should be resolved.

D.

The limitations of the guidance provided by general theories of intellectual property is perhaps easiest to see with respect to the last of the four approaches. Lawmakers who try to harness social-planning theory must make difficult choices at two levels. The first and most obvious involves formulating a vision of a just and attractive culture. What sort of society should we try, through adjustments of copyright, patent, and trademark law, to promote? The possibilities are endless.

The range of options is illustrated by my own effort in a recent essay to bring social-planning theory to bear on the question of the proper shape of intellectual-property law on the Internet. I offered, as the foundation for that analysis, a sketch of an attractive intellectual culture. A condensed version of that sketch follows:

Consumer Welfare. Other things being equal, a society whose members are happy is better than one whose members are, by their own lights, less happy. Applied to the field of intellectual property, this guideline urges us to select a combination of rules that will maximize consumer welfare by optimally balancing incentives for creativity with incentives for dissemination and use. That goal must, however, be tempered by other aspirations.

A Cornucopia of Information and Ideas. An attractive culture would be one in which citizens had access to a wide array of information, ideas, and forms of entertainment. Variety in this sense helps make life stimulating and enlivening. Access to a broad range of intellectual products is also crucial to widespread attainment of two related conditions central to most conceptions of the good life—namely, self-determination and self-expression—both by providing persons the materials crucial to self-construction, and by fostering a general condition of cultural diversity, which enables and compels individuals to shape themselves.

83 See Margaret Jane Radin, "Property and Personhood," *Stanford Law Review,* 34 (1982): 957, at 970.

A Rich Artistic Tradition. The more complex and resonant the shared language of a culture, the more opportunities it affords its members for creativity and subtlety in communication and thought. For reasons best explored by Ronald Dworkin, recognition of that fact points toward governmental polices designed to make available to the public "a rich stock of illustrative and comparative collections of art" and, more generally, to foster "a tradition of [artistic] innovation."

Distributive Justice. To the greatest extent practicable, all persons should have access to the informational and artistic resources described above.

Semiotic Democracy. In an attractive society, all persons would be able to participate in the process of making cultural meaning. Instead of being merely passive consumers of images and artifacts produced by others, they would help shape the world of ideas and symbols in which they live.

Sociability. An attractive society is one rich in "communities of memory." Persons' capacity to construct rewarding lives will be enhanced if they have access to a variety of "constitutive" groups – in "real" space and in "virtual" space.

Respect. Appreciation of the extent to which self-expression is often a form of self-creation should make people respectful of others' work.[84]

The controversial character of a vision of this sort is immediately apparent. Many of its components – for example, the criterion of distributive justice – have for centuries been the subjects of furious debate among political philosophers.[85] It is plainly implausible that theorists of intellectual-property could resolve controversies of this scale in the course of analyses of copyright or patent doctrine.

Unfortunately, the choice of a particular social vision by no means exhausts the difficulties associated with this fourth approach. Equally serious problems commonly arise when one tries to apply such a vision to a specific doctrinal problem. Take the problem of parody, for example. Intellectual products that make fun of other intellectual products are becoming increasingly common: "Don't leave home without it" on a condom container crafted to resemble an American Express card. Comic books depicting Mickey Mouse and Donald Duck participating in a drug-infested, promiscuous culture. Altered photographs of John Wayne suggesting that he was homosexual, embellished with the caption, "It's a bitch to be butch." Trademarks that allude humorously to

---

84 See Fisher, "Property and Contract on the Internet."
85 On distributive justice, see, for example, Aristotle, *Nicomachean Ethics,* Book V, Ch. 2; Bruce Ackerman, *Social Justice in the Liberal State* (New Haven: Yale University Press, 1980); Charles Fried, "Distributive Justice," *Social Philosophy & Policy,* 1 (1983): 45; John Rawls, *A Theory of Justice* (Cambridge, Mass.: Harvard University Press, 1971); Michael Sandel, *Liberalism and the Limits of Justice* (Cambridge: Cambridge University Press, 1982).

other trademarks ("Dom Popignon" popcorn; "Lardache" bluejeans). Should these be permitted? The particular social vision sketched above points in inconsistent directions. On one hand, permitting, even encouraging, parody of this sort would seem to facilitate semiotic democracy. Parody erodes the control over the meanings of cultural artifacts exerted by powerful institutions and expands opportunities for creativity by others. On the other hand, parodies (especially if effective) may cut seriously into the legitimate personhood interests of the artists who originally fashioned the parodied artifacts. Which of these two concerns should predominate must be determined by reflection on the cultural context and significance of individual cases. The social vision on its own does not provide us much guidance.

IV. The Value of Theory

The indeterminacy of the personality and social-planning perspectives has long been recognized. That recognition is reflected, for example, in the common accusation that those perspectives are "illiberal" insofar as they seek to regulate persons' behavior on the basis of necessarily controversial "theories of the good" – the sort of thing that governments ought not do.[86] A closely related, equally common charge is that the social-planning and personhood perspectives are "paternalistic" insofar as they curtail persons' freedom on the basis of conceptions of what is "good for them" with which they themselves may not agree.[87] By contrast, the utilitarian and labor-desert approaches, especially the former, have enjoyed an aura of neutrality, objectivity, and above all determinacy. That aura helps to explain why courts, when presented with difficult problems of statutory interpretation, have sought guidance most often from economic arguments and least often from social-planning arguments. One of the burdens of this essay has been to disrupt that pattern – to show that the prescriptive powers of all four arguments are sharply limited.

That conclusion, however, does not imply that the theories have no practical use.[88] In two respects, I suggest, they retain considerable value. First, while they have failed to make good on their promises to provide comprehensive prescriptions concerning the ideal shape of intellectual-property law, they can help identify nonobvious attractive resolutions of particular problems. Second, they can foster valuable conversations among the various participants in the lawmaking process.

A good example of the first of these uses of theory involves the recent history of the "right of publicity" – the entitlement of celebrities to prevent (or

---

86 See, for example, Ronald Dworkin, "Liberalism," in *A Matter of Principle* (Cambridge, Mass.: Harvard University Press, 1985), pp. 181–204.
87 For exploration of this argument, see Fisher, "Fair Use Doctrine," at 1762–66.
88 Cf. Weinreb, "Copyright for Functional Expression," at 1252–4 (suggesting that courts should cease trying to resolve complex copyright questions through efforts to ascertain and then apply underlying policies and should instead rely upon the traditional common-law interpretive techniques of "analogy and metaphor").

demand compensation for) commercial depictions or imitations of their faces, voices, distinctive turns of phrase, characteristic poses, and so on. Until quite recently, this right was widely thought by American courts and commentators to be "commonsensical." For example, the author of the principal treatise on the subject describes the right of publicity as "a self-evident legal right, needing little intellectual rationalization to justify its existence."[89] Sentiments of this sort prompted one state after another to recognize the entitlement – either through legislation or through common-law decisionmaking – and then give it generous scope.

In the mid-1990s, a small group of commentators began drawing explicitly on theories of intellectual property to criticize the right of publicity. None of the four major perspectives, they argued, provided support for such an entitlement. (a) From a utilitarian standpoint, the right seems senseless. It is not necessary to induce people to cultivate distinctive identities. It encourages people, once they have become celebrities, to coast on their endorsement incomes rather than continue to provide the public the services that made them famous. And it wastes social resources by inducing excessive numbers of adolescents to seek fame. (b) Nor is the right justified as a reward for labor. Often, fame results from luck, fickle public tastes, or the efforts of third parties more than it does from the efforts of the celebrity. In any event, celebrities are adequately remunerated in other ways for their labor. (c) If protecting personhood were one's goal, the right of celebrity would be a poor way to achieve it. The right protects the ability of celebrities to make money from their personae – an ability not particularly close to the heart of personality development – and does nothing to prevent disclosure of intimate details concerning celebrities' lives. (d) Last but not least, the right of celebrity exacerbates the centralization of semiotic power in the United States and undermines popular control over "popular culture."[90]

A few influential courts have begun to take notice. For example, in a recent decision, the Court of Appeals for the Tenth Circuit relied explicitly on this emerging body of critical commentary to turn aside a challenge by the Major League Baseball Players to the sale of a set of baseball cards that parodied the league's stars. The power of theory is especially evident in the following passage:

Parodies of celebrities are an especially valuable means of expression because of the role celebrities play in modern society. As one commentator explained, celebrities are

---

89 J. Thomas McCarthy, *The Rights of Publicity and Privacy* (New York: C. Boardman, 1992), Sec. 1.1[B][2], at 1–5. See also ibid., Section 2.1[B] ("The advocate of a Right of Publicity, when called upon to explain why such a right should exist at all, is not being illogical in simply challenging: 'Why not?'").

90 The three scholars most influential in developing these arguments are Jane Gaines, Rosemary Coombe, and Michael Madow. See Gaines, *Contested Culture: The Image, the Voice, and the Law* (Chapel Hill, N.C.: University of North Carolina Press, 1991); Coombe, "Objects of Property and Subjects of Politics"; and Madow, "Private Ownership of Public Image."

"common points of reference for millions of individuals who may never interact with one another, but who share, by virtue of their participation in a mediated culture, a common experience and a collective memory." Through their pervasive presence in the media, sports and entertainment celebrities come to symbolize certain ideas and values. . . . Celebrities, then, are an important element of the shared communicative resources of our cultural domain.

Because celebrities are an important part of our public vocabulary, a parody of a celebrity does not merely lampoon the celebrity, but exposes the weakness of the idea or value that the celebrity symbolizes in society. . . . In order to effectively criticize society, parodists need access to images that mean something to people, and thus celebrity parodies are a valuable communicative resource. Restricting the use of celebrity identities restricts the communication of ideas.[91]

A federal District Court recently employed a similar approach in rejecting a claim by Mayor Rudolf Giuliani that an advertisement describing *New York Magazine* as "possibly the only good thing in New York Rudy hasn't taken credit for" violated Giuliani's right of publicity.[92] If this style of analysis becomes more popular, the doctrinal tide may well turn.

Another example of the deployment of theory to suggest solutions to specific problems comes from my own work. Should the producer of an intellectual product be permitted to engage in price discrimination – that is, to charge prices that vary with consumers' ability and willingness to pay for access to the product? When it is feasible, producers frequently try to market their wares in this fashion.[93] Various doctrines in current intellectual property law limit (though certainly do not eliminate) their ability to do so. For instance, some kinds of patent license terms (e.g., agreements to purchase only from the patentee staple items of commerce for use in conjunction with the patented technology), though highly effective price-discrimination tools, are currently treated as "patent misuse." The first-sale doctrine in copyright law prevents a seller from prohibiting low-margin consumers from reselling the copies they purchase to high-margin potential consumers, thereby limiting the power of the seller to exploit the latter. And some aspects of current trademark law concerning "parallel imports" discourage trademark owners from charging less for their products in poor countries than in rich countries. Should these rules, or related doctrines in contract law, be modified?

91 *Cardtoons, L.C. v. Major League Baseball Players Association*, 95 F.3d 959, 972–73 (10th Cir. 1996).
92 *New York Magazine v. Metropolitan Transit Authority*, 987 F. Supp. 254, 266 (1997).
93 See, for example, Patricia M. Danzon, *Pharmaceutical Price Regulation: National Policies versus Global Interests* (Washington, D.C.: AEI Press, 1997) (geographic price discrimination for drugs); *ProCD, Inc. v. Zeidenberg*, 86 F.3d 1447 (7th Cir. 1996) (discrimination between commercial and noncommercial customers in sales of nationwide telephone directories); Michael Meurer, "Price Discrimination, Personal Use, and Piracy: Copyright Protection of Digital Works," *Buffalo Law Review*, 45 (1997): 845 (distribution of digital works on the Internet). For a useful taxonomy of types of price discrimination, see Scherer, *Industrial Market Structure*, pp. 315–34.

One's initial reaction is likely to be: no. Charging whatever the market will bear has an unsavory flavor. It smacks of greed and has no obvious social benefit. Impressions of that sort contributed to the Robinson–Patman Act[94] and have colored some courts' responses to price discrimination in the distribution of intellectual products.

Immersion in intellectual-property theory, however, suggests a different answer. At least two of the four approaches reviewed in this essay – utilitarianism and social-planning theory – converge to suggest that price discrimination in the sale of intellectual products may in some contexts be a good thing. Recall that one of the objectives of economic theorists is simultaneously to increase incentives for creative activity and to reduce the associated welfare losses. Price discrimination – by enabling producers to charge eager consumers more than less eager consumers – makes such an unlikely combination possible. By discriminating among subgroups of consumers, a producer is able both to increase his or her own monopoly profits and to reduce the number of consumers who are priced out of the market. In combination, these two effects sharply increase the ratio between incentives for creativity and welfare losses. Finally, price discrimination makes possible greater approximation of the ideal of distributive justice discussed briefly in Section III.D. Usually (though not always), the consumers able and willing to spend substantial sums for an intellectual product are more wealthy that the consumers able and willing to spend only a little. Because of that circumstance, price discrimination often enables a larger group of poor consumers to gain access to a product – and to pay less than their wealthy counterparts. Widespread adoption of this marketing strategy would thus enable us to approach the goal of providing all persons equal access to works of the intellect.[95]

To be sure, price discrimination in some contexts may have substantial disadvantages. The resources expended in establishing and administering price discrimination schemes represent social losses that at least partially offset the efficiency gains described above. Price discrimination sometimes requires the producer to obtain information about the tastes or habits of potential consumers, and the gathering of that information may invade their privacy. In the patent context, the gathering of analogous information concerning the business practices of licensees may facilitate the formation of cartels. Finally, price discrimination might sometimes result in pricing out of the market consumers interested in making transformative uses of intellectual products.[96] Only through careful analysis of the markets for specific sorts of intellectual

94 15 U.S.C. Sec. 13.
95 The argument is developed at greater length in Fisher, "Property and Contract on the Internet," at 1234–40.
96 These disadvantages of price discrimination are explored in Julie E. Cohen, "Copyright and the Jurisprudence of Self-Help," *Berkeley Technology Law Journal*, 13 (1998): 1089–143; Wendy Gordon, "Intellectual Property as Price Discrimination," *Chicago-Kent Law Review*, 73 (1998): 1367–90; Kaplow, "Patent–Antitrust Intersection."

products can it be ascertained whether these drawbacks exceed the economic and social benefits reviewed above. But a combination of utilitarian and social-planning theory creates a nonobvious *prima facie* case for the expansion of opportunities for price discrimination.

The other reason why intellectual-property theory retains value is that it can catalyze useful conversations among the various people and institutions responsible for the shaping of the law. More specifically, continued explicit discussion of the kinds of themes addressed in this essay would be valuable in three contexts. First, interaction among Congress, the courts, and administrative agencies (in particular, the Patent and Trademark Office) would be improved. Congress, when it adopts or amends intellectual-property laws, frequently fails to anticipate difficult interpretive questions. If the courts, when compelled in the context of individual disputes to resolve those questions, articulate a general theory they are using to guide their decisionmaking, they increase the likelihood that Congress, during the next general revision of the relevant statute, will be able thoughtfully either to endorse or to reject the courts' judgments. Much the same can be said of decision-making by administrative agencies that are then appealed to the courts.

Second, explicit reliance upon intellectual-property theories will improve conversations between lawmakers and their constituents. *Why* should the term of a copyright be extended from the life of the author plus fifty years to the life of the author plus seventy years? Because the additional time is necessary to encourage additional creativity? Because authors deserve greater rewards for their labors? Because the culture would be worse off if works like "Steamboat Willie" were released to the public domain? *Why* should it be possible to register as a federal trademark the sound made by motorcycles bearing a particular brand – thereby preventing other manufacturers from making motorcycles that sound the same? Because otherwise consumers will be confused concerning the manufacturers of the motorcycles they are buying? Because a culture in which motorcycles can be recognized from a distance by the noise they make is better than a culture in which they cannot? Because employees of the first company deserve a reward for the effort they invested in constructing a muffler that emits a distinctive guttural sound? By articulating and defending a theoretical rationale for each innovation, Congress (in the first example) or the courts (in the second example) would increase the ability of the public at large or, more plausibly, affected interest groups critically to appraise the change. Lawmakers, in short, would become more accountable.[97]

Finally, through continued conversations among scholars, legislators, judges, litigants, lobbyists, and the public at large, there may lie some hope of

---

97 It was largely for this reason that the Legal Realists urged lawmakers (including judges, whom the Realists insisted were as much lawmakers as legislators) to be more explicit concerning the policy bases of their decisions. See, for example, Felix Cohen, "Transcendental Nonsense and the Functional Approach," *Columbia Law Review,* 35 (1935): 809.

addressing the inadequacies of the existing theories. For the reasons sketched above, the analytical difficulties associated with the effort to apply the Lockean version of labor theory to intellectual property may well prove insurmountable, but there may be some non-Lockean way of capturing the popular intuition that the law should reward people for hard work. Only by continuing to discuss the possibility – and trying to bring some alternative variant of labor theory to bear on real cases – can we hope to make progress. Much the same can be said of the gaps in personality theory. The conception of selfhood employed by current theorists may be too thin and acontextual to provide lawmakers much purchase on doctrinal problems. But perhaps, through continued reflection and conversation, we can do better.

Conversational uses of intellectual-property theories of the sort sketched above would be different from the way in which such theories most often have been deployed in the past. Instead of trying to compel readers, through a combination of noncontroversial premises and inexorable logic, to accept a particular interpretation or reform of legal doctrine, the scholar or lawmaker would attempt, by deploying a combination of theory and application, to strike a chord of sympathy in his or her audience. The sought-after response would not be, "I can't see any holes in the argument," but rather, "That rings true to me."

Table of Cases

Index of Names

Index of Subjects